The Dynamics of Belief

PHILOSOPHICAL THEORY

SERIES EDITORS
John McDowell, Philip Pettit and Crispin Wright

The Dynamics of Belief: A Normative Logic
Peter Forrest

For Truth in Semantics
Anthony Appiah

Abstract Objects
R. L. V. Hale

Fact and Meaning
Jane Heal

Conditionals
Frank Jackson

Special Explanation: The Disunity of Science
Graham Macdonald

Probability and Causation
Peter Menzies

Abstract Particulars
Keith Campbell

A Statement of Fact
Huw Price

The Free Rider Problem
Richard Tuck

The Dynamics of Belief

A Normative Logic

PETER FORREST

Basil Blackwell

Copyright©Peter Forrest 1986

First published 1986

Basil Blackwell Ltd
108 Cowley Road, Oxford OX4 1JF, UK

Basil Blackwell Inc.
432 Park Avenue South, Suite 1503,
New York, NY 10016, USA

British Library Cataloguing in Publication Data

Forrest, Peter
The dynamics of belief: a normative
logic. – (Philosophical theory)
1. Inference (Logic)
I. Title   II. Series
160   BC199.147

ISBN 0-631-14619-9

Library of Congress Cataloging in Publication Data

Forrest, Peter, 1948 –
The dynamics of belief.

(Philosophical theory)
Bibliography: p.
Includes index.
1. Logic. 2. Belief and doubt. I. Title.
II. Series.
BC71.F66   1986   121'.6   86-6780
ISBN 0-631-14619-9

Phototypeset in 11/13 pt Baskerville by Dobbie Typesetting Service,
Plymouth, Devon
Printed in Great Britain by T. J. Press, Padstow, Cornwall

Contents

To Felicity

Preface

This book is the result of two deep convictions I have about logic. One is that logic concerns, among other things, *inferences*. And that inferences are made by people. They are not just sequences of propositions or of sentences. The other conviction is that logic is not merely a descriptive theory but is also a normative theory which stands to how we reason as ethics stands to how we act. Combining these two convictions I consider one of the central topics of logic to be a discussion of the right and wrong inferences to make. Since to make an inference is to undergo a change to one's beliefs this leads me to a normative theory of changes to systems of beliefs, and also of degrees of belief.

The dynamics of belief which I present in this book owes much to the statics of systems of beliefs presented in Brian Ellis's *Rational Belief Systems* (1979). The other intellectual debt which I would like to acknowledge, and which is not adequately captured by citations, is to David Stove, who supervised my doctorate at Sydney University on a related topic (Probabilistic Modal Inferences). To him I owe, among much else, my awareness of the importance of particular judgements of rationality. I would like to thank him and Jim Franklin of the University of New South Wales for their helpful comments on a draft, and Philip Pettit for some extremely valuable editorial advice. Lastly I would like to thank Hazel Gittins for her work on the word-processor, which involved much patient deciphering of my near-illegible writing, and repeated alterations.

Research School of Social Sciences
Australian National University

Introduction

I THE NEED FOR A NORMATIVE DYNAMICS

Twentieth-century logic has been dominated by the Fregean tradition that logic concerns laws of truth (Frege 1977, p. 1). But, on the other hand, logicians consider that they have something important to say about inferences.[1] However, inferences are there to be *made*, they are not just sequences of propositions. And to make an inference is, in part, to come to believe the conclusion as a result of believing the premises. So logic concerns changes to belief. Further, one obviously important thing about an inference-making is whether or not it is *rational*.

The moral I draw is that there are two autonomous but connected disciplines, positive logic and normative logic.[2] Positive logic concerns the descriptive laws of truth, in the tradition of Frege; normative logic the prescriptive laws of thought,[3] in the tradition of Husserl (1970, pp. 70–2) and Johnson (1921, Part I, pp. 224–6). As its subtitle indicates this work concerns normative logic. But I do not denigrate positive logic. Both are, I believe, necessary. I shall also be concerned with the connection *between* positive and normative logic. Thus, among other things, I shall discuss the question: Under what circumstances is a 'valid' (i.e. necessarily truth-preserving) inference a rational inference to make?

I draw that moral. But, I fear, few logicians do. For most of them condemn the normative to footnote status.[4] That is, they think that all the hard and interesting work is in positive logic. Normative logic, they think, is merely a matter of saying that 'valid' inferences are by far the best ones to make, but if you cannot get a 'valid' inference then 'invalid' ones with a high probability are better than ones with a low probability. One of my aims is to take normative logic out of the footnotes, by showing that there is a lot that can be said about it. And if you reject the theory I produce I hope you will construct a better one. If you do I wager it will not fit into a footnote.

The chief topic of normative logic is the rationality of *making* various inferences. And to make an inference is to undergo a *change* to one's system of beliefs. I am concerned, therefore, not just with the statics of systems of beliefs but with their dynamics. Hence the title. Because I see the dynamics of beliefs as the appropriate framework for normative logic, my interest in changes to belief is not merely the common one of wondering how beliefs should change given new evidence.[5] For when an inference is made a change occurs quite independently of new evidence. Likewise the problem of how to respond to inconsistency in one's system of beliefs can be handled independently of considering new evidence. I treat, then, the question of response to new evidence as but one problem among several.

I have two complaints, then, about modern logic. It tends to disregard the normative; and its interest in belief-change tends to be narrowed down to the problem of what happens when new evidence is acquired. The result is a gap between logic conceived of as the science of how we should reason, and logic as described by most logicians. Part of the justification for presenting my systematic normative logic is that it helps fill this gap. But I am not working on entirely virgin soil. To some extent the gap, and the need to fill it, have been recognized. So to show where I stand, I now briefly contrast my approach with those whose interests are closest to me. First, there is Brian Ellis's book, *Rational Belief Systems* (Ellis 1979), to which I am heavily indebted. Ellis's work is, for the most part, though, concerned with the *statics* of systems of belief. And I am developing a *dynamics*.

Isaac Levi in his *Enterprise of Knowledge* (Levi 1980) does consider the dynamics of systems of belief (*credal states* as he calls them), but he assigns a special role to knowledge claims (either actual ones or ones to which a person is committed). And the parts of his work most comparable to mine concern his account of changes to the corpora of knowledge claims rather than the changes to the credal states, which, in his account, depend on the knowledge claims. An approach somewhat like Levi's is that of the Gärdenfors School, as I call it. This comprises fairly technical papers by Peter Gärdenfors, Carlos Alchourron and David Makinson (see Makinson 1985). However the Gärdenfors School emphasizes belief rather than knowledge. In that respect I am closer to it than to Levi. But there are three respects in which I differ significantly from both Levi and the Gärdenfors School.

(1) They assume the logical closure of systems of belief. (Or in Levi's case of corpora of knowledge.) I do not.
(2) I treat as of central importance adjustments, whereby degrees of belief in given propositions are altered. But both Levi and the Gärdenfors School put the emphasis on contractions, whereby a proposition is totally eliminated from the set believed in. (Or, in Levi's case, from the corpus.)
(3) I attach great importance to compromises (especially in chapters 9 and 10).

The first difference, namely my not assuming logical closure, is simply a matter of not making a common idealization. The advantage of not making the idealization of logical closure is that it enables me to discuss inferences by deduction. In particular, the theory I develop could be applied much more easily to mathematical reasoning, both formal and heuristic, than can rival approaches. The second difference, discussed in detail in chapter 6, goes along with an emphasis on degrees of belief. Partly because I state my theory in terms of degrees of belief I am able to argue (in chapter 3) that adjustments cannot be reduced to other kinds of change, thus justifying the third difference.

My emphasis on degrees of belief is one respect in which I come close to the Bayesians or subjectivists such as de Finetti. But I reject the Bayesian approach in several ways. First, as I explain in chapter 4, I do not rely on Dutch Book Arguments. Secondly, I consider that the normative judgements concerning degrees of belief are far richer than those which the subjectivists extract from the Dutch Book Argument. Thirdly, as I argue in chapter 10, I think there is something suspect about the Principle of Temporal Coherence,[6] which is the one principle the Bayesians have which directly concerns change or lack of it.

II METHODOLOGY

My aim is to proceed in an empirical (but not necessarily empiricist) fashion. By that I mean that I rely heavily on *considered particular judgements* concerning rationality. These particular judgements will be of the form:

This change (or this lack of change) to this system of beliefs (or degrees thereof) is rational (or irrational).

But, for convenience, I often consider low-level generalizations, of the form:

Changes of type X (or lack of change) to systems of beliefs (or degrees thereof) are rational (or irrational) in circumstances of type Y.

In principle, however, I claim that we could always go back to particular judgements.

I call these considered particular judgements, *intuitive judgements*, or *intuitions*, and I think of them as data, analogous to scientific observations. I think of these intuitions as *a priori*, but not indefeasible. However, the reader may give her or his own account of, or replacement for, intuitive judgements, say, as well-entrenched beliefs, or beliefs one is reluctant to give up. Nothing much depends on my reliance on the *a priori*.

To derive a systematic theory from particular judgements I need to make inferences from them. Although the conclusions of these inferences are generalizations, the inferences made will be subject to particular judgements, namely that *these* inferences from data to generalizations are rational ones. So the particular judgements reign supreme. Because of my emphasis on particular, yet *a priori*, judgements, I call my position Empirical Rationalism. But as I have indicated it is the being empirical not the Rationalism which affects what I say in this work.

Intuitions are, as I have said, *considered* judgements. They are not just what comes off the top of one's head. To *consider* a judgement involves, I submit, putting it to the test. How should intuitions be tested? While I do not believe that there are any infallible tests, both Descartes' criteria of clarity and distinctness and Husserl's method of bracketing off presuppositions (Husserl 1970, pp. 263–6) suggest criteria. Thus, although I think that an intuition may be vague and yet reliable, intuitions that failed to survive the *attempt* at clarification were never reliable. So we should subject our intuitions to the discipline of such an attempt. Again, while I do not accept that we can free ourselves of all un-thought-out presupposition, intuitions should be subject to the attempt to make explicit that which we presuppose.

Because I base so much on intuitive judgements, I would like to emphasize the truism that people must find their intuitive bases themselves. Paradigms, dogmas, orthodoxies and consensus are all very well in their place, but their place is not philosophy. In philosophy, I submit, 'Egotism is true modesty' (Newman 1947, p. 384). In this work I systematize *my* intuitions. Who else's could I systematize?[7] But the interest of this work does not of course lie in my intuitions, it lies in how I systematize them. I offer this work to the reader in the hope that he or she may find my systematization interesting and be able to adapt all or some of it to his or her intuitions.

As part of my systematic theory I propose various general *principles* of normative logic. Where I can obtain results from those by means of fairly rigorous argument I call these results *theses*. I also consider various initially plausible but rejected conjectures, and explain why I do not rely on them. The explanation of my non-reliance is based on arguments which I do not think need be as rigorous as those used to derive theses. For I do not treat the negation of a rejected conjecture as itself a principle.

The rejected conjectures are generalizations. And typically they are ones which are not firmly grounded on particular judgements. Hence I believe they can be argued against by means of particular counter-examples even where they have high initial plausibility. However, if you attach greater weight than I do to general (*a priori*) principles, then you might back the conjecture against the counter-examples. So be it. At least I shall have produced grounds for some, perhaps slight, degree of doubt in the conjecture.

In order to show more clearly where I stand I shall now contrast my position with three approaches which are similar to it in various respects.[8] First I hope I have avoided Dogmatic Rationalism, by which I mean the sticking to *a priori* judgements, often of a general kind, come what may. That I come to 'know' something *a priori* does not preclude its being subsequently rejected on either *a priori* or *a posteriori* grounds.

Next I contrast my position with the extreme reliance on particular judgements. Advocates of situation ethics reject all general moral principles. Adapting this to logic, we would obtain the recommendation first to immerse oneself in positive logic and then make only particular judgements of rationality, relying on good sense, as Duhem calls it (1954, chapter 6). In that case general principles, if we could find any, could never result in the rejection of particular judgements. By contrast I believe they can, provided they are themselves based on other particular judgements. For in such situations we may have a clash between several particular judgements, those on which the generalization is based and that which is contrary to it. The outcome may well be the provisional rejection of that particular judgement. I say 'provisional' because I do not treat such a rejection as the failure to pass a test. There is nothing intrinsically wrong with such an intuition. And in different circumstances it should re-assert itself.[9]

Finally there is the method of reflective equilibrium, as Rawls calls it (1972, chapter 1, section 9).[10] This is so close to my own position that mine could properly be considered a mere variant of it. Rawls's considered judgements are those which stand up to various tests such as not being made when 'upset or frightened, or when we stand to gain one way or the other' (1972, p. 47). If a person then decides how these judgements should be altered to fit various proposed systematic accounts he or she may reject some considered judgements in order to fit some theory, or else to insist on the considered judgements and reject any theories inconsistent with them. Afterwards the person is said to have reached a state of reflective equilibrium.

The chief respect in which I differ from Rawls is my emphasis on particular judgements. As Rawls describes reflective equilibrium it could be achieved by someone who allowed considerations of theoretical simplicity to rule over the considered judgements. As I intend my methodology, general principles only serve to correct some particular judgement when and because there is a clash between that judgement and those on which the general principles are based. Another, but minor, point in which I differ from Rawls, concerns his suggestion that it is because of the 'likelihood that considered judgements are . . . subject to certain irregularities and distortions' that they may be rejected in the state of reflective equilibrium. No doubt that is one reason. But Rawls's remark suggests that being rejected is strong evidence of some intrinsic defect in the intuition. I disagree. All intuitions are, I believe, defeasible. And typically it is just bad luck, not an intrinsic defect, if an intuition is incorrect.

To sum up: my method is similar to that of reflective equilibrium, but with the emphasis on particular judgements; and it is part of a more general programme of non-dogmatic Empirical Rationalism.

III BROADER ISSUES

There are a few issues which are related to the topic of this book, but which I do not have space to discuss in detail. Partly to avoid suggesting to the reader I hold positions I do not, I shall mention them here.

Firstly I have done my best to avoid talk of truth. Thus, when introducing self-evidence in chapter 4, I do not use the natural phrase 'self-evidently truth-preserving'. My avoidance here is not because I intend to eliminate truth or reduce it to warranted assertibility. Rather it is simply to achieve maximum neutrality on the difficult topic of the connection between truth and rationality. For what it is worth I deny that truth can be defined in terms of, or replaced by, rationality. On the other hand, I deny that rationality is merely a means to the end of achieving true beliefs. For although I believe that rational changes are more likely to lead to true beliefs than irrational ones, I do not think that is what constitutes their rationality. And this is because I suspect that an analysis of 'likely' in this context will inevitably be in terms of rationality itself.

Secondly, nothing I say is directly relevant to the question of whether normative judgements express genuine beliefs and so can be assessed as true or false, or whether they express desires or emotive attitudes, as prescriptivists and emotivists would have it. I am inclined to believe that our mental life is far richer than our mental vocabulary. So perhaps judgements of rationality are expressions neither of beliefs nor desires nor emotional attitudes. However, given the usual classifications, I would claim that judgements of rationality, at least the comparative ones, express beliefs and, as such, are capable of being true or false. (And, of course, I believe of any one of mine that it is true.) My reason for this claim is that it seems on introspection that my judgements are beliefs, or at least, belief-like, and none of the sceptical arguments against the truth of judgements of rationality persuade me to reject this introspection.[11]

Another issue which is relevant to normative logic is whether the judgements of rationality, which are ostensibly normative, really are normative. According to Psychologism, principles of rationality would be construed as *descriptive* laws of thought. A *crude* Psychologism, according to which logic provides iron laws of thought (that is, laws which can have no exceptions)[12] is clearly untenable: fallacies do occur. But Ellis's more sophisticated version (1979) is based on the claim that the laws of a scientific theory need not hold without exception, and, indeed, need not hold at all. The laws indicate a sort of norm (in a non-normative sense of norm). And (further) explanation is required for departing from this norm. Ellis's theory, as I understand it, is that the principles of normative logic are to be understood primarily[13] as such 'norms' or as idealized descriptions, departures from which need further explanation.

Idealized Theory Psychologism, as I call Ellis's theory, does capture some of our intuitions. For there is a close connection between rationality and explanation. That a certain change is required for rationality explains that change.[14] So I agree with Ellis that the principles of normative logic do provide an ideal, departures from which require further explanation. But I deny that this gives an adequate account of them.

My chief objection to Idealized Theory Psychologism is that it is too egalitarian. Suppose, as I might well discover, that the vast majority of people reason in ways other than mine. This would disturb me, and make me reconsider my own intuitive judgements. But it should not imply that my judgements *must* be wrong. Yet an idealized theory must be an idealization of what is actually the case. And if I am the exception, or in a small minority, the only proper idealization will be to ignore me. So in case of such a discrepancy between me and the majority, on Ellis's theory I *must* be the irrational party. And that is counter-intuitive. So I reject Ellis's sophisticated version of Psychologism.

The last issue that I shall briefly touch on is the traditional dispute between rationalists and empiricists. Since I appeal to intuitive judgements, I have described myself as a rationalist. Does it follow that I reject the whole of Empiricism? There is much in Empiricism I need not reject. For instance, I accept the principle that violations of symmetry (believing that one particular is an *F* but some other is not) can only be arrived at rationally as a result of observations. And that has an empiricist, as well as an empirical, flavour to it. Another empiricist principle which I do not *have to* reject is one to the effect that *a priori knowledge* is always of necessary truths. For I am here concerned with rational belief rather than with knowledge.

IV SUMMARY

My chief aim in this work is to systematize our intuitive judgements of the rationality or irrationality of changes to beliefs, and by so doing to exhibit the richness of normative logic. But I have several subsidiary aims. One is to resist the influence of paradigms in philosophy, in Kuhn's sense of paradigm (1970). Paradigms, even dogmas, are fitting in the sciences, no doubt. For continual controversy hampers scientific enquiry. But I see no need for deference to paradigms in philosophy. In particular I do not defer to the current paradigm for logic, which is the (positive) logic of deductions. (It is the paradigm, I suspect, only because it is the branch of logic which has achieved greatest completion.) As a consequence of the dominance of this paradigm, there is a tendency to judge other branches of logic, especially the theory of probable inference, by the standards of the (positive) logic of deduction. At its crudest this results in the pronouncement of all probable inferences as *merely* invalid. But less crudely there is a tendency to treat probable inferences as second class when compared with deductive ones. And one of my aims is to show there is no such first class/second class distinction. Other subsidiary aims are to provide a satisfactory theory of proportional syllogisms; to discuss the problem of whether theory, observation or auxiliary hypotheses are to be rejected when they clash (the problem of the direction of the arrow of *modus tollens*, to use Lakatos's happy metaphor); and to discuss inferences by induction.

I am concerned with the rationality of inferences and other changes to systems of beliefs. And a belief has, I claim, some content which I call a proposition. In the first chapter I clarify what I mean by a proposition, by rationality and by an inference. I also discuss the sorts of idealizations I shall be making and some limitations of scope. In chapter 2 ('Doxastic Systems') I discuss degrees of belief. I do not assume that degrees of belief have an intrinsically numerical structure. So it is important to note what structure a system of degrees of belief does have and how this can be represented numerically. In addition I introduce some notation concerning degrees of belief.

The first two chapters will have prepared the way for an outline of the dynamics of systems of belief, which I provide in chapter 3 ('The Framework for a Dynamics of Belief'). In that chapter I discuss homeostatic models for rational change and consider how more complex changes may be analysed in terms of simpler ones.

It might seem curious that I begin the dynamics of belief before discussing the statics. I do so because I define the central normative concept of the statics, doxastic consistency, as being in a state such that no change is required for rationality, and hence in terms of the dynamics. In chapter 4, where my debt to Ellis is especially clear, I develop the statics of systems of belief. While this is somewhat similar to the accounts provided by subjectivists such as de Finetti, I do not consider the multiplication rule to be sufficiently justified and so do not rely on it. Furthermore, since I reject the Dutch Book Argument, a detailed justification is required of the principles which I assume.

In chapters 5 and 6 I provide a normative theory of deductions. In chapter 5 I examine the case of deductive *expansions*, that is deductions in which the conclusion has not previously been considered. In that case the conventional wisdom that 'valid' inferences are especially good is, for the most part, vindicated. But in chapter 6, where I consider deductive *adjustments*, that is deductions in which the conclusion has already been considered, the conventional wisdom is overthrown.

In chapters 7 and 8 I turn to probable inferences. I provide the basis for a theory of probable inferences in chapter 7 and discuss a special, and unduly neglected, case in chapter 8, that of proportional syllogisms. In addition I argue that probable inferences are not second class.

Chapters 5 to 8 have been concerned with a flat rational/irrational distinction. But we can have comparisons of rationality: some rational changes are more rational than others and some irrational ones are less irrational than others. In chapter 9 I introduce the comparative theory of rationality. One reason for so doing is that in some cases our comparisons of rationality are easier to systematize than our of flat rationality. An instance of this is that of inference by induction. In chapter 10 I examine inferences by induction, showing how we can derive the result that induction is required, at least for *maximal* rationality.

Starting with chapter 2 I star the more technical sections and put them at the end of each chapter.[15] This book is written in such a way that the technical sections may be omitted at a first reading.

1

Propositions, Rationality and Inferences

When I talk of propositions, rationality and inferences, what I say might perhaps need no interpretation. However, I shall make some preliminary remarks on those topics. These remarks are not intended as definitive studies so much as a prophylactic against confusion. In the same spirit I discuss idealizations and limitations of scope.

I   DOXASTIC ATTITUDES AND PROPOSITIONS

I call the attitudes of belief and disbelief, and all the degrees thereof, *doxastic* attitudes. Likewise I call changes to doxastic attitudes, *doxastic* changes. Now I shall make three, no doubt controversial, assumptions about such doxastic attitudes. The *first* is that we do have doxastic attitudes and that they form a natural kind, or if they do not then at least we can treat them as forming a natural kind for the purposes of normative logic. The alternative would be to posit different principles governing changes to purportedly different kinds of belief. Thus I assume, for instance, that beliefs about theoretical entities in science are subject to the same normative principles as beliefs about bank balances, or cookery. My *second* assumption is that a person's having a doxastic attitude is to be analysed as a relation between the person and the object of belief, which I call a *proposition*. I use the term proposition here, not in its traditional sense in which propositions are sentences or statements, but in its Cambridge sense, that is, in the way that Moore, Russell and Johnson used it (Prior 1976, chapter 1). In this Cambridge sense a proposition just is the object of the belief, whatever the object turns out to be. My *third* assumption is that propositions have a sentence-*like* structure,[1] so that we can talk of a proposition containing a predicate, or a name. In accordance with this I assume that propositions can be referred to by their linguistic manifestations as sentences. All these assumptions are controversial.[2] I admit that. But it would be too great a digression into the philosophy of mind to argue for them in detail. Instead I shall clear up some ambiguities in the assumptions I have made, and I shall explain why these assumptions could be treated as legitimate idealizations even if they turn out to be false.

The principal ambiguity in my account of doxastic attitudes is that between proposition-token and proposition-type. This is best illustrated by a prima-facie argument for propositions which I now sketch. (As I have said above I shall not go into the details.) This is a variant of the One Over Many argument. For instance, on 10 March 1984 I believed that some time on 11 March 1984 crimson rosellas would be in the gum tree outside my office. I believed *it*. I could have doubted *it*. Again I could have hoped *it*. And I could both have doubted and hoped *it*. Taking this at its face value, I conclude that there is a something which these attitudes are all attitudes towards. I call this something a *proposition-token* and I say that belief, doubt, hope etc. are all attitudes to such proposition-tokens.

But now consider the way two people – or one person at two times – can have the same belief. Should we say that this is the identical proposition-token or merely the same proposition-type? I believe the latter. And I believe the latter because as Lycan (1981) has pointed out it is not a trivial matter to decide when beliefs are beliefs in the same thing. We can classify proposition-tokens in at least two ways, functionally[3] and truth-conditionally.[4] Thus my belief which is expressed by saying 'It will be cold tonight' has much the same functional role this evening as yesterday evening. I shall, on both evenings, tend to put another log on the stove; I shall groan about the climate, and so on. Yet the truth-conditions are, intuitively, different. Conversely my belief this evening expressed by saying 'It will be cold tonight' and my belief tomorrow morning expressed by saying 'It was cold last night' have the same truth-conditions but different functional roles. It seems, then, that proposition-tokens can be classified into proposition-types in incompatible ways. Hence we should not treat any of the types as made up of a single token. And what we mean by the *same belief* will be belief in a token of the same proposition-type, with respect to the appropriate classification. Accordingly I stipulate that when I say 'proposition' I mean 'proposition-type', and I shall specify, once and for all, the appropriate classification for my purposes. That will be a classification in which the automatic updating of beliefs with the passage of time does not count as a doxastic change. Thus when the belief that today is Tuesday becomes, overnight, the belief that yesterday was Tuesday, I shall be said to undergo no doxastic change, that is, my attitude to proposition-types will be deemed unchanged. My reason for requiring this classification is that I do not want such automatic updating to be even discussed in a *normative* theory. They are not up for appraisal as rational or irrational. If you have the misfortune to update incorrectly you have some defect, but not one of rationality.

Functional types are not preserved by automatic updating. But truth-conditional ones are. I claim, however, that truth-conditional types are too coarse for a theory of inferences. For I want all inferences to count as changes, even those from a premiss (e.g. 'Some mammals have horns') to an equivalent conclusion ('Some horned things are mammals'). But in such cases the conclusion and the premiss are of the same truth-conditional type.[5]

I claim, then, that we need to consider suitable sub-types of the truth-conditional ones. For what it is worth, my classification is obtained by considering various *transformations* which are considered to be type-preserving. Then two proposition-tokens are of the same type just in case one can be obtained from the other by a sequence of type-preserving transformations. Among such transformations I include:

(1) Updating transformations due to the passage of time.
(2) Transformations due to change of spatial location. ('The clock is over there' and 'The clock is here' can express belief in the same proposition-type if I move.).
(3) Some elementary linguistic transformations such as that from active to passive.

If I were concerned with interpersonal comparisons I would also have to allow some transformations covering the preservation of type when the believer changes. But in that case it would, I suspect, become rather hard to stop at a finer classification than the truth-conditional one. I would draw the moral that a classification of proposition-tokens into types suitable for my present purpose is not suitable for the discussion of communication.

The propositions (that is, the proposition-types) which I consider are sub-types of truth-conditional types. That is, no two beliefs are considered belief in the same thing if the conditions in which they would be true differ. It follows that propositions can be considered to be bearers of truth. This is especially convenient when we consider those degrees of belief which do not constitute belief but rather agnosticism. If I have a degree of belief one half that True Love will win the Golden Slipper Stakes, and she does, then it is more natural to say that what I have that degree of belief one half *in* is true, rather than say that my degree of belief one half is true. Hence propositions rather than degrees of belief are to be taken as truth-bearers.

One final expository remark about belief: As Dennett has pointed out (1978, p. 45) there are things we might be said to believe, such as that no human being is larger than a mountain, which are not usually *stored* but are easily *generated*. Are we to count these as beliefs? *Pace* Ryle I assume that a belief is an *occurrent* state. Hence I shall treat 'beliefs' which are not stored not as beliefs but merely as dispositions to believe. But there is nothing to stop anyone modifying my theory by treating a disposition to believe that p (if asked whether p) as itself a belief.

What if my assumptions are incorrect? Firstly, consider those who either eliminate doxastic attitudes or insist they do not form a natural kind. Then, surely they will provide a replacement. Otherwise they would be denying all significance to our belief/disbelief distinction, which would lead to the absurdity that one might as properly say the eliminativist disbelieves as believes his or her theory. And it is reasonable to hope that much of what I say will be carried over to the replacement theory. So, even if I were convinced that some such replacement would occur, I could still keep my theory as a suitably idealized one. And similar remarks hold for the elimination of propositions: the prima facie argument I sketched was based on the judgement that we are on to some significant feature of doxastic attitudes when we talk of belief in the *same* thing. And even if that feature has been misdescribed it is reasonable to hope much of what I say can be preserved. Here the analogy with science is encouraging: a great deal survives scientific revolutions.

I would have a slightly different apologia for continuing to assume the sentence-like structure of propositions. Here I could concede that suitably primitive propositions fail to have such structure. But it would still be plausible that once we have learned a language many of our beliefs are stored as remembered sentences in a language. So I suspect that all I would need here is a limitation of scope. Those parts of my enquiry (especially the theory of the proportional syllogism) which make use of the sentence-like structure of propositions would then have to be limited to comparatively sophisticated contexts.

II RATIONALITY

I propose a normative theory. So I need some term of evaluation. I could use the very general term 'right'. But instead I shall use 'rational'. This is partly to exclude considerations of *moral* rightness. It is, I believe, morally wrong to indulge in irrationality. And, perhaps, this is the only way in which a belief can be morally wrong. But these are both non-trivial theses: initially at least, we should distinguish rationality from morality.[6] So in a work of logic, like this, I shall be considering rational and irrational changes to systems of beliefs.

Irrationality is one sort of defect in reasoning. But how are we to distinguish irrationality from lack of imagination, insight, or intelligence, all of which are limitations on our capacity to think, and hence to reason? There are, I think, several differences. First, irrationality can, I think, be deliberate and so blameworthy, whereas lack of intelligence, imagination or insight is a *mere* defect, for which we could be pitied but not blamed. Intelligence, imagination and insight are gifts, or abilities, whereas rationality is not. Moreover irrationality consists of fairly gross defects: rationality is not to be praised, lack of it is to be blamed. Irrationality may also be distinguished from other defects of reasoning by the intimate connection between it and the emotions. Too much or *too little* emotion[7] can make a person think irrationally, on some occasions, or, at least, make it hard for that person to be rational.

I now make four comments by way of the clarification of the concept of rationality I am using. First, when I say a doxastic change is rational I mean it is rationally permissible, namely not irrational. But someone else might mean that it is rationally obligatory, namely that failure to make that change is irrational. That there is this ambiguity is evidence of a tendency to conflate the rationally permissible with the rationally obligatory, as when we ask 'What is *the* rational change?', suggesting there is only one. It may turn out that there is only one rational change of a certain kind. But this is not to be presumed.

Secondly, I consider the rationality of a doxastic change to be supervenient on the change itself together with such considerations as what the person seems to observe or remember, but not to depend on factors independent of the person, such as the objective chance of the person's beliefs being true, or such as other people's beliefs.

Thirdly, although I consider rationality to be normative I am primarily concerned with the assessment and justification of changes as rational or irrational rather than giving counsel to those who are perplexed as to how to reason in a given situation. The best counsel, I believe, is to examine the relevant arguments and then just make up your mind. However, knowledge of normative logic might influence the way people do make up their minds.

Finally I consider rationality as a norm for doxastic *changes*. So to say a change is irrational is, in part, to say it is a change not to be undergone. We could develop a rather different account of rationality by considering the rational virtues. In such an account we would discuss virtues such as the proper degree of emotional involvement in thought, the proper extent to which we should take seriously arguments for seemingly outrageous positions and so on. This is not my present topic. And I see no rivalry between the two rather different concepts of rationality.

III   INFERENCES

Our concept of an inference is, I take it, derived from that of inferring. 'To make an inference' is synonymous with 'to infer'. So what happens when someone makes an inference? This much should not be too controversial: a necessary condition for S to have made an inference is that S comes to have a new belief, or degree of belief, which I call the doxastic conclusion, as a result of already having one or more beliefs, or degrees of belief (the doxastic premisses). I shall call the propositions towards which the doxastic premisses or conclusion is an attitude the *propositional premisses* or *propositional conclusion*. This will help to avoid confusion. Where convenient I shall abbreviate 'doxastic' to 'δ' and 'propositional' to 'π'. Hence I may talk of a δ-conclusion or a π-premiss.

The necessary condition for S to make an inference is clearly not sufficient. If I believe that Rigel is a blue giant and, *as a result of introspection*, come to believe that I believe Rigel is a blue giant, then I have not made the inference:

Rigel is a blue giant.
Therefore I believe Rigel is a blue giant.

For introspection is not an inference-making. Again suppose Alice has just proved Fermat's last theorem and she comes to believe by introspection that she is elated where the elation is caused by her belief that she has proved Fermat's last theorem. She has not made the inference:

I have proved Fermat's last theorem
Therefore I am elated.

I take it that in an inference-making the conclusion is reached as a result of a *reasoning* process from the premises. But what further account, if any, of that reasoning process can be given I do not know. Fortunately in a work of logic it suffices to consider simply the fact that a doxastic attitude has been acquired as a result of having other doxastic attitudes. The standards of evaluation I am considering *are* those for reasoning. So no explicit mention need be made of the fact that the process is one of reasoning. If it happens to be the result of some deviant causal chain it still gets evaluated as if it were the result of reasoning. In such cases the evaluation is inappropriate but not incorrect.

My emphasis on inference may cause some opposition. For it has been suggested that it is *arguments* (including apologias), namely something *public*, which are subject to the logicians' assessment, not the obscure workings of our minds.[8] Now I grant that one may properly use arguments or make apologias which do not correspond to the inferences, if any, actually used to arrive at one's position. But I claim that the standards of evaluation are the same. An argument or apologia is a good one only if it expresses an inference that could rationally be made. Hence I concentrate on inferences.

IV   IDEALIZATION

'No system without idealization.' I agree, but we may and should distinguish several different sorts of idealization to avoid confusion. First there is the sort of idealization you make merely because if you do not make it you cannot proceed with the theory. For example, it often happens in applied mathematics – or used to before the age of computers – that some mathematical function is simply assumed to have a smooth graph because otherwise the problem would be insoluble. I shall call this a *fudge idealization*. This is the hardest sort of idealization to justify, unless one's aim is merely to show that some data *can* be treated in a systematic fashion. So I avoid it. In particular, the assumption that degrees of belief are representable numerically, although it is almost[9] a necessary condition for theoretical progress is not an idealization of this sort. For it is capable of an independent though not entirely conclusive justification, which I provide in chapter 4.

Next there are idealizations which consist of a more or less arbitrary choice of one among several variants of a theory, where a choice has to be made for the sake of exposition. Here the justification is that a more general theory would be harder to grasp, but would not lead to significantly different results. I call this an *expository idealization*. In the course of presenting a comparative theory of rationality, in chapters 9 and 10, I frequently make idealizations of this sort.

More interesting are the sort of idealizations discussed by Ellis (1979, pp. 1–3) in which the ideal theory constitutes a 'norm', departures from which are to be *subsequently* explained. This is an important sort of idealization and one I resort to frequently. I shall call it a *first-approximation idealization*. For instance, one of the difficulties with a theory of normative logic is the way in which what is rational may depend on one's intelligence. Something which might be a failure of rationality for one person may merely be due to lack of intelligence for another. The way I handle this problem is to consider what is rational for a logically omniscient person, that is, someone like us except that he or she can survey all logical connections at a glance. I call that absolute rationality. So I am making the first-approximation idealization that rationality is absolute rationality.

V   LIMITATIONS OF SCOPE

One obvious way in which this enquiry is limited in its scope is that I fail to discuss things I might have discussed. For instance, apart from a few remarks in the next chapter, I do not discuss conditionals. Nor do I discuss implication and entailment except in barbarous stipulated senses.[10] Again I do not consider vague beliefs. Such limitations of scope cause no confusion. But there are three other limitations which I shall make explicit lest they do confuse. The first concerns my reliance in several places on an object-language/meta-language distinction for beliefs. For instance, I shall treat a person's judgements of rationality as themselves part of a meta-system separate from the person's system of (first-order) beliefs. I then ignore any changes to the judgements of rationality. In making a sharp distinction between system and meta-system I provide what I hope is merely an *expository* idealization. In ignoring the meta-system, I limit the scope of my enquiry, again chiefly for purposes of exposition.

A second limitation to the scope of my enquiry is that I concentrate on the rationality of changes to systems of beliefs, rather than the rationality of inference-making. Now since inference-makings are changes to systems of beliefs the distinction here may not be immediately obvious. To illustrate the distinction consider Mr Cigol who is certain that:

(1)   All animals with hearts have kidneys.
(2)   All animals with kidneys have arteries.
(3)   All animals with arteries have hearts.

Then we may suppose that Mr Cigol is in a position rationally to make an inference whose π-premisses are (2) and (3) and whose π-conclusion is:

(4)   All animals with kidneys have hearts.

In fact Mr Cigol does come to be certain that (4) but *his* reason is his certainty that (1). So he has come to believe the right thing for the wrong reason. Now the change to his system of beliefs, qua change, will satisfy all the requirements of rationality. Otherwise he was not even in a position rationally to infer (4) from (2) and (3). Yet his inference was irrational. In this work I shall judge inference-makings only as changes to doxastic systems. I do so because the extra requirement that the reasoner be making the inference for the right reason is one that I find hard to discuss. For I do not know what constitutes Mr Cigol's inferring (4) from (1) rather than from (2) and (3). I treat this as a limitation of scope. But it could also be treated as a first-approximation idealization. We could, as a first approximation, ignore the like of Mr Cigol and simply say an inference-making is rational if the corresponding change to the system of beliefs is rational.

The third limitation concerns rational predicaments. Does it ever happen that what is required for *rationality* is impossible for that person? Even more serious, does it ever happen that it is both irrational not to undergo some change to one's beliefs and irrational to undergo it? The Kantian dictum that 'ought' implies 'can' would suggest not. Yet I have argued elsewhere (Forrest 1985) that those awkward situations, which I call rational predicaments, can arise. However, while I think that judgements of rationality do express beliefs, their importance and interest derives in part from their use as appraisals, justification and, to some extent, guidance. And those uses are frustrated if what is required for rationality is not possible. Hence it is a proper limitation of scope to concentrate on what is of interest in judgements of rationality, and so to ignore rational predicaments, which in any case I believe to be rare. Since I am considering a logically omniscient person this amounts, I think, merely to the assumption that any change it is irrational not to perform must be rational.

2

Doxastic Systems

When you acquire a new belief you undergo a change *of* belief, but no belief of yours changes. What changes is a *system* of beliefs. So the subject-matter of my enquiry are changes to systems of beliefs. Furthermore, as I shall argue, beliefs admit of *degrees*. So to avoid suggesting degreelessness I shall not talk about systems of *beliefs*, but rather *doxastic systems*, by which I mean systems of degrees of beliefs. In this chapter I consider doxastic systems and their representation, in a purely *descriptive*, that is non-normative, fashion. The normative theory begins in the next chapter.

I DEGREES OF BELIEF

Do beliefs really have *degrees*? Would it not sound artificial, to put it mildly, to say 'I have a degree of belief 0.99 that God exists, but only a degree of belief 0.71 that Satan exists'? And is not there something badly wrong about saying 'I have a degree of belief 0.01 that dinosaurs are extant'? where this degree of 'belief' being near zero indicates *disbelief*?

These are genuine worries, not to be dismissed simply out of respect for the slick mathematical look of theories couched in terms of numerical degrees of belief. But these worries can be removed, or, at least, alleviated. I begin by considering comparisons of *confidence*. I believe that the next egg I boil for ten minutes will be hard. And I believe that in ten years' time I shall still be alive. But I am more confident of the former than the latter. Thus some of our beliefs are held with greater *confidence* than others. Nor need we rely on introspection here. Behaviour can indicate comparative confidence.

Not only do we have comparisons of order, we have judgements of equal confidence. I have the same confidence that the next coin I toss will land heads as I have that it will land tails. Sometimes, then, beliefs are *comparable* with respect to the confidence with which they are held. But I do not assume that any two beliefs are comparable. Perhaps my belief in the existence of God is neither greater nor equal nor less in degree of confidence than my belief in the existence of electrons. Nor shall I assume that comparisons of confidence are always transitive.[1] It may happen, perhaps even rationally, that someone is more confident of p than of q, more confident of q than of r, but more confident of r than of p.

I explicate disbelief not as the mere failure to believe (nor as belief in the negation), but as a positive rejection of belief. And such a rejection is sometimes more confident than at other times. Again, there can be comparisons among those propositions which are neither believed nor disbelieved, but to which I am agnostic.[2] Thus I neither believe nor disbelieve in the existence of life elsewhere in the galaxy, but I am more inclined towards belief than towards disbelief.

When I talk of degrees of belief I am not suggesting that beliefs come with an intrinsic numerical strength. Rather I am merely considering attitudes of belief, agnosticism and disbelief together with the comparisons already mentioned and other relevant structures. The resulting system I call a *doxastic system*. More precisely, I say that of two attitudes of belief the more confident has the higher degree, of two attitudes of disbelief the less confident has the higher degree, and of two attitudes of agnosticism the one tending more to belief has the higher degree. And, of course, I say that any attitude of belief has higher degree than any attitude of agnosticism which, in turn, has higher degree than any attitude of disbelief.

The word 'belief' in 'degree of belief' is a term of art. For degrees of belief include attitudes of agnosticism and disbelief.

Among other structures which a doxastic system has, some beliefs are singled out as being *certain*. These are the beliefs we are *sure* of. Now there is a possible ambiguity here. Someone might mean by certainty a degree of belief than which no greater is possible. Speaking for myself, I find no evidence for my having maximally *possible* confidence. So I shall ignore this feature, if it is one, of some doxastic systems. Again, in philosophical circles, certainty was often considered to entail unrevisability. That is not how I shall use the term. By *certainty* I mean *full* belief. I take the paradigms of *full* belief to be those beliefs which are the natural, pre-critical, outcome of normal perception. Thus I am certain I have two hands, even though I am even more confident that I have two hands or I am hallucinating. This is the sense of certainty that I am interested in. And there is nothing sophisticated about it. Sophistication arises when we come to see that rationality often requires a less than full belief, a belief compatible with significant doubt.

Not only may I believe with certainty, I may disbelieve, that is reject belief, with certainty. In that case I say that I am *contracertain*.

There are a couple of further structures a system of degrees of belief might have. One is a *nextness* relation. It might happen that while the degree of belief in p is less than that in q there *could* be no degree of belief between p and q. Like the maximally *possible* degrees of belief this would involve a modality. Again I have no evidence for such a structure. So I shall ignore it. More plausible is a vague dyadic relation of nearness, or a precise triadic relation of the degree of belief in p being nearer to that in q than that in r.

A person's doxastic system, then, is specified not just by what the person believes, disbelieves or is agnostic about, but also the additional structure such as certainty, contracertainty, the comparisons of degrees of belief, equality of degree of belief, and a vague nearness relation.

Any doxastic system which actually belongs to a human being would have to be *finite*. So the propositions occurring in it would not form a logically closed system. But we may need to consider infinite doxastic systems. Indeed it is often convenient to consider doxastic systems which contain attitudes to all the propositions in some language. In that case we may have logical closure.

Partly to illustrate some of the distinctions I have made, and partly to avoid confusion, I shall consider *doubt* and *non-belief*. There are three ways in which X could be said to doubt that p:

(1) X disbelieves p (as in doubting Thomas).
(2) X is agnostic about p.
(3) X believes that p but without certainty.

Likewise it is important to distinguish three cases of non-believing:

(1) X does not believe that p, because X disbelieves that p.
(2) X does not believe that p, because X is agnostic about p.
(3) X does not believe that p, because X has no attitude to p whatever. (Perhaps X has never considered p.)

Finally, not only may we sometimes compare the degrees of belief of a given person at a given time, but we may also sometimes compare the degrees of belief of a given person at different times, especially where the proposition is the same.[3] Thus the discovery of gravity waves increased my confidence that General Relativity is at least approximately correct.

II CONDITIONAL BELIEFS

As well as unconditional doxastic attitudes such as belief and disbelief there may be *conditional* ones. And I include these in a person's doxastic system. By a (degree of) belief in p conditional on q, I mean the (degree of) belief I have in p within the supposition of certainty that q. This need not be the (degree of) belief I would in fact have if I were to come to be certain that q. It reflects a thought-experiment rather than a counterfactual.

   Just as a degree of belief can manifest itself in willingness to take risks, or make wagers, so a *conditional* degree of belief can manifest itself in a willingness to take conditional risks or make conditional wagers. Here a wager on p conditional on q is a wager on p which becomes void unless q. So, for instance, a wager that a given horse will win a race would be conditional on that horse running if the withdrawal of the horse made the wager void. Philosophers of positivist or behaviourist inclination like F. P. Ramsey (1931, pp. 166–84) tried to use the disposition to wager, or more generally take risks, as an analysis of having degrees of belief. Hence they found conditional degrees of belief quite unproblematic. They would be dispositions to take conditional risks. But I do not grant that analysis. Nonetheless I consider the link between conditional degrees of belief and conditional risk-taking to be important. For the fact that they have behavioural manifestations helps to remove the suspicion that conditional beliefs are philosophers' myths. Another way in which conditional beliefs can be rendered familiar is by exhibiting the connection between them and indicative conditionals. It is widely claimed (see Adams 1965) that the degree of assertibility of an indicative conditional equals the subjective conditional probability. Now I dislike the phrase 'subjective probability', because I find the subjective/objective distinction confusing. But, as I understand it, a subjective probability is a numerical (representation of a) degree of belief. So the widespread claim is just that our willingness to assert (or accept) an indicative conditional 'If p then q' depends on the degree of confidence we have in q conditional on p. Provided we take 'even if' as merely a stylistic variant of 'if',[4] this seems a plausible enough hypothesis. And on this hypothesis to say 'If p then q' is to provide a linguistic *sign* of a (high enough degree of) belief in q conditional on p. This makes it plausible that conditional beliefs are in no way philosophers' myths; people actually do have them.

I conclude this section with a substantive claim:

The Supposition Postulate

If belief in p and belief in p conditional on q both occur in a doxastic system, then either they are equal or one is greater than the other. (So they are never non-comparable.)

Without this postulate I would have trouble when it came to the representation of doxastic systems considered in chapter 4. The evidence for it is simply our willingness to make the comparison mentioned.

III THE REPRESENTATION OF DOXASTIC SYSTEMS

A theory of degrees of belief is facilitated by representing them numerically. To do so we assign a number fom 0 to 1 to each doxastic attitude in the system. If the attitude is to proposition p, and we write the representing number as $d(p)$, then d is a credence function in Carnap's sense (1968 p. 260). Again if the attitude is to p but is conditional on q then the representing number is written as $d(p/q)$. The propositions (and pairs of them) occurring in the system then constitute the *domain* of d, written as $Dom(d)$. For a representation I require that if one degree of belief is greater than or equal to another, then the number representing the first is greater than that representing the second. I also require that certainty be represented by 1, belief without certainty by a number less than 1 but greater than ½, disbelief without contracertainty by a number less than ½ but greater than 0 and contracertainty by 0. Finally I require any attitude of agnosticism to be represented by a number less than those representing any attitudes of belief, but greater than those representing any attitudes of disbelief.

The cost of the representation is that *some* of the rich structure of doxastic systems may be lost. That is, we may not be able to retrieve all the information there is about the doxastic system from its representation. Now the typical constraint provided by a normative theory will be one which shows some changes to be irrational. Because I consider the credence functions rather than the doxastic systems themselves, I shall say the change of credence functions is irrational if none of the changes it represents are rational. As a consequence, among the changes not excluded by the principles some may still be irrational ones. For instance, some information about nearness could be lost in the representation. As a result a change to doxastic systems that irrationally altered the vague nearness relations might, in spite of that, be permitted by my theory. Consequently I treat my theory as a first-approximation idealization: if a change to a doxastic system is irrational, but it is not excluded by my theory, then we require an explanation of that deviance, in terms of the loss of information in the representation.

Among information lost in the representation we have, in addition to nearness, some comparisons. For I have not required that if the degree of belief in p is greater than that in q then $d(p)$ is greater than $d(q)$. I permit $d(p)$ to equal $d(q)$. One reason why I permit this loss of information is the already-mentioned possibility of failure of transitivity. If the degree of belief in p is greater than that in q which is greater than that in r which in turn is greater than that in p, then we are forced to represent these three degrees of belief by the same number. Another reason is that I believe there are comparisons among degrees of certainty, and among degrees of contracertainty. Yet I represent certainty by 1 and contracertainty by 0, thus obliterating those comparisons.

If any two degrees of belief in the system are taken to be comparable (i.e. one is greater than or equal to the other) then this is all the loss of information which need occur. But where we have non-comparability we can only infer from the fact that $d(p)$ is greater than $d(q)$ that *either* the degree of belief in p is greater than that in q *or* they are non-comparable. This is yet another loss of information.

However, we may take some comfort from one of the results of section VI (namely thesis 2.6.1). This shows that we can find special representations such that if the degree of belief in p is greater than that in q then $d(p)$ is greater than $d(q)$ unless we have one of the situations indicated previously. That is, unless we are comparing two attitudes of certainty, two attitudes of contracertainty or there is a failure of transitivity. In this connection it should be noted that, as I show in thesis 2.6.2, we do not have uniqueness even for these special representations. To get even an approximation to uniqueness we must bring in normative considerations (as in chapter 4).

IV WHY NOT IGNORE DEGREES OF BELIEF?

We have a richly structured doxastic system. But, I think, what really matters is what *beliefs* we have, and, to a lesser extent, which are certain. So why bother with degrees of belief and their numerical representations? Why not investigate normative logic by concentrating on systems of *beliefs*, which could conveniently be represented by sets of propositions?

My answer is that to do so would be *either* unduly to restrict our attention to beliefs we are certain of, *or*, ludicrously, to consider only inferences with a single premiss. For consider an inference from p and q to r. Typically the lack of confidence in p and that in q should combine to produce a lack of confidence in r. And typically the confidence in r will be less than that either in p or in q. For example, if the degree of belief in p is represented by ¾, and that in q by ¾, that in r might be represented by a number as low as ½. So we have no guarantee that the degree of belief in r will amount to *belief*. To investigate when it does and when it does not, we need to consider degrees of belief. And that, in turn, is facilitated by a theory of credence functions. The results we eventually obtain will then put constraints on the beliefs. Thus if we are constrained, on pain of irrationality, to have $d(p) \leqslant \frac{1}{2}$, then we should not believe p. Again if we are constrained to have $d(p) < 1$, then we should not be certain of p. Conversely, if we are constrained to have $d(p) = 1$, we should be certain of p. Moreover if we are constrained to have $d(p) \geqslant d(q)$, then we should not believe q if we disbelieve p.

V CREDENCE FUNCTIONS*

I represent doxastic systems by means of credence functions.[5] A credence function, d, is an assignment of real numbers[6] from 0 to 1 to various propositions and pairs of propositions, which constitute its *domain*, *Dom*(d). Throughout this work I use the letters d and e with suitable subscripts and superscripts (including *, − , 0, +) for credence functions. And I use d both for the monadic $d(\ )$ and the dyadic $d(/)$.

If d and e differ only in that e assigns values to some propositions which d does not assign values to, then I say d is a *restriction* of e, or equivalently, e is an *extension* of d. I write it thus: $d\mathcal{R}e$. I allow the degenerate case: $d\mathcal{R}d$. Clearly, if d represents S, then any restriction of d represents a subsystem of S, where a subsystem of S consists of a subset of the propositions occurring in S together with the structure inherited from S.

For a given set of propositions P in the domain of a credence function e there will be a unique credence function which has P for its domain and has the same values as e for propositions in P. I call this the restriction of e to P and I write it: $e\|P$.

My next piece of notation concerns the *meet* of two credence functions d and e. Its domain is $\{p\,|\,d(p) = e(p)\}$ and it assigns $d(p)$ to all p in this set. I write it: $d\wedge e$.

Sometimes we could have $d(p) = e(p)$ for no p. In that case there would strictly speaking be no meet. It is convenient to introduce the 'empty function' ϕ whose domain is the empty set. Then we may say that if $d(p) = e(p)$ for no p, $d\wedge e = \phi$.

We could define restrictions in terms of meet. For we have the obvious result:

Thesis 2.5.1

$d\mathcal{R}e$ if and only if $d = d\wedge e$.

The first requirement for a credence function d to represent the doxastic system S is:

CFO   The domain of d consists of all the propositions to which there is an attitude in S and all the pairs $<p,q>$ such that there is an attitude to p conditional on q.

I state the other five requirements first for the special case where we ignore conditional degrees of belief. We have:

CF1   If the degree of belief in p equals that in q, then $d(p) = d(q)$.
CF2   If the degree of belief in p is greater than that in q, then $d(p) \geqslant d(q)$.

CF3 $d(p) = 1$ if and only if the attitude to p is one of certainty. Likewise $d(p) = 0$ if and only if the attitude to p is one of contracertainty.

CF4 If p is believed, then $d(p) > \frac{1}{2}$. Likewise if p is disbelieved then $d(p) < \frac{1}{2}$.

CF5 If p is believed and the attitude to q is one of agnosticism, then not only do we have $d(p) \geqslant d(q)$ in accordance with CF2, but we also have $d(p) > d(q)$. Likewise if p is disbelieved and the attitude to q is one of agnosticism then $d(p) < d(q)$.

CF1 to CF5 are extended to conditional degrees of belief in the obvious way. For example, we have CF1:

(1) If the degree of belief in p equals that in q then $d(p) = d(q)$.

(2) If the degree of belief in p conditional on r equals that in q then $d(p/r) = d(q)$.

(3) If the degree of belief in p conditional on r equals that in q conditional on s then $d(p/r) = d(q/s)$.

We may also consider a finite, or even infinite, number of doxastic systems S_1, S_2 etc. such that, sometimes at least, a degree of belief in one of the S_1, S_2 etc. is comparable to one in another of the S_1, S_2 etc. (They may be the systems of a person at different times.) In that case I say that S_1, S_2 etc. are *jointly represented* by d_1, d_2 etc. if each of the d_i represents each of the S_i *and*:

CF1* If the degree of belief in p (in S_i) equals that in q (in S_j) then $d_i(p) = d_j(q)$; *and*

CF2* If the degree of belief in p (in S_i) is greater than that in q (in S_j) then $d_i(p) \geqslant d_j(q)$.

Once again these requirements are to be extended to cover conditional beliefs.

VI TWO REPRESENTATION THEOREMS*

The existence of infinitely many numerical representations for any given doxastic system is trivial. For given α, β, such that $0 < \alpha < \frac{1}{2} < \beta < 1$, d could assign 0 to contracertainty, α to disbelief

without contracertainty, ½ to agnosticism, β to belief without certainty
and 1 to certainty. However, I want there to be rather special
representations which do not wantonly obliterate information due to
the comparisons. To make this more precise I need a definition. If
the degree of belief in p is greater than that in q, I say that the
comparison is *non-representable* if:

(1) Both p and q are believed with certainty;
(2) Both p and q are believed with contracertainty; or
(3) There is some finite collection of degrees of belief, in $r_1, \ldots,$
     r_n where p is r_1 and q is r_n, but such that the degree of belief
     in r_{i+1} is at least as great as that in r_i, for $i = 1 \ldots (n-1)$.

It is easy to check that, for any representation d, if the degree of
belief in p is greater than that in q but the comparison is non-
representable, in my stipulated sense, then $d(p) = d(q)$. What I shall
show is that except for cases of non-representable comparisons we
can always require $d(p) > d(q)$.

Thesis 2.6.1

Any finite or countably infinite doxastic system has a numerical
representation d, such that for any propositions p and q, if there
is a degree of belief in p greater than that in q then $d(p) > d(q)$,
unless the comparison is non-representable in the sense I
stipulated.

Proof I begin by defining a transitive relation of comparison for the
doxastic system. I say that the degree of belief in p is τ-greater than
or τ-equal to that in q if it is either greater than or equal, or there
are propositions $r_1, \ldots, r_n$, for which p is r_1 and q is r_n, such that,
for all $i = 1 \ldots (n-1)$, there is a degree of belief in r_i greater than
or equal to that in r_{i+1}. Then if the degree of belief in p is τ-greater
than or τ-equal to that in q but not vice versa, I say it is τ-greater
than. Otherwise I say they are τ-equal. I shall represent the subsystem
B, consisting of beliefs without certainty, by numbers less than 1 but
greater than ¾, as follows: B contains at most a countable infinity
of attitudes. So let these be to the propositions P_1, P_2 etc. For each
P_i we select a corresponding real number α_i such that:[7]

(1)   The sum of all the α_i is less than ¼; and

(2)   No two subsets of $\{\alpha_1, \alpha_2 \ldots\}$ have the same sum.

Then let $d(p)$ be ¾ plus the sum of all those α_i such that the degree of belief in p is τ-greater than or τ-equal to the degree of belief in the corresponding P_i.

It is easy to check that if the degree of belief without certainty in p is greater than that in q then $d(p) > d(q)$ unless the comparison is non-representable. In a similar fashion I represent the subsystem of attitudes of agnosticism by numbers from ¼ to ¾, and the subsystem of degrees of disbelief without contracertainty by numbers greater than 0 but less than ¼. This specifies the required representation.

Next we have:

Thesis 2.6.2

If S is a doxastic system with finitely many attitudes in it, and p is a proposition to which the attitude is neither certainty nor contracertainty, then there are infinitely many representations of S which differ only in the value they assign to the degree of belief in p, and to those degrees of belief τ-equal to p.

Proof There is a representation d as in thesis 2.6.1. Let max $\{d(q) \mid$ the degree of belief in q is τ-less than that in $p\} = M(p)$. Let min $\{d(q) \mid$ the degree of belief in q is τ-greater than that in $p\} = m(p)$. Since S is finite, $m(p) < d(p) < M(p)$. So we may consider the infinitely many functions, e, obtained by allowing $e(p)$ to take the values between m and M. Of these, infinitely many will be compatible with CF3 and CF4. These will be representations.

It is easy to check that thesis 2.6.1 and 2.6.2 can be extended to cover the joint representation of up to countably many doxastic systems.

3

The Framework for
a Dynamics of Belief

The previous chapter was concerned merely with the description of doxastic systems. In this chapter I discuss the kinds of change doxastic systems undergo, and I consider those normative principles which are not concerned merely with a single kind of change. Notable among these are the principles concerning the composition of simpler changes into more complicated ones and the decomposition of more complicated changes into simpler ones.

I KINDS OF DOXASTIC CHANGE

We may classify changes to doxastic systems in two ways. First we may distinguish *internal* from *external* changes. By an *external change* I mean one which arises in some way other than by reasoning. Those due to reasoning I call *internal changes*. Some examples of external changes are deletions of beliefs due to physical damage to the brain, and total replacement of one system by a different one as a result of some fanciful science-fiction operation of brain re-programming. More prosaically, changes that are the immediate result of perception or introspection are external. External changes are not even candidates for judgements as rational or irrational, although perception can be appraised in other ways, for instance as reliable or unreliable. To call changes due to perception *external* and so not subject to judgement as rational or irrational, is not to advocate a totally passive attitude towards perception. We need not pretend to be *tabulae rasae*. For whether or not we *maintain* a system initially caused by an external change *is* a matter for judgement as rational or irrational. Unless I say to the contrary all changes are to be assumed internal.

Changes may also be classified in terms of the change to the set of propositions occurring in the system (i.e. to the domains of the credence functions). First, we have *contractions*.[1] A contraction is a change in which various propositions just cease to occur in the system.[2] (So if the change is represented by d^-/d^+ then $d^+ \subset d^-$). Spontaneous, and hence external, contractions are fairly common. Most of the trivia I believed a year ago I no longer believe. And that is not because I have come to disbelieve them. I no longer have any doxastic attitude towards them. But I am concerned with internal changes. So what would an internal contraction be? It would be a suspension of judgement in the strictest sense. For if we suspend judgement, strictly speaking, we suspend even the judgement of coming to have an *agnostic* attitude, that is one between belief and disbelief: it is as if we had never entertained the proposition.

The inverse of a contraction is an *expansion*. In an expansion no old degrees of belief are changed but new ones are acquired. (So $d^- \subset d^+$.)

The third basic kind of change is an *adjustment*. In an adjustment the set of propositions occurring in the system is unchanged. An adjustment, then, is represented by a pair of credence functions d^-/d^+ with the same domain.

There are more complicated kinds of change. We can consider, for instance, a change in which not only are new propositions considered (as in an expansion) but some of the attitudes to old ones are altered. We might call it an adjustment-cum-expansion. If a complex change such as an adjustment-cum-expansion is undergone, is it in fact the result of simpler changes, such as an adjustment followed by an expansion? That is an empirical question which I am not able to answer. But there are two related questions which I shall discuss. The first is whether the overall change could have been obtained as a result of simpler changes. The answer is that every change could be obtained as a result of a contraction followed by an expansion.[3] The second question is the more important for a normative theory. It is whether every rational complex change could be obtained as the result of a sequence of simpler rational changes. I discuss this normative question in section V.

I now illustrate the various kinds of change by means of an example. Harry is walking along Broadway, one evening, when a woman calls out, 'Beware of dangerous animals!' He considers but rejects that warning, which consideration results in his having an explicit high degree of belief that:

(1)   There are no dangerous animals on Broadway.

However he continues to muse on the theme of dangerous animals and comes to have a high degree of belief that:

(2)   Hyaenas are dangerous animals.

So he then makes an inference and comes to have a fairly high degree of belief in a proposition not hitherto considered:

(3)   There are no hyaenas on Broadway.

Presently he meets a hyaena. Under the influence of various olfactory, auditory and visual sensations he comes to be certain of:

(4)   There are hyaenas on Broadway.

and contracertain of (3). This change is an external one and not one of the internal ones being considered. But, as a consequence, Harry's system of degrees of belief requires further change. For he is certain that (4), while having high degrees of belief in (1) and (2); yet (1), (2) and (4) form an inconsistent triad. He adjusts by lowering his degree of belief in (1) to something near zero, thus restoring equilibrium. Next day he is thoroughly confused about the whole episode, recalls that he was intoxicated, and suspends judgement on (1) and (4). So he has made a contraction.

II   DOXASTIC CONSISTENCY

Some logical defects which a system may have are distinguished from others as:

(1)   Always capable of removal without irrationality; and
(2)   Independent of context.

These I call *doxastic inconsistencies*. When I say they are independent of context I mean that qualitatively identical defects (i.e. involving attitudes of the same type to propositions of the same type) in any other context constitute a defect.

By definition, doxastic inconsistency consists of defects which could always be removed without irrationality. So, if, as I shall argue in chapter 9, there are further sources of logical disvalue which cannot all be removed, then at least some of them will not amount to doxastic inconsistency. This is an important point, I think. For we are tempted to assume that because it is rational to maintain a system it must be free of all sources of logical disvalue. But that need not be the case. Sometimes we may just have to live with logical disvalue. For example, suppose I have an intuition that everything has an explanation, but it clashes with other intuitions. So I reject it. I might come to decide it was intrinsically defective as an intuition, being based, say, on wishful thinking. But that could well be over-reaction. A more sober assessment of the situation would be that the intuition is intrinsically in perfectly good order and that its non-acceptance is indeed a defect, which gives the system some logical disvalue. However, accepting it would give the system greater disvalue. It is, I submit, quite rational to maintain a system which violates the intuition without necessarily saying the intuition itself was intrinsically defective. Thus intuitions which are not accepted can still be alive and kicking, waiting to re-assert themselves in different circumstances.

Doxastic inconsistency, then, is not the only defect a system might have, but it plays a central role in normative logic. I shall discuss the principles governing doxastic consistency in the next chapter. Here it suffices to give some obvious examples. Either always or for the most part to believe p and also to believe $\sim p$ is, though possible, doxastically inconsistent.[4] Likewise, to be certain that q, certain that p conditional on q and to have a degree of belief less than certainty that p is to be doxastically inconsistent. Again to be certain that p, certain that q and to have a degree of belief less than certainty that $p\&q$ is to be doxastically inconsistent.

III   THE HOMEOSTATIC MODEL AND ITS VARIANTS

The logical disvalues which are not context relative and which may always be removed occupy, I suggest, a salient position in a theory of the dynamics of beliefs. And I have defined doxastic consistency as the absence of all sources of such disvalues. This suggests a simple *model* for rational changes. On this model a doxastic system is repeatedly disturbed away from doxastic consistency by external factors, such as perception, and doxastic consistency is repeatedly restored. Thus in the episode of Harry and the hyaena, Harry is certain there are no hyaenas on Broadway, but he then observes a hyaena and comes to be certain there is a hyaena on Broadway. This external change results in doxastic inconsistency between his certainty that there are no dangerous animals on Broadway, his certainty that hyaenas are dangerous animals, and his certainty that there is a hyaena on Broadway. He removes this doxastic inconsistency by coming to be nearly contracertain that there are no dangerous animals on Broadway. This is a consistency-restoring adjustment in response to a perturbation away from doxastic consistency.

Another possible response to loss of doxastic consistency is a contraction. We might be so bemused by the external influence, such as perception, that 'we don't know what to think'. In that case we contract. For example, suppose Mr Monotone had an experience which initially caused him to believe a wall was decorated with uniformly red, uniformly green round squares. Even a capacity to hallucinate such things might seem incredible to Mr Monotone. Perhaps he would not know what to think, and would simply 'forget about' the whole experience, or, more precisely, suspend judgement about it. In that case he would contract his system, excising the ill-fitting belief he had just acquired.

Internal expansions do not fit into this simple homeostatic model. Suppose I make an inference, and, as is often the case with inferences, suppose I previously had no attitude at all towards the π-conclusion. So the inference is an expansion. This change will not be a consistency-restoring response to a disturbance from consistency. But we could require it to *preserve* doxastic consistency. In this way we obtain a more complicated homeostatic model for rational doxastic change, with consistency-restoring adjustments (or contractions) and consistency-preserving expansions.

One advantage of this model, I submit, is that it enables us to avoid automatically assuming that we shall have a single theory for all inference-makings. For an inference-making could either be an adjustment (if I already have an attitude towards the π-conclusion) or an expansion (if I do not). But if adjustments typically *restore* and expansions typically *preserve* consistency we should not expect the same rules to apply in the two cases.

The other advantage of this model is that it raises a number of questions of which the following will be discussed in this chapter:

(1) Is the restoration of consistency a sufficient condition for an adjustment to be rational?
(2) Is the preservation of consistency a sufficient condition for an expansion to be rational?
(3) Is it ever rational to expand *before* consistency has been restored?
(4) When should consistency be restored by contraction, and when by adjustment?

Of these questions I shall consider (1) and (2) in this section. The conditions are not sufficient. That the restoration of consistency is not sufficient for the rationality of an adjustment is demonstrated by considering those cases where the immediate effect of perception is itself an *external* adjustment from a δ-consistent to a δ-inconsistent system. Then completely undoing this change and reverting back to the previous state would be an adjustment. If it were always rational to make this reverse adjustment as an *internal* change, then we could always rationally *ignore* those cases of perception whose immediate effect is the destruction of δ-consistency. But such ignoring of perception when it is inconsistent with what is already believed would be dogmatism in the pejorative sense. I conclude that it is not always rational to make any adjustment whatever which restores consistency. Another argument for this conclusion is to consider an adjustment to one or two degrees of belief which suffices to restore consistency. Now consider another adjustment which, quite gratuitously, also results in a change to a thousand other degrees of belief. I submit it is not a rational change even though it may well restore consistency.

Likewise an expansion may preserve consistency without being rational. Consider someone with just the usual knowledge of lotteries, who thinks for the first time about the proposition that Mrs Goodluck will win the next lottery, and comes to believe it. I submit that this expansion is irrational. Yet it could well preserve consistency. For we may consider an otherwise identical person making such an expansion as a result of reading in a newspaper that Mrs Goodluck had won. In the latter case the subsequent system might have no rational defect. *A fortiori* it would be δ-consistent. Hence, it should also be δ-consistent in the qualitatively identical situation under consideration. I conclude, then, that some consistency-preserving expansions are irrational.

That the restoration or preservation of consistency is not sufficient for rationality suggests a need for extra principles governing the rationality of adjustments and expansions, which have to be grafted onto the homeostatic model. In chapters 5 to 8, I provide some such extra principles, based on intuitive judgements. And that is the most straightforward approach to the dynamics of doxastic systems. But the homeostatic model also suggests a more unified, if somewhat more speculative, approach. Instead of discovering extra principles directly governing changes to belief systems, we discover logical values or disvalues other than doxastic consistency and inconsistency. Then we may make *comparisons* of rationality. Applying a variant of the homeostatic model, we obtain the requirement that, for maximum rationality, adjustments and expansions should minimize total disvalue. This more comprehensive, but more speculative, variant of the homeostatic model will be the inspiration for chapters 9 and 10, where I provide a theory of comparative rationality.

Notice that there need be no conflict between the two models. They inspire different research programmes, one for rationality the other for comparisons of rationality, but the results should, and I think will, be compatible.

IV   EXPANSIONS FROM INCONSISTENT SYSTEMS

The third question I listed in the previous section is whether it is ever rational to expand before restoring δ-consistency to a δ-inconsistent system (by means of a contraction or an adjustment). Notice that the definition of δ-inconsistency is such that it is irrational to delay restoring δ-consistency indefinitely. But I do not intend that, simply by definition, it will be irrational to postpone the restoration of δ-consistency for a while. Nonetheless, it is an interesting conjecture that we should never delay the restoration of δ-consistency, while undergoing expansions. So I consider:

The Primacy of Consistency-restoration Conjecture

It is conjectured that it is never rational to expand from a δ-inconsistent system.

Counter-argument Consider one Dr Trilobite, who is engaged on research into Palaeozoic global catastrophes and mass extinctions. He is certain of all four members of the inconsistent tetrad:

P_1: No non-physical item interacts with anything physical.
P_2: No mind is physical.
P_3: All bodies are physical.
P_4: Some minds interact with some bodies.

My judgement is that since the mind/body problem is in some sense *irrelevant* to Palaeozoic global catastrophes, it is not irrational for him to continue expanding, acquiring new propositions about extinction, before he sets about removing the doxastic inconsistency due to certainty in all four of P_1 to P_4. That can wait until Saturday afternoon. To this it may be objected that I should be considering what is rational for a *logically omniscient* person, and such a person could either simultaneously expand and restore δ-consistency, or restore δ-consistency so quickly as not to hold up his or her research. But that is to misunderstand the nature of the logical omniscience idealization. All I suppose is that a logically omniscient person can survey all possibilities and logical connections; in other respects the logically omniscient person is just like us. Now, in the case I describe, Dr Trilobite could well be aware of the doxastic inconsistency. So whether or not he is logically omniscient does not affect the issue.

However, I submit that we do need some principle to prohibit inferences in cases where there is some *relevant* doxastic inconsistency. For my particular judgements about such expansions are that they are irrational. Furthermore if we did not prohibit expansions from systems with relevant δ-inconsistencies we would endorse not merely the perpetuation but also the multiplication of δ-inconsistencies. For instance Dr Trilobite might infer from P_1, P_3 and P_4 that some minds are physical, thus exacerbating the inconsistency.

I explicate the requirement of irrelevance by saying that the inconsistency is irrelevant if an adjustment which eliminates it could have been made first without affecting the outcome of the expansion. In terms of the representing credence functions this amounts to:

The Principle of Relevant Adjustment

If an expansion represented by d^-/d^+ is rational even though the system represented by d^- is δ-inconsistent, then there must be a rational adjustment represented by d^-/d^*, and a rational expansion represented by d^*/d^+, such that d^* is δ-consistent.[5]

I concentrate on consistency-restoring adjustments rather than contractions because the requirement of irrelevance would be too weak otherwise. For instance, Dr Trilobite might contract away from P_1 and then expand to $\sim P_1$, or contract away from P_2 and then expand to $\sim P_2$, and so on, thus licensing a deduction from any three of P_1, P_2, P_3, or P_4 to the negation of the fourth. And that is, I submit, too weak a requirement.

V   COMPOSITION AND DECOMPOSITION

The *composite* of two or more doxastic changes is a single change which would have had the same initial and final doxastic states. Conversely a change is said to be *decomposed* into two or more changes if it is the composite of them.[6] In this section I am primarily concerned with the extent to which composition and decomposition preserve rationality. That is, if the individual changes are rational, would the composite have been? And which, if any, decompositions of a rational change would have given us two or more rational changes? Notice that, for the case of composition, I am not assessing a process made out of two or more rational changes. I take it to be obvious that such a *process* is rational.[7] What I am assessing is whether a single change with the same initial and final states as this process is rational. And that is by no means obvious. Indeed, but for the idealization of logical omniscience it would be incorrect. For consider a sequence of many adjustments to only a few attitudes at a time whose overall effect is an adjustment to many attitudes. Given only limited intelligence it might well be judged irrational to collapse the whole process to a single adjustment, even though each adjustment and hence the process is rational. However, I do make the logical omniscience idealization and I propose:

The Composition Principle

The composite of two rational doxastic changes would itself be a rational change.

Before I justify the Composition Principle I shall state the Decomposition Principle. For the two are justified together. I begin with a definition. Given any doxastic change we may decompose it into a contraction and/or an adjustment and/or an expansion, as follows.[8] First, if necessary, we contract away from any propositions occurring in the system before but not after the system. Then, if necessary, we adjust the subsystem to which belong the propositions occurring both before and after. Finally, if necessary, we expand, incorporating all the propositions occurring after but not before the change.[9] I call this the *canonical decomposition*. And I propose:

The Decomposition Principle

The parts of the canonical decomposition of a rational doxastic change are themselves rational.

The most straightforward way of justifying a general principle by means of particular judgements is to rely on a combination of:

(1) Its elegance or simplicity.
(2) The lack of particular counter-examples.
(3) A profusion of instances of it, which are intuitively firm particular judgements.

The Composition and Decomposition Principles satisfy (1) and (2) (given logical omniscience). But (3) is tricky. It is tricky because I think we often cannot discern whether what seems to be a single change really is a single change and not a process made up of two or more changes performed rapidly. For instance, often when we reconstruct arguments – our own or others' – we speculate that extra steps should be interpolated. Therefore I propose a less direct justification for the Composition and Decomposition Principles. In place of (3) I rely on:

(4) Being a nonredundant member of a set of principles which jointly systematize particular judgements.

In this case, the Composition and Decomposition Principles, taken together, provide a striking result. Consider a sequence of a contraction and/or adjustment and/or expansion, but not in that order, which are individually rational. Then composing them and decomposing them in the canonical order (contraction, adjustment, expansion) still gives us rational changes. Consider the case where you expand from a δ-inconsistent system. I claim (see the next section) that δ-consistency may always be rationally restored by an adjustment. First compose the expansion and the consistency-restoring adjustment. Then decompose it into an adjustment and an expansion. By the Composition and Decomposition Principles the adjustment prior to the expansion and the expansion from the now δ-consistent system should both be rational. And that implies the Principle of Relevant Adjustment, and is supported by the same particular judgements as that principle. Again consider someone who adjusts or expands first and then contracts. For these to be rational changes it must have also been rational to have contracted first. And that is intuitively correct. Otherwise the rationality of the adjustments or expansion would seem to depend on having various doxastic attitudes which are subsequently excised. And, intuitively, if you could have predicted that you would be in a position subsequently to excise them, then you should not have relied on them earlier. But a logically omniscient person could have made that prediction. Hence, in this case too, the Composition and Decomposition Principles have systematized our intuitions. In addition, the special case of the Composition Principle for expansion is nonredundant in the theory of proportional syllogisms developed in chapter 8.

Taken together the Composition and Decomposition Principles show that the rationality of any doxastic change is determined by that of its components in the canonical decomposition. Hence we may concentrate on the rationality of contractions, adjustments and expansions, ignoring more complex changes. This is an important result. It would be equally important if we could further decompose changes. In particular, Levi, considering corpora of knowledge, considers that we may decompose what he calls *replacements* (analogues of adjustments) into a contraction followed by an expansion. Levi's argument (1980, p. 13) is that anything incompatible with a corpus of *knowledge* is to be rejected as impossible. So we cannot even consider $\sim h$ until we have contracted away from h. This argument depends critically on the way Levi is considering *knowledge*. Having even full belief, let alone a lesser degree of belief, is no grounds for dismissing alternatives as impossible. Hence it is no criticism of Levi that I reject the following Levi-inspired conjecture:

The Radical Decomposition Conjecture for Adjustments

Given an adjustment we may consider all the propositions to which the attitude changes. It is noted that the adjustment is the composite of a contraction away from all those propositions followed by an expansion back to them.[10] The conjecture is that the contraction and expansion would be rational if the adjustment is.

If this conjecture were correct then we need only consider contraction and expansion in a theory of doxastic change. But I am confident it is incorrect.

Counter-argument I have two criticisms of the conjecture. The first is that the contraction will often be far too drastic. The second, related criticism is that after the contraction there will sometimes be no reason for the subsequent expansion. To make these criticisms I consider an example. A theory T is supported by many observations $O_1, \ldots, O_n$. And a new piece of evidence E throws doubt (perhaps only to a very small degree) not only on T but on $O_1, \ldots, O_n$ as well. Acquiring this new piece of evidence is an external change which results in a δ-inconsistent system, with high degrees of belief in all of $T, O_1, \ldots, O_n$ and E.[11] There is a rational adjustment, I submit, which restores δ-consistency by lessening the degrees of belief in all of $T, O_1, \ldots, O_n$ a bit. (I am not claiming this is the only rational way of restoring δ-consistency). But if we decompose this adjustment into a contraction followed by an expansion, the contraction would excise any attitude to $T, O_1, \ldots, O_n$, and, no doubt, E as well. Firstly this is too drastic a response to the new evidence. For the adjustment might only have required the slightest degree of doubt in each of the $O_1, \ldots, O_n$. And, secondly, once the contraction has been made, what reason have we to expand back to a high degree of belief in T and $O_1, \ldots, O_n$? Usually the memory of the observations. But, I submit, the adjustment would be rational even if we had forgotten why we had the high degree of belief in $O_1, \ldots, O_n$. And in that case the subsequent expansion would be irrational.

We cannot, then, avoid a detailed theory of adjustment. But we might hope to decompose rational contractions, adjustments and expansions into rational changes which only involve a single proposition at a time.

In the case of contractions I have no opinion as to whether this can be done. However I shall argue against the following:

The Expansion One at a Time Conjecture

Given a rational expansion in which more than one new proposition occurs, the conjecture is that this expansion is the composite of rational expansions for which only one new proposition occurs at a time.

Counter-argument Suppose I believe O_1, O_2 etc., as a result of observation. I expand, coming to believe a theory T which explains O_1, O_2 etc. Then I expand again, coming to believe a prediction P as a result of believing T, where P would not have been antecedently plausible. By the Composition Principle, an expansion to both belief in T and belief in P would be rational. So by the conjecture I could have expanded to belief in P first, and then to T. But the expansion to belief in P first is intuitively irrational. This is a counter-example.

Now it might be replied that what I have is rather a counter-example to the Composition Principle, on the grounds that it is irrational to expand simultaneously to T and P. But I disagree. We may notice logical connections without undergoing any doxastic change, except at a meta-level. So our coming to believe T and its consequence could be simultaneous, even if we noticed the explanatory power of T before we *noticed* its consequence P.

Finally I consider:

The Adjustment One at a Time Conjecture

Given a rational adjustment in which the attitude to more than one proposition is altered, the conjecture is that it can be decomposed into rational adjustment for which the attitude to only one proposition is altered at a time.

Counter-argument Consider an inconsistent chiliad, consisting of the propositions $P_0, \ldots, P_{999}$. P_0 is the proposition that in a given lottery there are tickets numbered 1 to 999 of which precisely one will be selected. P_n is the proposition that ticket number n will not be selected. Suppose someone, perhaps irrationally, comes to be certain of all of P_0, . . ., P_{999}. I have a firm intuition that there is a rational adjustment in which some slight degree of doubt is had in all of P_0, . . ., P_{999}, thereby restoring δ-consistency. (If the change is represented by d^-/d^+, we might have $d^+(P_n) = 0.999$ for all n). By the conjecture this could be decomposed into adjustments to one proposition at a time. Consider the first of these and suppose it is to P_k. The only adjustment to P_k alone that is within sight of rationality would be that in which we become contracertain of P_k. But having become contracertain of P_k I cannot see how any further adjustment would be rational in which eventually the degree of belief in P_k rises again to near certainty. But that is what it must do if the composite is to be the adjustment under consideration.

I draw the conclusion that even if it is possible to adjust rationally to one proposition at a time, not every rational adjustment is the composite of rational one-at-a-time adjustments.

VI THE THEORY OF CONTRACTIONS

Contractions differ from adjustments and expansions in that once one knows what propositions are involved one knows the contraction. That reduces the theory of contractions to an answer to the question: When is it rational to contract away from the propositions in a given set?

Spontaneous contraction away from trivia is common enough. And it is in perfectly good order. But it is not an internal change, and so not up for appraisal as rational. What we have to consider is the deliberate suspension of judgement. I propose three principles governing contraction. I shall state them all before discussing them.

The Inconsistency Requirement for Contractions

If a system is doxastically consistent it is irrational to contract it.

The Principle of Minimal Contraction

If a contraction away from a set of propositions P would restore doxastic consistency, then it is irrational to contract away from Q, where P is a proper subset of Q.

The No Obligation Principle for Contractions

A contraction is never required for rationality.

The first principle could be thought of as a special case of the second, by taking not changing a system as a contraction away from an empty set. The No Obligation Principle (together with the definition of doxastic consistency and the Decomposition Principle) implies that it is always rational to remove an inconsistency by means of an adjustment.

These principles systematize my particular intuitive judgements. But, in addition to relying on my intuitions, I shall defend them against a couple of objections. The chief of these is based on Foundationalism. It is often claimed that, with the exception of some class of epistemically basic beliefs (e.g. those directly due to perception) no belief may be rationally held unless it is justified by other beliefs. Granted an extension of that thesis to attitudes even of agnosticism, it would follow that if my attitude to some proposition *P* is not basic, and if it cannot be justified by my basic beliefs, then it is irrational not to contract away from it. And that would hold even if the attitude to it did not contribute to doxastic inconsistency; say the system is doxastically consistent. This would provide a counter-example to all three principles. But Foundationalism is incorrect. Not only are there well known difficulties in displaying which are the basic beliefs, but it also runs counter to our particular judgements of rationality, precisely because it advocates too much contraction. For example, consider the amnesiac who finds him or herself with many beliefs but no memories of accepting those beliefs. Such an amnesiac will, presumably, have very few basic beliefs and so would be required by the foundationalist to undergo a massive contraction. Yet my intuition here is that the amnesiac should not give up the old beliefs before better ones have been found. So instead of relying on Foundationalism in order to reject the principles for contractions, I rely on particular judgements of rationality to reject Foundationalism. Furthermore, even if Foundationalism for belief (and disbelief) were accepted, there would still be little warrant for extending it to agnosticism. So adjustments resulting in agnostic attitudes would be available as substitutes for contractions.

Another objection to the first two principles is that defects other than doxastic inconsistency might be sufficient to warrant contraction.

In that case there would be defects which it would be rational to remove by contraction even from a δ-consistent system. But my intuitive judgement is that other defects are not gross enough to warrant the surgery of contraction.

As a result of the failure of the Radical Decomposition Conjecture for Adjustments and as a result of the No Obligation Principle for Contractions, I am entitled to concentrate on adjustments rather than contractions in giving an account of consistency-restoration. That is not to say that I think the further theory of contractions pointless. It is just not my present concern.[12]

4

The Principles of
Doxastic Consistency

In the previous chapter I provided a framework for the dynamics of belief. As part of this I introduced doxastic consistency, the key notion of the statics. The principles of doxastic consistency are some but not all of the standard principles of probability. For instance, I do not rely on the Multiplication Rule, namely $d(p\&q) = d(p/q) \times d(q)$. In addition there is one principle (Completability), due to Ellis (1979), which is not a standard principle of probability, nor derivable therefrom, and is required precisely because I do not assume doxastic systems are closed under the elementary logical operations.

I THE PARTLY NORMATIVE,
PARTLY STIPULATIVE CHARACTER OF THE PRINCIPLES

I shall state the principles for δ-consistency in the form of constraints on credence functions. But there are infinitely many credence functions representing a single system. This complicates matters. Is a constraint on a credence function, say the Addition Rule $[d(p\&q) + d(p\lor q) = d(p) + d(q)]$, to be thought of as a stipulation about how we represent the doxastic system, narrowing down the range of allowed representing functions? Or is it a normative constraint on the system being represented which must be satisfied for δ-consistency? In some cases at least the principles are a bit of both. Many representations of δ-consistent systems fail to satisfy the principles.[1] However, many systems cannot be represented so as to satisfy the principles. (They will, of course, be δ-inconsistent.) For example, if the degree of belief in $p\&q$ is the same as in p, but that in $p\lor q$ is greater than that in q, then no representation could satisfy the Addition Rule.

What we must do is to state various principles directly governing the δ-consistency of doxastic systems. And we must then show that any system satisfying those principles may be represented by a credence function satisfying the familiar principles to be stated in the next few sections. Finally we stipulate that they *are* so represented.

A quick route to such justification would be to require (as a principle directly governing systems of degrees of belief) that every δ-consistent system be representable in such a way that, for instance, the Addition Rule holds. But that principle is not, I submit, intrinsically plausible. It has an *ad hoc* feel about it. Theft fails, then. Rather than resort to honest toil I shall go begging. Koopman (1940, pp. 283–92) and Ellis (1979, pp. 12–16) have shown how to justify the Addition Rule using principles directly governing systems of degrees of belief. And I shall adapt their method.

The details of my adaptation will be found in section VIII. Here I merely present the basic idea behind the procedure. Most doxastic systems contain equal degrees of belief in a large number of pairwise incompatible alternatives, whose disjunction is believed with certainty. Thus I may be certain that precisely one of tickets number 1 to N will be selected, and have equal (small) degrees of belief that ticket number m will be selected, for $m = 1 \ldots N$. Call these propositions $u_1, \ldots, u_N$. Then, given δ-consistency, we may stipulate that $d(u_1) = \ldots = d(u_N) = 1/N$. Furthermore, for $m = 2, \ldots, N$, there may be an attitude to the disjunction $u_1 \vee \ldots \vee u_m$, that is, there may be an attitude to the proposition that one of the first m tickets will be selected. Assume there is. Then I further stipulate that $d(u_1 \vee \ldots \vee u_m) = m/N$. This provides a scale against which other degrees of belief can be measured. So, for instance, if the degree of belief in p is between that in $u_1 \vee \ldots \vee u_m$ and $u_1 \vee \ldots \vee u_{m+1}$, then $d(p)$ must be between m/N and $(m+1)/N$. If N is large this fixes $d(p)$ to within a negligible margin. At least it does so for those attitudes which are comparable to the disjunctions of the u_i. So, at least in that favourable case, the procedure gives us an approximately unique representation. When I discuss the general case in section VIII I am not, however, able to ensure even approximate uniqueness.

For two reasons I require not merely the representation of a single system but the joint representation of several δ-consistent systems. The first is that the Koopman/Ellis procedure only works for δ-consistent systems. But I am concerned not just with δ-consistent systems but also with δ-inconsistent ones. As a constraint on their representation I require that the principles hold for the credence

functions representing their δ-consistent subsystems. Hence I need
to show the joint representability of all the δ-consistent subsystems
in such a way that the principles hold. The second reason is that I
am concerned with doxastic changes, and so I must jointly represent
the systems before and after the change. For the special case of
expansions which preserve δ-consistency there is no difficulty: all that
is required is the representation of the final system. But in general,
I need to establish joint representability (see section VIII).

The overall result of section VIII is that we may concentrate on the
credence functions when considering δ-consistency. Accordingly I talk
about a δ-consistent credence function. In addition, I shall often not
bother with circumlocutions such as 'a credence function representing
the degree of belief'. Instead, where it causes no confusion, I shall
talk *as if* degrees of belief were themselves numerical.

II   SELF-EVIDENCE

Positive logic provides us with various schemata for axioms, theorems
and inferences. Some of the axioms and theorems will be *self-evident*
(abbreviated to 's-e') in the sense that we can *intuit* them with certainty.
By that I mean that we come to believe them with certainty and this
certainty requires no further justification. Clearly the axioms for a
logical system should be chosen from the self-evident propositions.
But many others may be self-evident as well. Similarly there are what
I would like to have called *self-evidently truth-preserving inferences*. But
to avoid begging questions as to the connection between rationality
and truth I call them *self-evident inferences*. The inference schemata in
positive logic will be chosen from these s-e inferences, and include
rules such as *modus ponens* and universal generalization. If a proposition
is derivable by means of a chain of s-e inferences from s-e propositions
I say it is *provable*. If r is derivable by such a chain from s-e propositions
and some further propositions $p_1 \ldots , p_n$, then I say that the inference
'$p_1, \ldots , p_n$; therefore r' is *provable*.

Although s-e propositions are intuited with certainty it may not
be irrational subsequently to revise them. But this is a possibility I
shall ignore until I consider the Comparative Theory of Rationality.

Without engaging in any controversies about the concept of
implication, I shall *stipulate* that if 'p; therefore q' is a s-e inference
then p is said *self-evidently to imply* q.

I now present the three principles concerning self-evidence. The first tells us to represent s-e propositions by 1. The second tells us that if q s-e implies p then we should have $d(p/q) = 1$. The third tells us that if p s-e implies q and vice versa then $d(r/p) = d(r/q)$. More precisely we have:

The Principle of Self-evident Propositions

If p is a s-e proposition in $Dom(d)$, then either $d(p) = 1$ or the system is δ-inconsistent.

The Principle of Self-evident Implication

If q s-e implies p, and if $<p,q>$ is in the $Dom(d)$, then either $d(p/q) = 1$ or the system is δ-inconsistent.

I take it that p s-e implies p. Hence as a special case we require $d(p/p) = 1$ whenever $<p,p>$ is in $Dom(d)$.

The Principle of Self-evidently Equivalent Suppositions

If p s-e implies q and vice versa, and if $<r,p>$ and $<r,q>$ are both in $Dom(d)$, then either $d(r/p) = d(r/q)$ or the system is δ-inconsistent.

Related to the principles of self-evidence is a principle which might seem redundant to many. A theory of positive logic may contain some anti-axioms. These will be *self-refuting propositions*, that is, ones for which intuition leads to contracertainty. For p to be self-refuting it is neither obviously necessary nor obviously sufficient for $\sim p$ to be self-evident. It is not obviously sufficient, for if it is ever the case that both p and $\sim p$ are true,[2] then it might conceivably also be the case that both p and $\sim p$ are self-evident and neither self-refuting. Likewise it is not obviously necessary, since if, as I believe, sometimes neither p nor $\sim p$ is true, then it might be the case that p could be self-refuting without $\sim p$ being self-evident. It is the threat of failure of straightforward bivalence that should make us consider self-refuting propositions as well as self-evident ones. I require that self-refuting propositions be represented by 0. More precisely:

The Principle of Self-refutation

If p is a self-refuting proposition and if p is in $Dom(d)$, then either $d(p) = 0$ or the system is δ-inconsistent.

In the previous chapter I talked rather loosely of inconsistent triads, tetrads, etc. Is an inconsistent polyad a set of propositions which cannot all be true? Or is it a set of propositions at least one of which must be false? If we assume bivalence it does not matter. But I do not, and anyway it does no harm to be more precise. Accordingly I define a *s-e inconsistent polyad* to be a set of propositions whose conjunction is self-refuting.

I say a proposition is *disprovable* if there is a provable inference from it to a self-refuting proposition. Likewise I say a set of propositions is *provably inconsistent* if there is a provable inference from that set to a self-refuting proposition.

I anticipate two objections to my talk of self-evidence and self-refutation. The first is that I have left these concepts rather vague. Can they bear the weight I put on them? Yes, they can, because all I require is that we either agree about the extensions of the concepts or know why we disagree. So instances of the truth-schemata and inference schemata of a positive deductive logic will be treated as s-e propositions and s-e inferences *by those* who accept that positive theory, *provided* they are simple enough for them to be suitable candidates for axioms or basic rules of inference. And if we disagree about self-refuting propositions it will probably be because we disagree about how much, if at all, bivalence fails. So at least we shall know *why* we disagree.

The second objection is that, since I have already idealized my theory by considering logical omniscience, I do not need to bother with the distinction between self-evident and other provable propositions. For all provable propositions should be self-evident to a logically omniscient person. In reply to this objection I admit that it is tempting to make a further idealization and to allow that everything provable is self-evident to a logically omniscient person. But I resist this temptation. For the extra idealization is neither necessary nor negligible. It is not necessary since the principles stated are strong enough for my theoretical purposes. It is not negligible because, as I understand it, logical omniscience is simply a matter of having a superlative degree of human abilities, such as being able to survey possibilities, and make the deductions of positive logic. But just to be able to 'see' what is to us merely provable, would be to have a quite different sort of epistemic access to logic from ours; it would be to be god-like rather than merely pre-lapsarian.

III SOME FURTHER PRINCIPLES

I rely on, and, in section VIII, go to some length to justify, the Addition Rule, namely that the (numerical representative of) the degrees of belief in $p\&q$ and in $p\lor q$ should add up to the sum of the degrees of belief in p and q. We have:

The Addition Principle

If p, q $p\&q$ and $p\lor q$ are all in $Dom(d)$, then either $d(p\&q) + d(p\lor q) = d(p) + d(q)$ or the system is δ-inconsistent.

Notice that if $p\&\sim p$ is self-refuting and $p\lor \sim p$ is self-evident (and provided both are in $Dom(d)$ – a proviso we will be able to remove) we obtain the requirement that $d(p) + d(\sim p) = 1$. If $p\&\sim p$ is self-refuting but $p\lor \sim p$ fails to be self-evident then we may have, without δ-inconsistency, $d(p) + d(\sim p) < 1$. Likewise if $p\lor \sim p$ is self-evident but $p\&\sim p$ fails to be self-refuting we could have $d(p) + d(\sim p) > 1$.

In chapter 9 I offer some justification for the Multiplication Rule [that $d(p\&q) = d(p/q) \times d(q)$]. However I do not think it sufficiently justified to rely on it. So I shall merely assume the special cases where $d(p/q)$ and/or $d(q)$ are equal to 1, thus:

The Restricted Multiplication Principle

Suppose $p\&q$, $<p,q>$ and q are all in $Dom(d)$. In that case:

(1)   If $d(q) = 1$, but $d(p\&q) \neq d(p/q)$ the system is δ-inconsistent.
(2)   If $d(p/q) = 1$, but $d(p\&q) \neq d(q)$ the system is δ-inconsistent.

This brings us to a discussion of the principles concerning conditional degrees of belief. I have already stated the Principle of Self-evidently Equivalent Suppositions. To state the next principle

I shall introduce some new terminology. I shall say that p s-e implies q *relative* to r if p&r s-e implies q. Likewise I say that q is self-evident *relative* to r if r s-e implies q. Again I say that p is self-refuting *relative* to r if p&r is self-refuting. And similarly for whatever is defined in terms of self-evidence, s-e implication and self-refutation.

Here the principle is that whatever holds for unconditional beliefs holds for conditional ones within the scope of some fixed supposition. So we have:

The Principle of Conditionalization

Suppose r is not disprovable. Let d_r be defined by:

(1) $Dom(d_r) = \{p \mid <p,r> \in Dom(d)\}$; and
(2) $d_r(p) = d(p/r)$ if $<p,r> \in Dom(d)$.

Then given any δ-consistent credence function d, d_r is also δ-consistent, and moreover satisfies the principles of self-evidence and self-refutation even when these are interpreted as relative to r.

This principle tells us that we cannot have consistency unless we have it within the scope of the supposition of anything not disprovable. However, if r is disprovable and if d_r is δ-consistent then we will be able to show that $d_r(r) = 0$. So if the principle were generalized to cover disprovable r we would have a rational predicament requiring that $d_r(r) = 0$ and $d_r(r) = 1$.

IV   BOOLEAN NEGATION AND
THE PRINCIPLE OF ALTERNATIVE SUPPOSITION

I have taken – and I shall go on taking – 'not' (abbreviated to ' $\sim$ ') in its conventional sense. Hence it is an open question whether $p \vee \sim p$ is always self-evident and p& $\sim p$ always self-refuting. But in logic it is convenient to close this open question. Accordingly I say that a proposition p has a Boolean negation q if p&q is self-refuting and $p \vee q$ self-evident. A proposition may have many Boolean negations, but I shall abuse terminology in a harmless way and write ' $\neg p$ ' for any Boolean negation of p. In many cases, of course, $\neg p$ will be $\sim p$.

Where it is not, we may hope that 'p fails to be true', [i.e. $\sim(p$ is true)] will be a Boolean negation of p. This is tantamount to assuming that the predicate 'is true' applies bivalently to propositions. If necessary I could stipulate that this is so by denying entry into the object-language to propositions which are neither true nor not true. Anyway, by fair means or foul, I shall assume every proposition has a Boolean negation, though not necessarily that this is its ordinary negation.

We may generalize the concept of a Boolean negation to obtain that of a *set of alternatives*. By a set of alternatives I mean a finite or infinite collection of propositions whose disjunction is self-evident and whose pairwise conjunctions are self-refuting. So I say that $\{p_1, p_2, \ldots\}$ is a *set of alternatives* if:

(1)[3]   It is self-evident that $p_1 \lor p_2 \lor \ldots$; and
(2)   if $i \neq j$, then $p_i \& p_j$ is self-refuting.

I am now in a position to state a generalization of Koopman's Axiom of Alternative Presumption.[4] This is a principle which could have been *derived* if I had assumed the Multiplication Rule. A special case is that $d(p)$ should be between $d(p/r)$ and $d(p/\neg r)$. More generally for any finite set of alternatives $r_1, \ldots, r_n$ we require that $d(p)$ be between the smallest and largest of the $d(p/r_i)$. More precisely:

The Principle of Alternative Supposition

Suppose $\{r_1\ r_2 \ldots r_n\}$ is a *finite* set of alternatives. In that case if p and $<p, r_i>$ $i = 1, 2 \ldots, n$ all occur in $Dom(d)$, but *either* $d(p) > d(p/r_i)$ for all i *or* $d(p) < d(p/r_i)$ for all i, then the system is δ-inconsistent.

V   COMPLETABILITY[5]

If I had assumed that all doxastic systems were closed under various logical operations then the principles I have already stated would be enough. But, as it is, one more is needed. For consider P, the proposition that 1 June 1979 is a Friday. Someone who is certain that P and certain that $\sim P$ and who maintains his or her system unchanged is, surely, irrational. So the system is δ-inconsistent. And this is something to do with the self-refuting character of $P\&\sim P$. But none of the principles I have stated demonstrate this δ-inconsistency *unless* the person has some attitude to $P\&\sim P$. Intuitively the requirement that there be some attitude to $P\&\sim P$ is unnecessary. Not to have considered the conjunction is at best an excuse for simultaneous certainty that P and certainty that $\sim P$. It is not a justification.

Following Ellis (1979, pp. 9–16) I introduce a *completability principle* designed to enable us to remove all the intuitively unnecessary requirements that various propositions occur in the doxastic system. To state this principle I assume that the language consists of some countable set of propositions. I then excise from this set any propositions about rationality judgements, and, perhaps, some other meta-linguistic propositions. I call the resulting set of propositions the object-language. And throughout the remainder of this work I shall be considering attitudes to members of this object-language. The idea behind the Completability Principle is that if however you expand to various propositions the system becomes δ-inconsistent, then it already is δ-inconsistent. We have:

The Completability Principle

If d is δ-consistent then d has a δ-consistent extension to the whole object-language.

If the requirement that the extension be to the whole object-language seems too strong, I note that in section VIII when I justify this principle I rely on an analogous principle which involves extension only to one proposition at a time.

As it stands this principle is reflexive; but harmlessly so. The Completability Principle together with the previously stated principles amounts to a single requirement for δ-consistency, namely capacity to be extended to a credence function satisfying the previously stated principles.

The Completability Principle rests on the idealization that we are considering what is rational for a logically omniscient person. Otherwise we should only expect a system to be extendable to the results of some fairly small number of fairly elementary operations on the propositions in the domain of d (see Forrest 1981, p. 47).

VI   RULES I DO NOT ASSUME

It is worth noting three common rules which I do not assume.

The Multiplication Rule

If $p\&q$, q and $<p,q>$ all occur in $Dom(d)$ then either $d(p\&q) = d(p/q) \times d(q)$ or d is δ-inconsistent.

As I have already mentioned I do not think the justification for this rule is strong enough. Another rule which I think lacks sufficient justification,[6] is:

Countable Additivity

Suppose we have a set $\{p_1, p_2 \ldots\}$ of propositions all of which occur in $Dom(d)$, together with their disjunction. And suppose that if $i \neq j$ $p_i\&p_j$ is self-refuting. Then, even if the set is countably infinite, we require for δ-consistency that $d(p_1 \vee p_2 \vee \ldots) = d(p_1) + d(p_2) + \ldots$

Finally, inspired by Carnap (1971, p. 15) we might suppose:

Regularity

If p is in $Dom(d)$ and d is δ-consistent, then either $d(p) < 1$ or p is provable.

I could have ensured regularity by introducing infinitesimals and allowing certainty without provability to be represented by one minus an infinitesimal. But without infinitesimals regularity would force upon us the sceptical position that certainty, namely full belief, is warranted only for provable propositions. And I reject that.

VII   AGAINST THE DUTCH BOOK ARGUMENT

Suppose you undertake either to make or accept a wager (for any amount in some range) that q, for any proposition q in some set. And suppose you specify the betting quotient before you are told whether you are going to make a wager or accept one. Then it can be shown (Ramsey 1931, p. 182, de Finetti 1974, pp. 87–9, 99–101) that if $Pr(q)$ is the betting quotient, Pr should satisfy various principles of probability, including the Addition and Multiplication rules, or else a Dutch book can be made against you. That is, unless those principles are satisfied, you could be forced to make and accept wagers in such a way that you are bound to lose. If, as we may assume, you value what you are betting for (e.g. money), then we judge it irrational to make or accept a system of wagers which will inevitably result in your loss. In this way, it has seemed to many, we could justify what I have called the principles of δ-consistency, and the Multiplication Rule as well.

This is a beautifully simple argument. But it is open to a number of objections. In the first place, as Ellis has argued (1973, pp. 125–52), where there is some uncertainty that the outcome will ever be decided, rational betting quotients diverge from degrees of belief. This point is supported by the more elementary point that we can have degrees of belief on topics which it is absurd to bet on, because we know they will never be decided. For example who would bet on the truth of the Axiom of Choice?

Secondly, consider the Dutch bookie him or herself. He or she is out to get you. To do this the Dutch bookie *ignores* his or her own initial degrees of belief, which are quite irrelevant. What is relevant is *our* betting behaviour. So to make the Dutch book the bookie has to have a system of betting quotients that fails to correspond to his or her initial degrees of belief. Surely the Dutch bookie's system of betting quotients is rational. But if it has to reflect the bookie's doxastic system, the Dutch bookie would have to revise his or her degrees of belief to make them fit the betting quotients, which in turn are determined by the behaviour of the quite possibly *irrational* punters. Something has gone wrong. And what, I submit, has gone wrong is the assumption that rational systems of betting quotients necessarily reflect δ-consistent systems of degrees of belief. Rational betting *behaviour* need not mirror rational doxastic attitudes.

Finally, even if we waive these objections, it can be shown that the Dutch book argument is parasitic on something like the Koopman/Ellis procedure. For consider how one would decide on a system of betting quotients intended to represent one's degrees of beliefs. Presumably one would make comparisons such as: I believe p to a greater degree than I believe I shall get a 1, 2, 3 or 4 in the throw of a fair die; so the betting quotient should be greater than $\frac{2}{3}$. But such comparisons are the stuff of the Koopman/Ellis procedure. So if there is some hitch which prevents that procedure from working then the procedure for finding the better quotients also fails. Therefore, I submit, even if the Dutch Book Argument were not open to serious objections, it would still be no substitute for the detailed considerations of the next section.

VIII JUSTIFICATION OF
THE PRINCIPLES OF CONSISTENCY*

Because of their partly stipulative, partly normative character the justification for the principles governing credence functions must depend on principles directly governing systems of degrees of belief. The latter principles may then be used to show that there exist representations by credence functions such that if the system is δ-consistent the credence function satisfies the former principles. We then stipulate that the appropriate representation is one of those whose existence has just been demonstrated.

My first step is to assume that the comparisons of degrees of belief are transitive. If not I introduce the τ-ordering as in section VI of chapter 2. And I write '$D(p) \geqslant D(q)$' as an abbreviation for 'The degree of belief in p is either τ-greater than or τ-equal to that in q'. So $D(p) \geqslant D(q)$ just in case for some integer n and propositions $r_1, \ldots, r_n$, $p = r_1$, $q = r_n$, and the degree of belief in r_i is greater than or equal to that in r_{i+1}. If there are no failures of transitivity then this is just the ordinary comparison of degrees of belief. And I say that $D(p) > D(q)$ if $D(p) \geqslant D(q)$ but not $D(q) \leqslant D(p)$. In this notation '$D(\ )$' is just an abbreviation, not a function.

I now state two principles directly governing systems of degrees of belief.

The Disjunction Principle[7]

Suppose $p\&q$ and $p^*\&q^*$ are both self-refuting. If $D(p) \leqslant D(p^*)$, if $D(q) \leqslant D(q^*)$ and if $D(p \vee q) > D(p^* \vee q^*)$ then the system is δ-inconsistent. Likewise if $D(p) < D(p^*)$ and $D(q) \leqslant D(q^*)$ but $D(p \vee q) \geqslant D(p^* \vee q^*)$ the system is δ-inconsistent.

The Boolean Negation Principle

If $D(p) \leqslant D(q)$ and $D(\neg p) < D(\neg q)$ then the system is δ-inconsistent.

In order to represent the system I shall follow Koopman and Ellis and rely on the existence of what I call sets of n *δ-equal* alternatives. Here a set of n alternatives $\{u_1, \ldots, u_n\}$ is said to be δ-equal (with respect to a given system) if $D(u_1) = \ldots = D(u_n)$. The basic strategy is to consider the disjunctions $u_1, u_1 \lor u_2, u_1 \lor u_2 \lor u_3, \ldots, u_1 \lor \ldots \lor u_{n-1}, u_1 \lor \ldots \lor u_n$. These provide a scale for measuring the degree of belief in p. We assign to p (approximately) the value k/n where k is the smallest integer such that $D(p) \leqslant D(u_1 \lor \ldots \lor u_k)$. For this measurement procedure to succeed we need there to be enough sets of n δ-equal alternatives. I state:

The Equal Alternatives Principle

For any integer n and any δ-consistent finite doxastic system S there is a δ-consistent extension of S which contains a set of n δ-equal alternatives.

Typically for any finite system there should be some predicate 'G' which can apply to any number (including 0) of objects up to $n-1$ and such that the person has no information relevant to the number of Gs. Then we could take u_i to be the proposition that there are $i-1$ Gs. Notice that I do not require that the person actually come to have attitudes to the u_i.

Except for the Addition Principle it is possible to state coherently a D-transform of the principles governing credence functions. By the D-transform I mean a principle obtained by replacing d by 'D', interpreting '$D(p) = 1$' as '$D(p)$ is certainty', and interpreting '$D(p) = 0$' as '$D(p)$ is contracertainty'. I shall assume the D-transforms of all these principles except completability. In addition I assume:

Doxastic Modus Ponens[8]

If $D(p)$ and $D(q)$ occur in the system, if p s-e implies q and if the system is δ-consistent, then $D(p) \leqslant D(q)$.

In place of the D-transform of Completability I assume a principle which is weaker in one respect but stronger in another. It is weaker in that it only warrants extension to one proposition at a time. It is stronger in that it specifies that in the extension any two doxastic attitudes are comparable. It is:

The Extension Principle

(1) If S is any finite δ-consistent system of degrees of belief, then S can be embedded in a δ-consistent system S^*, in which the same propositions occur, and in which any two attitudes are comparable.

(2) If S is any finite δ-consistent system of degrees of belief and p is a proposition not occurring in S, then S can be extended δ-consistently to include some attitude to p.

Finally to ensure that the Koopman/Ellis procedure results in a *representation* in my sense, I require:

The Archimedean Principles for Systems of Degrees of Belief[9]

Suppose S is a δ-consistent system of degrees of belief. Then:

(1) $D(p)$ is greater than contracertainty just in case in some δ-consistent extension of S there is a set of δ-equal alternatives $\{u_1, \ldots, u_n\}$ such that $D(p) \geqslant D(u_1)$.

(2) $D(p)$ is less than certainty just in case in some δ-consistent extension of S there is a set of δ-equal alternatives $\{u_1, \ldots, u_n\}$ such that $D(p) \leqslant D(u_2 \vee \ldots \vee u_n)$.

(3)[10] If p is believed, then in some δ-consistent extension of S there is a set of δ-equal alternatives $\{u_1, \ldots, u_n\}$ such that $D(p) \geqslant D(u_1 \vee \ldots \vee u_m)$ where $2m > n$.

(4) If p is disbelieved then in some δ-consistent extension of S there is a set of δ-equal alternatives $\{u_1, \ldots, u_n\}$ such that $D(p) \leqslant D(u_1 \vee \ldots \vee u_m)$ where $2m < n$.

Of the Archimedean Principles (1) and (2) can be seen as partly normative but partly an explication of what is meant by certainty and hence contracertainty. Part of the normative component, in the case for certainty, is that if $D(p)$ is definitely certain then for no extension and no finite set of δ-equal alternatives $\{u_1, \ldots u_n\}$ do we have $D(p) \leqslant D(u_2 \vee \ldots \vee u_n)$. Again if $D(p)$ is definitely not certain then there should be δ-equal alternatives $\{u_1, \ldots, u_n\}$ such that $D(p) \leqslant D(u_2 \vee \ldots \vee u_n)$. But where it is vague whether a degree of belief constitutes certainty, there the Archimedean Principle provides an explication, which can be put less formally thus: If you can get into a lottery paradox then your belief is not full belief (i.e. it is not certain). The Archimedean Principles (3) and (4) express the conviction that agnosticism is not a razor-edged path. I assume that there is a certain *width* to the range of attitudes which are neither belief nor disbelief. Hence for some large n and some set of n δ-equal alternatives, the attitude towards both the disjunction of slightly less and the disjunction of slightly more than half the n members should be neither belief nor disbelief.

These principles, which directly govern systems of degrees of belief, are justified not by thinking hard about them in isolation from instances and 'seeing' that they are correct, but by a combination of their intrinsic plausibility, the intuitive correctness of many instances, the lack of intuitive counter-examples and the role they play in my more general systematic theory.

We are now in a position to prove the required representation theorem (thesis 4.8.2). I shall, however, omit most of the details of the proof which is neither short nor interesting. We begin with a preliminary result.

Thesis 4.8.1

If $p\&q$ is self-refuting, and $D(p)$ is certainty, then either $D(q)$ is contracertainty or the system is δ-inconsistent.

Proof-sketch Suppose the contrary. By the Archimedean Principle we can ensure that:

(1) $D(q) \geqslant D(u_1)$, where $\{u_1, \ldots, u_n\}$ is a set of δ-equal alternatives.

Now $p\&q$ is self-refuting. So:

(2) $p \vee \neg(p \vee q)$ is a Boolean negation of q.

From (1) and (2) using the Boolean Negation Principle and the Principle of Self-evidence:

(3) $D(p) \leqslant D[p \vee \neg(p \vee q)] \leqslant D(u_2 \vee \ldots \vee u_n)$.

This contradicts the Archimedean Principle.

The representation theorem is:

Thesis 4.8.2

If S is any finite δ-consistent system, then S has a representation satisfying all the principles governing the δ-consistency of credence functions.

Proof-sketch For simplicity I concentrate on unconditional degrees of belief. Similar considerations hold for conditional ones. Given any finite δ-consistent system of degrees of belief S, we may, by the Archimedean Principles, extend it δ-consistently so that if $D(p)$ is greater than contracertainty in the original system then in the extension, $D(p) \geqslant D(u_1)$ where $\{u_1, \ldots, u_n\}$ is a set of n δ-equal alternatives.

And we may ensure that similarly appropriate conditions hold if $D(p)$ is less than certainty, if p is believed or if p is disbelieved. Call the system so obtained S_o^*. Then, using the Extension Principle and the Principle of Equal Alternatives, starting with the system S_o^* we can find a sequence of completely ordered δ-consistent systems, S_1^*, S_2^*, etc., where:

(1)   Every proposition occurs in some S_n^*.
(2)   If p occurs in S_n^* so does some Boolean negation of p.
(3) S_n^* is an extension of S_{n-1}^*.
(4)   In S_n^* there is a set of n δ-equal alternatives $\{u_1, \ldots, u_n\}$.

I now define a corresponding sequence of functions e_1, e_2, etc., where $Dom(e_n)$ consists of all the propositions occurring in S_n^*. I put $e_n(p) = 1$ if $D(p)$ is certainty, otherwise $e_n(p) = k/n$ where k is the smallest integer such that $D(p) \leqslant D(u_1 \vee \ldots \vee u_k)$, and $\{u_1, \ldots, u_n\}$ is the set of n δ-equal alternatives mentioned in (4). I next obtain some lemmas concerning the e_n. I omit the straightforward but tedious proofs, which rely on thesis 4.8.1.

Lemma 1: If p and q both occur in S_n^* and $D(p) \geqslant D(q)$ then $e_n(p) \geqslant e_n(q)$.

Lemma 2: If p and q both occur in S_n^* and $p\&q$ is self-refuting, then $e_n(p \lor q) \leqslant e_n(p) + e_n(q)$.

Lemma 3: If p and q both occur in S_n^* and $p\&q$ is self-refuting, then $e_n(p \lor q) > e_n(p) + e_n(q) - 1/n$.

Lemma 4: If $n \geqslant 3$, if both $(n-1)$ and $(n+1)$ divide N, and if p is in S_n^*, then $e_N(p)$ differs from $e_n(p)$ by at most $2/(n+1)$.

I now return to the proof of thesis 4.8.2:

If $n > m \geqslant 3$, we can find some N divisible by $(n-1)$, $(n+1)$, $(m-1)$ and $(m+1)$. Then by lemma 4, if p occurs in S_n^*, $e_N(p)$ differs from $e_m(p)$ by at most $2/(m+1)$ and it differs from $e_n(p)$ by at most $2/(n+1)$. So $e_n(p)$ and $e_m(p)$ differ by at most $4/(m+1)$. Hence the $e_n(p)$ converge as n increases. Let the limit be $e(p)$. Then every proposition is in $Dom(e)$. From lemma 1, if $D(p) \geqslant D(q)$, taking limits, $e(p) \geqslant e(q)$. From lemmas 2 and 3, taking limits, if $p\&q$ is self-refuting then $e(p \lor q) = e(p) + e(q)$, which is a special case of the Addition Principle. It is easy to check using the Archimedean Principles that e is a representation. It is also easy to check that e satisfies all the principles governing the δ-consistency of credence functions with the possible exception of the Addition Principle. (Completability is vacuous since $Dom(e)$ is the whole object-language.) Also e satisfies Doxastic *Modus Ponens* for credence functions, namely: If p s-e implies q then $e(p) \leqslant e(q)$.

Hence if p and q are provably equivalent $e(p) = e(q)$. To show that the Addition Principle holds in general, consider p and q where $p\&q$ is not self-refuting. We have to show that $e(p \lor q) + e(p\&q) = e(p) + e(q)$. But:

(1) $p\&(\neg p\&q)$ is self-refuting.

So:

(2) $e[(p\&(\neg p\&q)) \lor p] = e(p) + e(\neg p\&q)$.

Similarly:

(3) $(p\&q)\&(\neg p\&q)$ is self-refuting.

So:

(4) $e[(p\&q)\vee(\neg p\&q)] = e(p\&q) + e(\neg p\&q).$

Combining these two equations, we have:

(5) $e[(p\&(\neg p\&q))\vee p] + e(p\&q) = e(p) + e[(p\&q)\vee(\neg p\&q)].$

But $p\vee q$ is provably equivalent to $[p\&(\neg p\&q)]\vee p$, and q is provably equivalent to $[(p\&q)\&(\neg p\&q)]$. Therefore:

(6) $e(p\vee q) + e(p\&q) = e(p) + e(q).$

So e satisfies all the principles. Let d be the restriction of e to the propositions occurring in S. It is the required representation.

I now turn to the joint representation of several δ-consistent systems. I do not have an entirely satisfactory result. What I can provide is an argument to show that in typical cases we do have joint representability. I shall also provide a more formal sufficient condition for joint representability, without, however, claiming that this condition is always satisfied.

Typically, the systems considered will not depart far from δ-consistency. So we should expect the maximal δ-consistent subsystems to be large and to have a large intersection. Moreover, typically, there will not be doxastic changes to many propositions. So we should expect there to be a large intersection of all the δ-consistent systems to be represented (i.e. a large subsystem containing comparisons of degrees of belief only where all the systems agree on the comparison). Let us represent this by a credence function d. Then if $D(p)$ in some system S to be represented is not in this large central part of the system we should expect there to be propositions q and r in the central part such that $D(p)$ lies between $D(q)$ and $D(r)$ and the difference between $d(q)$ and $d(r)$ is small. In that case, suitable representations of S cannot vary by much in the assignment being made to p. Hence although we might not strictly speaking have joint representability we would have various representations which diverged by only a small amount from being joint representations. So we may idealize the situation by assuming joint representability in such a way that the Addition Rule holds. In this way we have grounds for assuming that we indeed have joint representability as required.

Finally I provide the sufficient condition:

Thesis 4.8.3

Given a finite set of finite δ-consistent doxastic systems, the following two conditions are jointly sufficient for there to be joint representations by credence functions satisfying the principles stated in this chapter:

(1) *Joint Extension*: The systems can be extended to completely ordered δ-consistent systems in which all the propositions of the object language occur and in such a way that any two attitudes, even taken from different systems, are comparable.

(2) *Joint Disjunction*:[11] Suppose S and S^* are any two members of the collection and that $p\&q$ and $p^*\&q^*$ are both self-refuting. If $D(p) \leqslant D^*(p^*)$ and $D(q) \leqslant D^*(q^*)$, then $D(p \lor q) \leqslant D^*(p^* \lor q^*)$. Likewise if $D(p) \leqslant D^*(p^*)$ and $D(q) < D^*(q)$, then $D(p \lor q) < D^*(p^* \lor q^*)$.

Proof Let the systems be $S_1, \ldots, S_n$ and for every proposition p in the object language consider the pairs $<p,S_i>$, for $i = 1 \ldots n$, which I shall write as p^i. Then the set of all the p^i, for a given i is a copy L_i of the object-language. Let $L = L_1 \cup L_2 \cup \ldots \cup L_n$. Then we may think of L as itself a language and consider the supersystem S, which consists of attitudes to members of L, where $D(p^i) = D_i(p)$.[12] Because of Joint Extension and Joint Disjunction, S itself satisfies the principles of δ-consistency. So by thesis 4.8.2 it has a representation d satisfying the principles of δ-consistency. Then we can jointly represent $S_1, \ldots, S_n$ by $d_1, \ldots, d_n$ where $d_i(p) = d(p^i)$.

IX RESULTS ABOUT DOXASTIC CONSISTENCY*

I conclude this chapter by collecting some theses derived from the principles of δ-consistency. These are selected either because of their intrinsic interest or because they will be required later. Relying on Conditionalization I shall prove results for unconditional degrees of belief but help myself to the analogous ones for conditional degrees.

Thesis 4.9.1 (The Material Conditional Rule)

If $\lnot p \lor q$ and $<p,q>$ are both in $Dom(d)$, then either $d(\lnot p \lor q) \geqslant d(p/q)$ or the system is δ-inconsistent.

Proof Assume δ-consistency and extend to a δ-consistent *e* whose domain is the whole object-language. We have:

(1) $e[(\neg p \vee q)/\neg p] = 1 = e(p/p)$; and
(2) $e(\neg p/p) = 0 = e(\neg p \& q/p)$.

By the Addition Principle:

(3) $e(q/p) + e(\neg p/p) = e(\neg p \vee q/p) + e(\neg p \& q/p)$.

From (1), (2) and (3):

(4) $e(\neg p \vee q/p) = e(q/p)$.

From (1) and (4), by the Principle of Alternative Supposition:

(5) $e(\neg p \vee q) \geqslant e(q/p)$.

Hence:

(6) $d(\neg p \vee q) \geqslant d(q/p)$.

Thesis 4.9.2

If $\neg p \vee q$ is in $Dom(d)$ and p s-e implies q, then either $d(\neg p \vee q) = 1$, or the system is δ-inconsistent.

Proof An immediate consequence of thesis 4.9.1

Thesis 4.9.3 (Doxastic Modus Ponens)

If p s-e implies q and if both p and q are in $Dom(d)$, then either $d(p) \leqslant d(q)$ or the system is δ-inconsistent.

Proof Assume δ-consistency; extend to *e*.

Then, by thesis 4.9.2:

(1) $e(\neg p \vee q) = 1$.

So, by the Addition Principle:

(2) $e(\neg p) + e(q) = e(\neg p \& q) + 1$.

Principles of Doxastic Consistency

Again, by the Addition Principle:

(3) $e(p) + e(\neg p) = 1$.

From (2) and (3):

(4) $e(q) = e(\neg p \& q) + e(p)$.

Therefore:

(5) $d(q) = e(q) = e(\neg p \& q) + e(p) \geqslant e(p) = d(p)$.

Thesis 4.9.4 (The Equivalence Rule)

If p and q are s-e equivalent (i.e. s-e imply each other) and both occur in $Dom(d)$, then either $d(p) = d(q)$ or the system is δ-inconsistent.

Proof An immediate consequence of thesis 4.9.3.

Thesis 4.9.5 (The Disjunction Rule)

If p, q and $p \lor q$ all occur in $Dom(d)$, then *either* $|d(p \lor q) - d(q)| \leqslant d(p)$ *or* the system is δ-inconsistent. In particular if $d(p) = 0$, and the system is δ-consistent then $d(p \lor q) = d(q)$.

Proof This follows from the Addition Principle and Completability.

Thesis 4.9.6 (The Conjunction Rule)

If p, q and $p \& q$ all occur in $Dom(d)$, then *either* $|d(p \& q) - d(p)| \leqslant 1 - d(q)$ *or* the system is δ-inconsistent. In particular if $d(q) = 1$, and the system is δ-consistent then $d(p \& q) = d(p)$.

Proof This follows from the Addition Principle and Completability.

Thesis 4.9.7 (The General Addition Rule)

Suppose $p_1, \ldots, p_n$ are n propositions all in $Dom(d)$, and such that if $i \neq j$ then $p_i \& p_j$ is in $Dom(d)$ and $d(p_i \& p_j) = 0$. Suppose

$p_1 \vee \ldots \vee p_n$ is also in $Dom(d)$. In that case either $d(p_1 \vee \ldots \vee p_n) = d(p_1) + \ldots + d(p_n)$ or the system is δ-inconsistent.

Proof By induction on the number of disjuncts, using the Addition Principle, the Equivalence Rule and Doxastic *Modus Ponens*.

I now consider inferences with several premises. I call $1 - d(p)$ *the measure of doubt* in p. Then we have:

Thesis 4.9.8

Consider an inference '$p_1, \ldots, p_n$, therefore r'. If $p_1 \& \ldots \& p_n$ s-e implies r, and if $p_1, p_2, \ldots, p_n$ and r are all in $Dom(d)$, then either the measure of doubt in the conclusion r is no greater than the sum of the measures of doubt in the premises or the system is δ-inconsistent.

Proof Assume δ-consistency and extend to e. It is elementary algebra that

(1) $\quad 1 - d(p_1 \& \ldots \& p_n) \leqslant |1 - e(p_1)| + |e(p_1) - e(p_1 \& p_2)| + \ldots + |e(p_1 \& \ldots \& p_{n-1}) - e(p_1 \& \ldots \& p_n)|$.

By repeated application of the Disjunction Rule we have:

(2) $\quad 1 - d(p_1 \& \ldots \& p_n) \leqslant [1 - d(p_1)] + \ldots + [1 - d(p_n)]$.

The required result now follows from (2) by Doxastic *Modus Ponens*.

Thesis 4.9.8 covers only the case of s-e truth-preserving inferences. I shall argue that if r is provable from $p_1, \ldots, p_n$ then the measure of doubt in r should not exceed the sum of the measures of doubt in $p_1, \ldots p_n$. This result is not obtainable simply by repeated application of thesis 4.9.8, since some of the p_i might appear more than once in the chain of inferences. But it can nonetheless be obtained quite easily.

Thesis 4.9.9 (The Subadditivity Rule)

If r is provable from $p_1, \ldots p_n$ and if $p_1 \ldots p_n$ and r all occur in $Dom(d)$, then either the measure of doubt in r does not exceed the sum of the measures of doubt in the p_i or the system is δ-inconsistent.

Proof Assume δ-consistency and extend to e if necessary. I first show that $e(\neg(p_1\& \ldots \&p_n)\lor r) = 1$. To show this I consider two cases. The first is that in which $p_1\& \ldots \&p_n$ is not self-refuting. In that case we may apply Conditionalization to thesis 4.9.8 and obtain:

(1) $1 - e(r/p_1\& \ldots \&p_n) = 0$.

So, by thesis 4.9.1:

(2) $e[\neg(p_1\& \ldots \&p_n)\lor r] = 1$.

The other case is that in which $p_1\& \ldots \&p_n$ is self-refuting. In that case we have, by the Addition Principle:

(1)* $e[\neg(p_1\& \ldots \&p_n)] = 1$.

So, by Doxastic *Modus Ponens*, we have again:

(2) $e[\neg(p_1\& \ldots \&p_n)\lor r] = 1$.

So in either case we have (2).

Next I rely on that notorious inference, disjunctive syllogism. Whatever its other faults I claim that '$\neg(p_1\& \ldots \&p_n)\lor r, p_1, \ldots, p_n$; therefore r' is a self-evident inference.[13] So by thesis 4.8.9:

(3) $1 - e(r) \leqslant 1 - e[\neg(p_1\& \ldots \&p_n)\lor r] + [1 - e(p_1)] + \ldots + [1 - e(p_n)]$.

From (2) and (3):

(4) $1 - e(r) \leqslant [1 - e(p_1)] + \ldots + [1 - e(p_n)]$.

Therefore:

(5) $1 - d(r) \leqslant [1 - d(p_1)] + \ldots + [1 - d(p_n)]$.

This is the required result.

Next I consider *provably inconsistent polyads*.

Thesis 4.9.10 (The Polyad Rule)

If $\{p_1, \ldots, p_n\}$ is a provably inconsistent polyad and $p_1 \ldots p_n$ all occur in $Dom(d)$ then *either* $d(p_1) + \ldots + d(p_n) \leqslant (n-1)$ *or* the system is δ-inconsistent.

Proof Assume d is δ-consistent and extend to e. Let the derivable self-refuting proposition be r. Then by thesis 4.9.9:

(1) $1 - e(r) \leqslant [1 - e(p_1)] + \ldots + [1 - e(p_n)] = [1 - d(p_1)] + \ldots + [1 - d(p_n)]$.

But $e(r) = 0$, so:

(2) $1 \leqslant [1 - d(p_1)] + \ldots + [1 - d(p_n)]$.

Therefore:

(3) $d(\mathrm{p}_1) + \ldots + d(p_n) \leqslant n - 1$.

Finally I record a result which will be required in the theory of proportional syllogisms.

Thesis 4.9.11 (The Multilemma Rule)

Suppose for $1 \leqslant i < j \leqslant n$ that q, $<q,p_i>$, p_i, and $p_i \& p_j$, are all in $Dom(d)$. Suppose $d(p_i \& p_j) = 0$ if $i \neq j$, and $d(p_1 \vee \ldots \vee p_n) = 1$. Then if $d(q) < d(q/p_i)$ for all i the system is δ-inconsistent.

Proof I suppose that $d(q) < d(q/p_i)$ and show that e, an extension to various propositions, must be δ-inconsistent. Hence by Completability d is itself inconsistent. To do this I assume e is δ-consistent and obtain a *reductio*.

Let r be the conjunction of $p_1 \vee \ldots \vee p_n$ and all the $\neg(p_i \& p_j)$ for $i \neq j$. Then by the Conjunction Rule:

(1) $e(r) = 1$.

Hence by the Restricted Multiplication Principle:

(2) $e(q) = e(q/r)$.

By the Restricted Multiplication Principle and Conditionalization:

(3) $e(q/p_i) = e(q/p_i\&r)$.

But $d(q) < d(q/p_i)$ for all i. So from (2) and (3);

(4) $e(q/r) < e(q/p_i\&r)$ for all i.

But $\{p_1, \ldots, p_n\}$ is a set of alternatives relative to r. So we have a violation of the Principle of Alternative Supposition (given Conditionalization). This is the required *reductio*.

5

Deductive Expansions

I have considered the framework for the dynamics of belief. I am now in a position to discuss inferences by deduction, beginning in this chapter with the case of deductive expansions. Here our particular judgements are in fair agreement with the conventional wisdom that validity is good.

I PROVABILITY VERSUS NECESSITY

Traditionally, logicians have been concerned with what they call *valid* inferences. This word 'valid' is a terminological disaster. For validity is often considered to be a descriptive term and, furthermore, to be a *term of art*, whose use is largely determined by philosophical tradition. But wherever any inference fails to have this attribute of validity it is called *invalid*, which is a *suggestio falsi*. For 'invalid' suggests 'bad'. Now if that were all that were wrong with the term invalid, it would not matter much; we could get used to and ignore the *suggestio*. But the situation is made worse by the way normative considerations have shaped the tradition which in turn has generated the term of art 'validity'. For the most part, logicians have been concerned, among other things, with the *right* sort of inference to make. So, potentially at least, the terms 'valid' and 'invalid' are viciously equivocal between a *partially* stipulated term of art and an evaluative term. I shall, therefore, refrain from using the term. Instead I shall provide a synonym for 'validity'. In mainstream logic, a π-inference is valid if the premises *strictly imply* the conclusion, which is *stipulated* to mean that, of necessity, either at least one premiss is not true or the conclusion is true. I shall say that such inferences are necessarily truth-preserving, avoiding any further use of the term 'valid'.

I now argue that necessary truth-preservation is not that characteristic of the π-inference which, intuitively, is connected with the rationality of making the δ-inference. For the sake of definiteness, I consider someone who is making an inference from certainty in the π-premisses to certainty in the π-conclusion. And I concentrate on the case where the δ-premisses are δ-consistent. We are looking for a class of π-inferences such that it is rational to make the inference from certainty in the premisses to certainty in the conclusion. (At least such that it is rational to do so in suitable circumstances.) I shall argue that necessary truth-preservation is in one way too weak and in another way too strong a condition for entry into this class.

It is too weak because there may be necessary truths which are not provable. A theist like myself might well propose 'God exists' as a necessary truth of this sort. Likewise some atheists might propose 'God does not exist' as a necessary truth of this sort. Nor need we confine ourselves to theological examples. Statements of origin, such as 'Saul Kripke was not born in the nineteenth century' are arguably non-contingent. So if true they are necessary. Yet they are not provable.

But in another respect necessary truth-preservation might be too strong a condition. For suppose, as seems coherent although peculiar, that some of the laws of truth discovered by logicians are contingent even though knowable *a priori*. Then there would be inferences which self-evidently preserve truth, but the world might have been such that they did not. Such a π-inference is just as suited for rational inference-making as a necessarily truth-preserving one. So there is no need to bring necessity into the picture at all (unless the π-inference happens to be one in modal logic). There are good reasons then, for concentrating on provability rather than necessary truth-preservation.

II DEDUCTIONS AND RELATED INFERENCES

I relied on our intuition about the case of inferences from certainty to certainty to justify concentration on the class of provable π-inferences. This gives us the paradigm of deduction, namely inferences from certainty in the premisses of a provable π-inference to certainty in its conclusion. But δ-inferences may be sufficiently like the paradigm to count as deductions even if the attitude to the π-premisses is not one of certainty. For example the *contrast* between the following cases is recognizably a deductive/non-deductive contrast:

Case One

I am certain that Socrates is a man.

I have a high degree of belief that all men are mortal.

So I come to have a high degree of belief that Socrates is mortal.

Case Two

I am certain that Socrates is a man.

I am certain that the vast majority of men are mortal.

So I come to have a high degree of belief that Socrates is mortal.

There are two salient differences between the cases. One is that the first of the π-inferences is provable, but the second is not. The other is that in the second, but not the first, the degree of doubt in the conclusion exceeds that of the premisses.

To make the second contrast more precise I call one minus the (numerical representation of the) degree of belief in p the *measure of doubt* in p. And I say that an inference-making is *conservative* if the measure of doubt in the π-conclusion does not exceed the sum of the measures of doubt in the π-premisses. I then explicate our notion of a deduction as a conservative inference-making whose π-inference is provable.

Related to the concept of a deduction is that of a *contra-deduction*. I begin with *contra-inferences*. To make a contra-inference is to come to disbelieve some proposition (the π-conclusion) as a result of believing various π-premisses. Typically we do not bother to distinguish a contra-inference to disbelief in p, from an inference to belief in $\sim p$. But there is a difference, as is most clearly seen where we suspect there is a truth-value gap. For then disbelief may well be in order where belief in the negation is not. By a *contra-deduction* I mean the making of a contra-inference where:

(1)   The δ-inference is *anti-conservative*, in the sense that the degree of belief in the π-conclusion is no greater than the sum of the measures of doubt in the π-premisses; and

(2)   The π-premisses and π-conclusion form a provably inconsistent set.

I shall not discuss contra-deductions further. The results for them are analogous to those for deductions.

III   THE PRESERVATION OF CONSISTENCY

An expansion to some given proposition or set of propositions is represented by a pair of credence functions d^-/d^+, where the given proposition or set of propositions occurs in the domain of d^+ but not in the domain of d^-. For the case where d^- is δ-consistent I say that d^-/d^+ preserves consistency if d^+ is also δ-consistent. (I shall extend the definition in the next section.) While this definition might seem obvious, it should be noted that it has an element of stipulation. For some expansions from δ-consistent *systems* to δ-inconsistent ones may also be represented by d^-/d^+ where both d^- and d^+ are δ-consistent credence functions. This is because of the inevitable loss of information in the representation.

I now state:

The Existence of Rational
Consistency-Preserving Expansions (from consistency)

Consider any δ-consistent credence function d^- and any proposition r not in the domain of d^-. If there is a consistency-preserving expansion to r then there is some rational consistency-preserving expansion.

This says that if it is possible to expand in a way which preserves δ-consistency then it is possible to do so rationally. And by Completability the antecedent is automatically satisfied.

The justification for this principle is best postponed until we have considered the conjecture that it is not merely rational to expand so as to preserve δ-consistency but irrational not to. This conjecture would express a prejudice in favour of deductions over other inferences, since it will turn out that it is only the deductions that preserve δ-consistency. More precisely we have:

The Obligation to
Preserve Consistency Conjecture

If d^-/d^+ is a rational (internal) expansion and d^- is δ-consistent, then it is conjectured that so is d^+.

Counter-argument This conjecture would seem to derive some support from the way δ-inconsistency is of disvalue in a system. Hence there is a presumption in favour of preserving δ-consistency. But, I claim, this presumption is sometimes overcome. It is overcome if some benefit outweighs the cost of introducing δ-consistency. A benefit which would do so is the discovery of some truth, or something which is likely to be true. This could easily happen for an *external* expansion. An observation might well change a δ-consistent into a δ-inconsistent system. Further, I submit this could happen even for an *internal* expansion as a result of an inference from data to a theory ('inference to the best explanation'). Consider, for example, Dr Methodos who considers for the first time a daring hypothesis, T, that splendidly explains observations $O_1 \ldots O_n$, but, unfortunately is inconsistent with O_{n+1} & H, for some background assumption H. Perhaps he is certain of $O_1 \ldots O_{n+1}$ and H, or nearly so. It is, I claim, rational for him to come to have a high degree of belief in T, even if that destroys δ-consistency. Discovering T is *like* making an observation, it can (temporarily) override considerations of consistency. I support this claim by criticizing the alternatives. One is to adjust first, and then expand. But that is absurd: it is not until one believes T that one needs to adjust. Another alternative is to deny the rationality of coming to believe T at all. And that is even worse. The only other alternative is to insist that a simultaneous expansion-cum-adjustment be made. But human beings are not like that. We are seldom able to adjust and expand simultaneously, and it would, therefore, be an idealization to insist upon that. Furthermore it would be a foolish idealization to make, because if I made it I would have to abandon the Decomposition Principle stated in chapter 2. For that tells us that such an adjustment-cum-expansion would only be rational if the adjustment were already rational. And I have denied it is. I conclude, then, that some internal expansions are rational even though they destroy δ-consistency.

This counter-argument illustrates the way in which the presumption in favour of the preservation of consistency may be overcome. But my discussion of it also shows that to overcome the presumption requires something rather out of the ordinary, like an inference to the best explanation, something which should not be *demanded* of people. To consider a new hypothesis is, I suggest, a work of rational supererogation. So, I submit, it is always rational to preserve consistency even though not always demanded for rationality. And that is what the Existence of Rational Consistency-preserving Expansions states. To be sure, I could idealize the situation by demanding rather more of the logically omniscient person. But no good purpose would be served by such an idealization. So I rely on the Existence of Rational Consistency-preserving Expansions.

The previous conjecture was that consistency-preservation was necessary for rational expansion. And I argued that it is not. Another interesting conjecture is that it is sufficient. So I now consider:

The Rationality of
All Consistency-preserving Expansions Conjecture

If d^-/d^+ is an expansion, and if both d^- and d^+ are δ-consistent, then it is conjectured that d^-/d^+ is rational.

Counter-argument Suppose Paul has never considered the proposition P: the next Australian dollar coin to be tossed will land heads. Suppose further that he has only the sort of information about coins we all have. Then, I suggest, an expansion whose result is belief in P would preserve δ-consistency. For a δ-consistent system could have resulted from the observation that P. But the expansion is intuitively irrational. Or again, consider an expansion whereby Paul, who has not previously thought about these matters, comes to believe that God annihilated the Earth ten years ago and recreated a facsimile five years ago (so five years are missing). This might well preserve δ-consistency, but would scarcely be rational. To these sorts of counter-examples it might be replied that I beg the question against sceptics about non-deductive inference. To that reply I have two rejoinders. The first is: Why not beg the question? Some things have to be taken for granted in philosophy and I am under no obligation to silence sceptics. The second is more eirenic. Recall I am systematizing our *intuitive* judgements and these, surely, are not as the sceptics would have us judge. (If they were we would not call the position a *sceptical* one.)

IV   DEDUCTIVE EXPANSIONS FROM
CONSISTENT SYSTEMS

Consider a provable π-inference whose premisses are $p_1, \ldots, p_n$, and whose conclusion is r. If one already has attitudes to $p_1, \ldots, p_n$

but not to r then one is in a position to make an inference to some degree of belief in r. This will be an expansion. To be more specific, suppose the doxastic system is initially represented by d^-, which is δ-consistent. Then one is in a position to make a δ-inference from degrees of belief $d^-(p_1)$, . . . $d^-(p_n)$ to some degree of belief $d^+(r)$ in r. If this expansion d^-/d^+ is consistency-preserving, then, since d^+ will have to be consistent, we have, by the Subadditivity Rule (thesis 4.9.9), that the measure of doubt in r cannot exceed the sum of the measures of doubt in the p_i. That is:

$$1 - d(r) \leqslant 1 - d(p_1) + \ . \ . \ . \ + 1 - d(p_n)$$

So, by the definition of a deduction, the only consistency-preserving expansions are deductions. If I had assumed the conjecture that consistency-preservation is necessary for rationality this would have established the strong result that the only rational expansion to r is the making of a deduction. However I rejected the conjecture. Therefore I have the weaker result that some deduction from the degrees of belief in p_1, . . . p_n to one in r is rational. But even this establishes a satisfactory connection between deductive expansion and rationality. Formally we have:

Thesis 5.4.1

Consider a provable π-inference 'p_1, p_2 . . ., p_n; therefore r'. And suppose p_1, p_2, . . ., p_n but not r are in the domain of d^- where d^- is δ-consistent. Then:

(1) The only expansions d^-/d^+ to r which preserve consistency are the makings of a deduction from $d^-(p_1)$, . . ., $d^-(p_n)$ to $d(r)$.
(2) Some such deduction is rational.

Proof Part (1) follows immediately from the Subadditivity Rule (thesis 4.9.9) and the definition of a deduction. Part (2) then follows from the Existence of Rational Consistency-preserving Expansions.

Thesis 5.4.1 is rather weak in two respects. The first, which I have already noted, is that there might be rational expansions which fail to preserve consistency. The second is that the requirement that

$$1 - d(r) \leqslant 1 - d(p_1) + \ . \ . \ . \ + 1 - d(p_n)$$

typically underdetermines $d(r)$. So there are many possible deductions. But since I rejected the conjecture that consistency-preservation is sufficient for rationality I have only the result that at least one of these deductions is rational. I have not said which. One case in which this underdetermination does not occur is where $d(p_1) = \ldots = d(p_n) = 1$. In that case we must have $d(r) = 1$ for a deduction. That is, the only expansion from certainty in the premisses to some attitude to r which preserves δ-consistency is that to certainty in r. And that expansion will be rational. Formally we have:

Thesis 5.4.2

Consider a provable π-inference 'p_1, p_2, . . ., p_n; therefore r'. And suppose p_1, . . ., p_n, but not r are in the domain of d^- where d^- is δ-consistent. Further suppose one is certain of the π-premisses. Then:

(1)   The only expansion to r which preserves δ-consistency is the inference to certainty that r; and
(2)   That expansion is rational.

Proof Thesis 5.4.2 is just a special case of thesis 5.4.1.

In an effort to remove the underdetermination of deductive expansion by rationality one might propose that it is always rational to be as cautious as possible. Indeed there may even be those who would say it was irrational not to be cautious. So we have:

The Cautious Deduction Conjecture

In the circumstances of thesis 5.4.1 it is rational to expand to the smallest degree of belief in r which preserves δ-consistency.

Counter-argument Counter-examples occur because non-deductive considerations often further determine the proper degree of belief in the conclusion. For example, if you are certain that at least 99 per cent of people in a certain group will die before age 100 and you have a high degree of belief, say 0.8, that 100 per cent will, but know no further relevant information, then the cautious inference is to a degree of belief 0.8 that a given person in the group will die before age 100.

That will indeed preserve δ-consistency. But considerations of non-deductive logic as discussed in chapter 8 require one to have a much higher degree of belief (0.99) in the conclusion.

I have, then, obtained a connection between rationality and the making of deductions. I have also shown that various natural attempts to strengthen my result fail.

There is one way in which my results can be generalized, however. We do not need to assume the δ-consistency of the initial system. And that is a relief, because very often we do not have δ-consistent systems. I say that an expansion from a δ-inconsistent system *preserves consistency* if it preserves the consistency of all δ-consistent subsystems. With that definition analogues of thesis 5.4.1 and 5.4.2 hold given various provisos. One proviso is that the δ-premisses are themselves δ-consistent. The second is that the Principle of Relevant Adjustment, stated in chapter 3, is satisfied by some consistency-preserving expansion. Of the two provisos it might seem as if the first is redundant. For surely if the δ-premisses themselves are δ-inconsistent then they would be affected by any consistency-restoring adjustment. So the reasons for making the deduction would be undermined. No doubt this is so. But, as I explained in chapter 1, I am not considering the rationality of inferences *qua* inferences but simply *qua* doxastic changes. So the Principle of Relevant Adjustment does not automatically preclude the rationality of inferences from δ-inconsistent premisses. The details of the case of deductive expansion from δ-inconsistent premisses will be found in section VI.

V DISJUNCTIVE SYLLOGISM AND
EX IMPOSSIBILE QUODLIBET

There are two reasons why my project comes into rather little contact with that of the relevance logicians (see Anderson and Belnap 1975 and Routley et al. 1982). The first is that I have not been concerned much either with conditionals or implication (except in a stipulated sense). The second is that I consider the rationality of inferences *qua* doxastic changes. Hence I ignore the dimension of irrationality in which you come to the right conclusion for the wrong reason. So Church's *use criterion* (Church 1951) that requires every premiss to be used and so condemns various kinds of redundancy, is not up for discussion.

There are, however, two pet hates of the relevance logicians which I shall discuss, disjunctive syllogisms and the rule of *ex impossibile quodlibet*. The former consists of π-inferences of the form '$p \lor q$, $\sim p$; therefore q'. The latter consist of π-inferences of the form '$p \& \sim p$; so q'. These two hates are connected, for *ex impossibile quodlibet* is derived using disjunctive syllogism.[1]

Some relevance logicians may also be di-alethic logicians and believe that both p and $\sim p$ could both be true. In that case neither disjunctive syllogism nor *ex impossibile quodlibet* would even be truth-preserving. However the intuitive objection to inferences based on these two rules is not restricted to any special cases in which there are true contradictions. So I shall suppose we ignore that possibility. Then I claim that both disjunctive syllogism and *ex impossibile quodlibet* are provable inferences. There is nothing wrong with them as π-inferences. Yet the relevance logicians are onto something. But, I submit, what they are onto concerns δ-inferences, not π-inferences. I shall concentrate on expansions because that is the case where deductions are most commonly rational. First consider *ex impossibile quodlibet*. If one infers belief in q from belief in p and belief in $\sim p$ one has made a deduction. It is intuitively an irrational one, except for carefully chosen p and q. But it may well be consistency-preserving in the extended sense considered in the previous section. For the subsystem comprising belief in p and belief in q might be consistent as might that comprising belief in $\sim p$ and belief in q. However the theory I have stated fails to apply because the δ-premisses are not consistent. Moreover by the Principle of Relevant Adjustment, it would be rational only if we could first rationally restore δ-consistency and then rationally expand to certainty that q. But on restoring δ-consistency we cannot be certain of both p and $\sim p$. (Recall that we are here ignoring the di-alethic position.) Hence we are no longer in a position rationally to expand to certainty that q. In this way, we can see that what goes wrong with *ex impossible quodlibet*, as stated, is at the level of δ-inferences not π-inferences.

Disjunctive syllogisms are not so straightforward. For sometimes they are intuitively rational. For instance if I have been told on good authority that either p or q but not which, and I already believe that $\sim p$ then it is rational to come to believe q. The suspect cases are those in which the only reasons for believing $p \lor q$ are reasons for believing p but not reasons for believing q. In those cases something is wrong with the system prior to the inference by disjunctive syllogism, namely that one believes $\sim p$ while having good reason to believe p. The case where the good reasons are merely probable ones is more difficult to discuss, and it is not clear to me that making a disjunctive syllogism in that case is irrational, so much as less than maximally rational. Hence I concentrate on the case where one either already believes p or one is in a position to deduce p. In both these cases the system prior to the inference is δ-inconsistent. Hence by the Principle of Relevant Adjustment an expansion to belief in q is rational only if it would have been rational if we had already adjusted to restore δ-consistency. But in the case being considered a consistency-restoring adjustment would either remove the belief in $\sim p$ or the belief in p (or the attitudes from which belief in p could be deduced). Hence the person would no longer be in a position to come to believe q as a result of making the disjunctive syllogism. Therefore the expansion to belief in q would be rational only if the expansion to belief in q could be justified on other grounds. In that case the change which is the making of the disjunctive syllogism would indeed be rational *qua* change. Whether or not it is rational *qua* inference-making is not determined by my theory. But it suffices to say that it would exhibit the defect of coming to believe the right thing for the wrong reason. I conclude, then, that where disjunctive syllogisms are irrational that is not because of any defect in the π-inference, which is provable, but because in various ways it is not always rational to make a deduction, even as an expansion.

VI   DEDUCTIVE EXPANSIONS FROM INCONSISTENT SYSTEMS*

In chapter 3 (section IV) I argued against the conjecture that it was always irrational to expand from a δ-inconsistent system. But I provided a principle putting a constraint on such expansions. A *necessary* condition for the expansion d^-/d^+ to be rational where d^- is δ-inconsistent is that for some rational consistency-restoring adjustment d^-/d^0, d^0/d^+ would be rational. In this section I provide a *sufficient* condition for the special case where d^-/d^+ is the making of a deduction.

First I extend the definition of consistency-preservation to cover the case where d^- is δ-inconsistent. I say an expansion from a δ-inconsistent system *preserves consistency* if it preserves the consistency of every consistent subsystem. More precisely the expansion d^-/d^+ resulting in attitudes to $r_1, r_2 \ldots$ preserves consistency if for every δ-consistent restriction e^- of d^-, $d^+ \parallel R$ is δ-consistent, where $R = Dom(e^-) \cup \{r_1, r_2, \ldots\}$.

I now propose:

The Existence of Rational Consistency-preserving Expansions (from Inconsistency)

Consider any credence function d^- and any proposition r not in $Dom(d^-)$. If there is a consistency-preserving expansion to r which satisfies the Principle of Relevant Adjustment, then there is a rational consistency preserving expansion to r.

Using this principle we may easily generalize thesis 5.4.1 obtaining:

Thesis 5.6.1

Consider a provable π-inference '$p_1, p_2, \ldots, p_n$; therefore r'. And suppose $p_1, \ldots, p_n$ but not r are in $Dom(d^-)$, where $d^- \parallel \{p_1, \ldots, p_n\}$ is δ-consistent (i.e. the δ-premisses are consistent). Then:

(1)	The only expansions d^-/d^+ to r which preserve consistency are deductions from $d^-(p_1), \ldots d^-(p_n)$; and
(2)	If there is a consistency-preserving expansion to r which satisfies the Principle of Relevant Adjustment, then some such deduction is rational.

Proof This is as for thesis 5.4.1. Part (1) follows from the Subadditivity Rule (thesis 4.9.9) and the definition of deduction. Part (2) then follows by the Principle of the Existence of Rational Consistency-preserving Expansions.

6

Towards a Theory
of Adjustments

Not all inferences are expansions. For I can infer from what I believe something which I previously disbelieved. And that is an adjustment. In this chapter I begin my investigation of adjustments, including a discussion of those which are inferences by deduction. I also take the opportunity to discuss the connection between 'validity' and rationality.

I TWO BASIC PRINCIPLES

One principle is implicit in the No Obligation Principle for Contractions. It is:

The Possibility of Rational Adjustment

If d^- is δ-inconsistent then there is some rational adjustment d^-/d^+ which restores δ-consistency.

I now rely on the idealization of logical omniscience and state:

The Preservation of Consistency by Adjustments

If d^-/d^+ is an adjustment, and d^- is δ-consistent but d^+ is δ-inconsistent then d^-/d^+ is irrational.

Notice that this is analogous to a rejected conjecture, namely that every rational expansion should preserve δ-consistency. The counter-argument to that relied on an inference to the best explanation. But the analogous counter-argument fails here. For the sake of definiteness, consider Dr Methodos again, who has observed $O_1 \ldots O_{n+1}$, makes background assumption H, and notices that theory T explains $O_1, \ldots, O_n$ but that O_{n+1}, T and H form a provably inconsistent triad. Initially, because of Popperian inclinations, Dr Methodos rejects T for that reason. Subsequently he adopts a more relaxed attitude, and comes to believe T because of its explanatory power. In this case he adjusts his degree of belief of T upwards and thereby destroys δ-consistency. Now ordinarily we might judge Dr Methodos to be rational. But recall that we are to consider him to be logically omniscient. As in the previous case, then, it is *possible* for a logically omniscient Dr Methodos to preserve δ-consistency. All he has to do is to adjust his degrees of belief in O_{n+1} and T simultaneously. And unlike the previous case there are good reasons for requiring this for rationality. The *first* is that either there is no departure from what is typical of human beings, or it is much less drastic than for the previous case. For in the previous case we would have required complicated adjustments-cum-expansions, but here we require only an adjustment to more than one proposition, which is something we often do. The *second* is that in the previous case we would have had to reject the Decomposition Principle, and so, *for the sake of an idealization*, we would have *complicated* our theory. But we have already rejected the Adjustment One at a Time Conjecture, so there is no such cost in this case. The *third*, and most important, reason is that if one adjustment which destroyed δ-consistency were allowed, it would be *ad hoc* not to allow a sequence of them. For example, suppose $O_1, \ldots O_{n+1}$ and T now provide evidence for a higher order theory T_2, which unfortunately is inconsistent with a few of the O_i. $O_1, \ldots O_{n+1}$ and T_2 now provide evidence for T_3, again unfortunately inconsistent with some more of the O_i, and so on. This could go on until we arrive at an especially splendid theory T_m which is, regrettably, consistent with none of the O_i. Once we allow an adjustment which leads to δ-inconsistency, I see no way of judging it irrational to come to believe T_m. To prevent this we should not even allow the first adjustment.

The Preservation of Consistency Principle, then, systematizes our particular judgements, in the sense that it is a first approximation based on the idealization of logical omniscience. Actual departures from it may be excused, or even justified, by appeal to our human limitations.

More problematic is whether a rational adjustment from a

δ-inconsistent system must *restore* δ-consistency. I have no firm intuition here. So I merely record the rather weak:

The Progress Towards Consistency Principle

If d^- is δ-inconsistent then an adjustment d^-/d^+ is irrational unless d^+ is nearer δ-consistency than d^-.

I defer any explication of being nearer δ-consistency until section VI.

II MINIMAL ADJUSTMENTS

An interesting class of adjustments are those which adjust by only as much as is required to restore δ-consistency; I call these *minimal adjustments*. (I explicate minimality in section VI.) If the only logical disvalues were those of inconsistency then only minimal adjustments would be rational. As a special case we would have the result that if d^- is already δ-consistent, then there is no rational adjustment d^-/d^+, even if d^+ is also δ-consistent (except the degenerate case of no change, if you call that an adjustment). However I believe there are logical values other than δ-consistency, which I discuss in chapter 9. Hence it will be quite rational to adjust from one δ-consistent system to another for the sake of those values. Nonetheless, minimal adjustments are important for two reasons. The first is because there is a simple answer to the question 'Why did you make that adjustment?', where it is minimal. The answer is 'Precisely to restore consistency'. But for any *further* adjustment some additional answer is required. The second is that while the total logical value may well be maximized by an over-adjustment (i.e. an adjustment beyond the minimum required to restore δ-consistency), I take it that such over-adjustments are works of supererogation. My intuitive judgements support the claim that some minimal adjustment is rational in the circumstances. Accordingly I propose a strengthening of the Possibility of Rational Adjustment, namely:

The Existence of Rational Minimal Adjustments

If d^- is δ-inconsistent there is some rational adjustment d^-/d^+ which is minimal.

This principle presupposes that there is a minimal adjustment from any δ-consistent system. I prove that result in section VI (thesis 6.6.1).

Because over-adjustments for the sake of logical values other than δ-consistency are works of rational supererogation, it might seem that any minimal adjustment would be rational. So I shall consider:

The Conjecture of the Rationality of
Any Minimal Adjustment

If d^- is δ-inconsistent and d^-/d^+ is a minimal adjustment, then it is conjectured that d^-/d^+ is rational.

Counter-argument Consider the inconsistent chiliad $P_0, \ldots, P_{999}$, where P_0 is the proposition that one of the tickets number 1 to 999 will be selected, and P_n, for $n = 1, \ldots, 999$, is the proposition that ticket number n will not be selected. Now suppose that initially one is certain of all thousand propositions. Further suppose one has only the usual information about lotteries. Then the system is δ-inconsistent: it violates the Inconsistent Polyad Rule (thesis 4.9.10). Which consistency-restoring adjustments are intuitively rational? I submit that rationality requires symmetrical adjustment to the attitudes to $P_1, \ldots, P_{999}$. I judge it irrational, for instance, to restore δ-consistency by coming to be contracertain that P_1 while remaining certain that $P_2, \ldots, P_{999}$. Yet that symmetry-breaking adjustment would be minimal. I conclude that not all minimal adjustments are rational.

III   DEDUCTIVE ADJUSTMENTS

In the previous two sections I was able to obtain some principles governing the rationality of adjustments. While these have intrinsic interest, they do not help us much when it comes to a theory of deductive adjustment. For, as I shall argue, there is not much one can say about deductive adjustments except by way of counter-example to conjectures. However, I begin with a positive result. Consider the situation where δ-consistency could be restored by contracting away from the proposition r. So the attitude to r is the only obstacle to δ-consistency. And suppose r is the conclusion of a provable π-inference, and there are attitudes to the π-premises $p_1, \ldots, p_n$. Then there is a deduction from the degrees of belief in the premises $p_1, \ldots, p_n$ to some new degree of belief in r, which is a minimal consistency-restoring adjustment. The proof of this result (thesis 6.6.2) I defer until section VI.

I now turn to the question of whether there are rational deductive adjustments. In some circumstances there are. Suppose there is a provable π-inference '$p_1, \ldots, p_n$; therefore r', and I have various degrees of belief in $p_1, \ldots, p_n$ and r. Suppose also that the measure of doubt in r is too little, that is, it is less than the sum of the measures of doubt in the p_i. Then (by thesis 4.9.9) my system is δ-inconsistent. Further suppose that my attitudes to $p_1, \ldots, p_n$ are based on observations or on very good reasons, but that my attitude to r was the result of mere caprice – I have no reason whatever for it. In that case, my intuition is that it is rational to adjust by increasing the measure of doubt in r so as to restore δ-consistency, without altering my degrees of belief in $p_1, \ldots, p_n$. Further my intuition is that this is the only rational adjustment which restores δ-consistency. This adjustment is the making of a deduction. However, the circumstances in which the attitude to the π-conclusion is quite without justification are not typical.

Can our result be strengthened? If I had accepted the rationality of any minimal adjustment then the previous result (thesis 6.6.2) would have proved the following conjecture, which, however, I shall argue against.

The Conjecture of the Existence of Rational Deductive Adjustments

If it is possible to restore δ-consistency by means of a deduction then, it is conjectured, it is possible to do so rationally.

Counter-argument Consider again a lottery situation. P_0, as before, is the proposition that precisely one of tickets number 1 to 999 will be selected. In this example, the person does not consider P_i but rather Q_i, the proposition that ticket number i will be selected, for $i = 1 \ldots 999$. (So $P_i = \sim Q_i$). Suppose the person is initially certain of P_0 because he or she has been told, and contracertain of all the P_i but for no good reason. Then δ-consistency can be restored by means of a deduction to certainty in one of the Q_i. But it cannot be rationally restored by a deduction. For by symmetry the person would have to come to be certain of all of the Q_i, but that also violates δ-consistency.

Furthermore δ-consistency cannot even rationally be restored by means of the contra-deduction to contracertainty in P_0. To be sure, that is not excluded by symmetry. But since the person has been told that P_0 it is intuitively too drastic.

IV   WHAT IS SO GOOD ABOUT VALID INFERENCES?

I am now in a position to discuss some general questions about deduction. So I shall interrupt my theory of adjustments, and digress. First, as I noted in chapter 5, section I, it is not validity in the sense of necessary truth-preservation, but rather provability that is interesting and important. Granted that, we may say that provable π-inferences are important because they form the basis for deductions. And deductions occupy a special place in the theory of expansions. As thesis 5.4.2 shows, if the doxastic system is already δ-consistent and the π-conclusion has not already been considered, then a deductive expansion from certainty in the π-premises to certainty in the π-conclusion is bound to be rational. Where we do not have certainty in the π-premises, there will still be *some* deduction which is rational. And even where d^- is δ-inconsistent, thesis 5.5.1 tells us that analogous results hold in suitable circumstances. All these results are in accordance with the orthodoxy that being valid is good. But that is the end of the vindication of orthodoxy. Firstly, as I argued in chapter 5, section III, there are rational expansions which destroy δ-consistency. Hence we should not assume that where a deduction can be made it is the most rational inference to make. A non-deductive consistency-destroying inference might be more rational, as the example of Dr Methodos suggests. Secondly, and even more impressively, is the failure of deduction to be central to a theory of adjustments. To be sure, in suitable circumstances, some deduction will be a minimal adjustment. But as I argued in the previous section, we cannot in general assume that because δ-consistency can be restored by a deduction it can be rationally restored by one.

I conclude that the connection between validity and rationality is by no means as straightforward as is often assumed: 'validity' is not all it is cracked up to be.

V   THE PROBLEM OF THE DIRECTION OF THE
ARROW OF *MODUS TOLLENS*

The failure of adjustment to have much to do with deduction, which occasioned the digression of the last section, leads naturally to a problem which adjustments have a great deal to do with, that of how δ-inconsistency is rationally to be removed. Using Lakatos's happy metaphor I call this the Problem of the Direction of the Arrow of *Modus Tollens*. And it has been discussed most widely in the context where one or more observations $O_1, \ldots, O_n$ have been made, where there is a theory T, and where there is an auxiliary hypothesis H, consisting of common-sense or background theories. If, as sometimes happens, $O_1, \ldots, O_n$, T and H form a provably inconsistent polyad, then someone who believes (to a suitably high degree) all of $O_1, \ldots, O_n$, T and H has a problem. For his or her doxastic system is δ-inconsistent. The problem, then, is which of $O_1, \ldots O_n$, T and H to abandon. Now if n is fairly large, maybe we can rationally believe all the members of the inconsistent polyad, but without full belief, that is certainty. For we could have a suitable lack of *confidence* in all of them, where that lack is compatible with belief. So the problem presents itself most crucially for the case where n is small. So, for definiteness, I shall consider a provably inconsistent triad O, T, H. By the Inconsistent Polyad Rule we require the sum of the degrees of belief in O, T and H to be no greater than 2. I shall assume, again for the sake of definiteness, that the person happens to be agnostic about some proposition P for which his or her degree of belief is at least ⅔.[1] (Perhaps he or she is agnostic about whether the next throw of some die will lead to a 1, 2, 3 or 4.) Hence we cannot dodge the issue by suggesting that belief in all three of O, T and H, with diminished confidence, can restore δ-consistency. For degrees of belief less than ⅔ cannot in the present case be beliefs.

There are some cases where the direction of the arrow of *modus tollens* is totally unproblematic, namely where *on other grounds* we should reject one of O, H, and T. Suppose, as is common, that O is a second-hand observation. And suppose I discover evidence that the observer was a fraud. Then O should be rejected. Again, suppose that T is a mere conjecture, but O and H are more firmly based. Then, intuitively, we should reject T. The problem is a *problem* only where all three of the degrees of belief in O, T and H properly resist change. Thus, we may suppose the observation is by a reliable observer, the theory has been previously well confirmed and to deny *H* would be *ad hoc*. The problem in this case is to discover what is the rational change.

Having now set up the problem, let us examine various responses to it, beginning with an option left open by Quine (1953). We could come to reject the hitherto-accepted principles of positive logic. I suggest that is only for the desperate. In the typical case, at least, the principles of positive logic are safe.[2]

Another response to the problem is to resort to *conventions*. Popper, for example, in *Conjectural Knowledge*, says that he soon realized that '*empirical refutations could always be avoided*' because it was always possible to ' "immunize" any theory against criticism' (Popper 1972, p. 30). Here he is alluding to the fact that the observation does not directly refute the theory but rather the theory conjoined with the auxiliary hypothesis. So empirical refutation is avoided if we reject the auxiliary hypothesis instead of the theory. Popper goes on to say:

> Thus I was led to the idea of *methodological rules* and of the fundamental importance of a *critical approach*; that is, of an approach which avoided the policy of immunizing our theories against refutation. At the same time, I also realized the opposite: the value of a *dogmatic* attitude: somebody had to defend a theory against criticism, or it would succumb too easily, and before it had been able to make its contribution to the growth of science.

In this passage Popper explicitly talks of 'methodological rules', and he talks about a critical *approach*, about avoiding a certain *policy* and about the value of a dogmatic *attitude*. All of which shows that Popper, faced with the Problem of the Direction of the Arrow of *Modus Tollens*, proposes *methodological conventions* about *strategies* to be adopted in putting forward theories. Lakatos's response is of the same sort – an appeal to methodological conventions. According to Lakatos, 'all scientific research programmes may be characterised by their "hard core"' (Lakatos 1970, p. 133). The hard core consists of some theory for which we have made the *provisional* methodological decision that it is not to be rejected; we decide instead to modify the auxiliary hypothesis. The methodological decision is a provisional one, because we may, and should, appraise the research programme itself. But this appraisal is not in terms of whether the theory that constitutes its hard core is supported by the evidence; *research programmes* are appraised according to the *progressive* or *degenerating* character of the problem-shifts they generate. We may say, then, that Lakatos proposes, as a methodological convention, a *provisional dogmatism*. Conventions never solve problems; they merely settle them. So this appeal to methodological conventions is not a solution to the problem of the Direction of the Arrow of *Modus Tollens*. Rather, it would seem appropriate, if at all, only *after* we had concluded that the problem was insoluble.

By contrast Quine's response (1953, p. 43) to the Problem of the Direction of the Arrow of *Modus Tollens* does not require conventions. He says, of our belief systems, 'Any statement can be held true come what may, if we make drastic enough adjustments elsewhere in the system'. And he says that we have a 'natural tendency to disturb the total system as little as possible'. Quine's talk about having a *natural tendency* has the conversational implication that *all* we have is a natural tendency. So his response amounts to this:

> Let us admit that it is arbitrary whether we reject the theory or the auxiliary hypothesis. But notice that people have a natural tendency to make one decision rather than the other, depending on which results in the least disturbance to the total system.

This response is, I suggest, a sceptical one which runs counter to our intuitive judgement. It is not arbitrary whether we reject theory T, auxiliary hypothesis H (or observation O). For if it were, there would be nothing rationally to prevent our sticking with the theory T regardless what observations were made which clashed with T, and regardless of how well confirmed the auxiliary hypotheses were. But we recognize the value of being empirical, that is, of testing theories against observations. Quine's thesis is incompatible with this intuition: it licenses an *obstinate dogmatism*. But it also licenses the opposite error, that of *rash scepticism*. Quine's thesis would warrant an Herodian policy of massacring infant theories by the score. For it is quite typical of new-born theories to come into conflict with a combination of observation and auxiliary hypothesis.[3] There would *be* no problem of the Direction of the Arrow of *Modus Tollens* except that intuitively we reject both obstinate dogmatism and rash scepticism.

However, if we remove its scepticism, this passage from Quine suggests a more constructive solution to the problem. I shall call this:

The Quinean Conjecture

The rational adjustments for the restoration of δ-consistency are conjectured to be those which alter the system by as little as possible.

Counter-argument The Quinean conjecture licenses too high-handed a response to 'recalcitrant phenomena'. If you make a disturbing observation *O*, which conflicts with your dearly loved and well-developed theory *T*, then by far the least disturbance results from coming to disbelieve *O*. And that is, of course, a *natural* tendency. But it is, we sometimes judge, irrational. Yet it is a minimal adjustment in my sense.

Now I might be charged with a simplistic interpretation of the Quinean Conjecture. Perhaps we should read 'altering the system as little as possible' as 'altering the system as little as possible taking into consideration the epistemic importance of the beliefs'. In that case we could obtain what is essentially one of Gärdenfors' (1984, pp. 136–57) accounts of what I call adjustments.[4] The basic idea is that in choosing which of *T*, *H* and *O* to disbelieve we pick out the one which is of least epistemic importance. I grant this as a friendly amendment to the Quinean Conjecture, and I assume we have a good enough grasp of epistemic importance. But I still reject the conjecture. I reject it because of its all or nothing character. For, I claim that where belief in *T*, *H* and *O* are all *independently justified* (i.e. where but for the δ-inconsistency, no adjustment would be called for) one should come to have a lower degree of confidence in all three. Suppose *T* is less epistemically important than *H*, which is, in turn, less important than *O*. Then rather than totally rejecting *T* while retaining full confidence in *H* and *O*, we should reduce our degree of belief in *T* by a lot, in *H* by less and in *O* by even less. This will involve coming to disbelieve *T* but not with contracertainty. And it might involve no longer believing *H*, or even *O*.

My discussion of the Quinean Conjecture has implicitly been a defence of the Compromise Solution, which I espouse.[5] The Compromise Solution tells us that, where there was a genuine problem, we should diminish the degree of belief in all three of *T*, *H* and *O*, by an amount depending on other considerations, namely the sort we have in mind when we talk of epistemic importance. And *as part* of this overall diminution of degrees of belief we shall no longer believe all three of T, H and O. Notice the intimate connection between the Compromise Solution and the lack of much connection between deduction and adjustment. For to reject T, while maintaining the complete degree of belief in H and O, would have been to make a contra-deduction from belief in H and O to disbelief in T. And it would typically be accompanied by the deduction from belief in H and in O to belief in $\sim T$.

An additional advantage of the Compromise Solution is that it enables us to give due consideration to the number of (independent) observations made. For suppose O_1, the first observation, is of less epistemic importance than H and T. Further suppose we successively make similar observations O_2, O_3 . . ., none of which taken individually are of as great epistemic importance as H and T. Then if we always completely reject the least important belief we shall disbelieve O_1, then disbelieve O_2, and so on, always retaining belief in H and in T. Yet intuitively, at some stage the combination of O_1, O_2, . . . O_n might be more important than T. On the Compromise Solution, each time we observe an O_i the degree of belief in T will be reduced a little more. So eventually we shall no longer believe T at all.

The Compromise Solution, then, has much to recommend it. But there is an objection to it, which needs consideration. It is that I have not shown by *what amount* the degree of belief in O, in T and in H should be lowered. All I have done is indicated that the amount should vary in ways obscurely covered by the concept of epistemic importance. To this I give what I call the *modified Duhem response*. The *unmodified* Duhem response is to appeal to *good sense* (Duhem 1954, chapter VI). And I take it that Duhemian good sense is much the same as what I call our intuitive judgements. So the unmodified Duhem response is to brazen it out and insist that our intuitive judgements need no further justification.

If driven to it I would brazen it out with Duhem. But if I did then I would take a risk. The risk, as I understand it, is that there will be an especially elegant systematic theory which requires the rejection of a few of our intuitions. By analogy with scientific method – or by appeal to *a priori* knowledge – we might consider that the theory should win here over the data (the intuitions). Indeed the unmodified Duhem response amounts to giving complete precedence, at the meta-level, to the data over the theory. If such precedence is justified there, why should it not be justified at the lower level, when discussing the Problem of the Direction of the Arrow of *Modus Tollens*? In that case we would obtain the hyper-Popperian thesis that theories always give way to observations. The very occurrence of the Problem of the Direction of the Arrow of *Modus Tollens* should make us wary of adopting an unmodified Duhem response to it. I suggest, then, that it is better to systematize our intuitive judgements as elegantly as we can. If we can do so without rejecting them, then, I say, the intuitive judgements are more secure than they would otherwise be. The modified Duhemian response, then, is to rely on a combination of our intuitive judgements and a systematic theory.[6] The required systematization will have to wait, though, until I develop the comparative theory of rationality, when I shall discuss which adjustments are the *most* rational. Until then no further progress can be made in the theory of adjustments. For the next two chapters I shall develop the theory of expansions to cover the case of non-deductive inferences.

VI   EXPLICATIONS AND PROOFS*

In section II I considered the case in which one system is *nearer δ-consistency* than another. I also considered *minimal* adjustments. In this section I explicate these related notions. In addition I show that there are minimal consistency-restoring adjustments (thesis 6.6.1). Finally I prove a result (thesis 6.6.2) (stated informally in section III) which shows the occurrence of minimal consistency-restoring adjustments which are deductions.

What it is for one system to be *nearer δ-consistency* than another? We might try to measure how far a credence function is from δ-consistency by introducing a *metric* or *distance-function* on the set of all credence functions with a given domain. Two well-known distance-functions are:

(1) $\text{dist}(d_1, d_2) = \sqrt{\Sigma} \, [d_1(p) - d_2(p)]^2$
(2) $\text{dist}(d_1, d_2) = \Sigma |d_1(p) - d_2(p)|$

In both cases the sum Σ is taken over all members of the (common) domain of d_1 and d_2. But I fail to see any reason for picking out one rather than another of these, or the infinitely many other, distance formulae. Furthermore, there is no guarantee that the representations of a doxastic system are unique, even when we require, as I do, that for δ-consistency the Addition Principle holds. So the distance function might depend on the choice of representation.

I propose, then, a more qualitative approach. First I say that credence function e is *between* credence functions d_1 and d_2 if:

(1) e, d_1 and d_2 all have the same domain;
(2) e is not identical to either d_1 or d_2; and
(3) For all p in that domain $e(p)$ is either equal to or between $d_1(p)$ and $d_2(p)$.

I then say that d^+ is at least as *near* δ-consistency as d^0 if:

Either d^+ is δ-consistent, or, for some δ-consistent e, d^+ is between d^0 and e.

Then d^+ is *nearer* δ-consistency than d^0 if d^+ is at least as near δ-consistency as d^0 and the converse does not hold.

It is easy to check that there is a partial ordering of credence functions with respect to nearness to δ-consistency.

To explicate what it is for an adjustment to be *minimal* I rely on the notion of betweenness. I say an adjustment d^-/d^+ is minimal if d^+ is δ-consistent and there is no d also δ-consistent between d^- and d^+. The Existence of Rational Minimal Adjustments, then, pre-supposes:

Thesis 6.6.1

For any d^- which is δ-inconsistent there is some minimal adjustment d^-/d^+.

Proof Here I assume I have stated all the principles of δ-consistency. Choose any suitable distance function for $\{d \mid Dom(d) = Dom(d^-)\}$. If $Dom(d^-)$ is finite, $dist(d_1, d_2) = \Sigma \mid d_1(p) - d_2(p) \mid$ will do. If $Dom(d) = \{p_1, p_2 \ldots\}$ is countably infinite, $\Sigma(\frac{1}{2})^i \mid d_1(p) - d_2(p) \mid$ will do. Then we find some member, call it d^+, of $\{d \mid Dom(d) = Dom(d^-)$ and d is δ-consistent$\}$ for which $dist(d^-, d^+)$ minimizes the distance between d^- and members of that set.[7] If d is between d^- and d^+ it is easy to check that $dist(d^-, d) < dist(d^-, d^+)$ so d is not δ-consistent. Hence the adjustment d^-/d^+ is indeed minimal.

Finally I state:

Thesis 6.6.2

Consider a provable π-inference 'p_1, p_2, . . ., p_n; therefore r'. And suppose that all of p_1, p_2, . . ., p_n and r are in $Dom(d^-)$. Suppose further that d^- is δ-inconsistent, but that the credence function obtained by excising r from $Dom(d^-)$ is δ-consistent. Then there is a deduction from $d^-(p_1)$ . . . $d^-(p_n)$ to some degree of belief $d^+(r)$ which is a minimal consistency-restoring adjustment.

Proof Once again assume I have stated all the principles of δ-consistency. Let d^* be the credence function obtained by excising r from $Dom(d^-)$. Then, since d^* is δ-consistent, by completability there is a consistent extension of d^* back to r. So there is a non-empty set of real numbers: $\{d(r)|d$ is a consistent extension of d^* back to $r\}$. It is easy to check that this has a maximum and a minimum member. Let whichever is nearer to $d^-(r)$ be $d^+(r)$. Then d^-/d^+ is minimal. Since d^+ is δ-consistent, and since $d^+(p_i) = d^-(p_i)$, $i = 1$ . . . n, it follows by the Subadditivity Rule (thesis 4.9.9) that coming to have $d^+(r)$ as a result of having $d^-(p_1)$ . . . $d^-(p_n)$ is indeed a deduction.

7

Probable Inference

In the last two chapters I discussed the normative theory of those changes which are deductions. In this chapter and the next I turn to other sorts of inferences, namely those in which the π-inference is not provable but is probable. I shall concentrate on rational consistency-preserving expansions to the conclusion of a probable π-inference, where there are already attitudes to the premisses.

Although one of my aims is to provide a detailed theory of some probable inferences (namely proportional syllogisms) using my normative theory, another of my aims is to show that the logic of probable inferences *is* purely normative, in the sense that the positive logic involved, if any, concerns provable inferences. That is, there is no need, or even opportunity, for a positive probabilistic logic. To show this I compare some different approaches to probable inferences. I call them the Factual, the Logical, the Subjectivist and the Normative theories of probable inferences. I argue by elimination that only the Normative Theory of Probable Inferences could be adequate. I then argue for the superiority of one of the variants of the Normative Theory.

By itself this discussion provides grounds for saying that the only approach to probable inferences which *could* provide a satisfactory systematic theory is the one I adopt. But in the next chapter I show that the normative approach does indeed provide a satisfactory systematic theory, at the very least, for a theory of proportional syllogisms. Together these considerations provide an argument for the thoroughly normative character of the logic of probable inferences.

I   REJECTED THEORIES OF PROBABILITY

Here is a paradigm of the making of a probable δ-inference:

I am certain that the urn contains one black and 99 white balls
and that the ball I shall select is in the urn. So I come to have
a high degree of belief (0.99) that the ball I select will be white.

There are two features of this inference-making which clearly
distinguish it from a deduction. *First* it is not conservative. I do not
come to be certain of the π-conclusion but merely have a high degree
of belief (0.99) in it. *Secondly*, the π-inference, namely:

The urn contains one black and 99 white balls.
The ball I shall select is in the urn.
Therefore the ball I shall select is white.

is not provable. Nor is it necessarily truth-preserving: I *might* select
the one black ball.

I now consider various approaches to probable inference-making,
illustrating them by means of the paradigm I have mentioned. *First*,
there is what I call the Factual Probability Theory. On this approach
some non-logical, non-normative, *facts* about the situation determine
the rationality of making the inference in question. On one variant,
the factual probability of an inference-schema is identified with the
proportion of its instances which are truth-preserving. Alternatively,
(Reichenbach 1949) the inference-schema is assumed to have an
infinite sequence I_1, I_2, etc. of instances. In that case the probability
is identified with the limit of the relative frequencies of truth-preserving
inferences (provided that limit exists). This variant of the factual
approach is not suited, and was not intended,[1] to apply to individual
inference-makings. And since we are concerned with the rationality
of making a given inference on a given occasion, it is not a very
promising approach. Far more promising is the propensity variant.
On this variant, some *propensity* or *objective chance*[2] of my selecting a
white ball would be posited. And it might be said that if I knew this
propensity or chance then it would be rational for me to have a degree
of belief that a white ball will be selected equal to it.

The attempt to rely exclusively on factual probabilities meets very
grave difficulties. The chief one, I think, is that we seldom, if ever,
know the factual probability. We have to *estimate* it. But the process
by which we estimate it is itself one of probable reasoning. So we should
not, on pain of circularity, give a factual probability account of
probable inference. For instances, suppose I used a specified probable

inference-schema on 100 occasions and had extremely good reasons to believe the premisses were true in all 100 cases and that the inference preserved truth on 99 of those 100 occasions. To come to a belief about the proportion of *all* the instances of the schema which preserve truth I have to make an inference from a *sample* of the inferences to the whole population of the inferences. And *that* is itself a probable inference, and one which is more problematic than the paradigm which I am considering. There is a similar difficulty with propensities.

I now turn to what I call the Logical Theory. This is the attempt, notably by Carnap at one time (Carnap 1962), to extend positive logic to provide an account of probable inferences. On this approach there will be a conditional probability $P(p/q)$ defined for any p and any consistent q. $P(p/q)$ is a measure of *partial entailment*, in the sense that q entails p if and only if $P(p/q) = 1$, and p and q are inconsistent if and only if $P(p/q) = 0$. So if $P(p/q)$ is between 0 and 1 (and, on a modification to Carnap's theory, it might be *infinitesimally* different from 0 or from 1) q *partially* entails p. The probability of the π-inference, then, could be identified with the logical probability of the conclusion relative to the conjunction of the premisses. Given a suitable theory of logical probabilities, all we would need is some fairly simple connection between logical probabilities and rational degrees of belief. Then we could obtain a theory of probable inference-making whose normative component is trivial, or nearly so.

On a modification of this approach we could follow Kyburg (1974, p. 247) and treat a probability as an interval of real numbers rather than a precise number. But, for our present purpose we may ignore this development and concentrate on a simpler Carnapian approach.

It is generally conceded that the rational degree(s) of belief in the π-conclusion of a probable inference may depend not just on the degrees of belief in the π-premisses but on other relevant degrees of belief. Thus, consider the π-inference:

> There are 100 balls in the urn, 99 of which are white, one of which is black.
> I shall select one ball.
> So I shall select a white one.

The probability of this π-inference will turn out to be 0.99. But even if I am certain of the π-premisses I should not come to have a degree of belief 0.99 in the π-conclusion, if I also believe the black ball is bigger than the white ones, and that I shall select the biggest ball I can feel in the urn. On the Logical approach then, we rely on the Requirement of Total Evidence. This tells us to have a degree of belief in the π-conclusion equal to the logical probability of the π-conclusion relative to *all* the evidence available.[3] If we stipulate that the premisses of the probable π-inference express *all* the empirical information, then it is initially plausible that the degree of belief in the conclusion should be equal to the logical probability of the inference itself (or, following Kyburg, within the indicated range).

I have two objections to the Logical Theory. The less serious is that the distinction between evidence and other beliefs is somewhat problematic.[4] Much more serious is that the evidence may itself be merely probable, that is, not believed with certainty. There can be cases where it is quite proper to have a high degree of belief less than certainty in the result of an observation. For instance, when I look at the Pleiades I am certain I see six stars, but there are two or three others which I am not sure I see (see Jeffrey 1968, section 2). Nor do we always have further evidence with respect to which these observations are probable.[5] If that is granted, then we need to know what degree of belief it is rational to have in some proposition r, given *varying* degrees of belief in the empirical observations. This could seem a mere quibble. For typically observation does result in full belief. So why not ignore the other cases, at least as a first approximation? One answer is that most evidence is not due to direct observation. Most is the result of memory and testimony.[6] And while I usually believe what I seem to remember, or what people tell me, often it is with less than perfect confidence. Moreover, frequently we build up one probable inference on another, where the conclusion of an earlier inference is a premiss (a piece of 'evidence') for a later one. It is preferable not to exclude this by demanding that one always go back to evidence in the strict sense. To all this it might be replied that we can graft a normative theory of probable inference onto the logical approach, provided we do not expect a totally trivial normative component to the theory.

But how can this be done? I fail to see what the principle would be. Perhaps something very complicated would work but simple suggestions fail. For instance suppose we require that:

$$\mathrm{d}(r) = P(r/p_1 \& \ldots \& p_n) \times \mathrm{d}(p_1 \& \ldots \& p_n)$$

Here I take it that r is the conclusion of a probable π-inference and that all the (relevant) evidence is included in the π-premisses $p_1, \ldots p_n$. That is a simple enough conjecture, but it should be rejected. For sometimes the pieces of evidence cannot all be correct. (They form an inconsistent polyad.) Then δ-consistency requires $d(p_1 \& \ldots \& p_n) = 0$. But it is far too strong to require that if the (relevant) evidence is inconsistent then we should be contracertain of the conclusion, or even that we should fail to believe it. Suppose Mr H. I. Till is charged with embezzlement. The prosecution has ten independent witnesses, and the evidence of even one or two would, by itself, be enough to commit Mr Till. But his lawyer, a good logician, shows that they cannot all be telling the truth although any nine could. I maintain a jury should still convict. And, more to the point, I maintain it is irrational to come to be certain that Mr Till is innocent simply because *all* the (relevant) evidence forms an inconsistent decad. This example also shows that replacing equality by an inequality

$$d(r) \geqslant P(r/p_1 \& \ldots \& p_n) \times d(p_1 \& \ldots \& p_n)$$

is too weak a requirement. Likewise the requirement that

$$d(r \& p_1 \& \ldots \& p_n) = P(r/p_1 \& \ldots \& p_n) \times d(p_1 \& \ldots \& p_n)$$

is too weak. I admit that rejecting a simple conjecture shows very little. But I give it as an illustration of the sort of difficulties that arise. And I doubt that any tolerably simple principle can be found that will do better.

In spite of a considerable admiration for Carnap's achievement I abandon the Logical approach. The remaining non-normative (or, I believe, limitedly normative) approach enjoying currency is that of the subjectivists, or Bayesians, such as Savage (1954) and de Finetti (e.g. 1974). They require only that credence functions be 'coherent' in the sense that betting quotients representing the degrees of belief are proof against a Dutch book. This 'coherence' requirement amounts, roughly, to the requirement that the system be δ-consistent. What is characteristic of the subjectivist theory is its insistence that, once we have restricted our attention to coherent systems, it is purely *descriptive*. No further normative judgements are made. In their place, the subjectivist simply notes that people have various tendencies. For instance, often credence functions have a certain symmetry.[7] That is, whatever is believed of a is also believed of b, for two names 'a' and 'b'. Or more generally, for various permutations of proper names 'a_1', . . ., 'a_n', $d[F(a_i)] = d[F(a_j)]$, where $F(x)$ is a suitable predicate. Again, often credence functions satisfy various independence constraints, that is: $d(p/q) = d(p)$, for various p and q.

Now, not making various judgements will not lead the subjectivist into error. But subjectivists, such as de Finetti, are not merely limiting the scope of their enquiries. They deny the propriety of making normative judgements (other than that of coherence). Such a denial is understandable, though not acceptable to me, as a *critical* response to normative logic, one expressing scepticism about the normative judgements usually made. But my present task is to systematize our intuitive judgements of rationality. So such scepticism is premature. For example, consider one Mr Gamble, who is certain the urn contains 100 balls, one black and 99 white. He is certain he shall select a ball from the urn. And he has no information which we lack. But unlike the rest of us he is certain that he shall select the one black ball, and takes bets accordingly. All the subjectivist should say to Mr Gamble is: '*If* you had the same degree of belief that any one ball is black as that any other is, *and if* you have the same degree of belief that any one ball is selected as that any other is, *then*, assuming coherence, you could not be certain that you shall select a black ball.' To that Mr Gamble would reply: 'Of course I do not assign the same degree of belief to any one ball being black as any other and to any one ball being selected as any other; for I know I am going to select a black ball and I am being coherent.' Intuitively, Mr Gamble is irrational. Whereas, someone who comes to have a degree of belief 0.99 that a white ball will be selected is rational. The moral I draw from the case of Mr Gamble is that the Subjectivist Theory needs supplementing by various normative principles, such as one telling us that, in some circumstances, it is irrational to come to have different degrees of belief in $F(a)$ and $F(b)$, where 'a' and 'b' are two names.

Neither the Factual, nor the Logical, nor the Subjectivist Theories of probability is satisfactory. Accordingly, I shall develop an approach to probable inferences based on various non-trivial *normative* principles.

II THE NORMATIVE THEORY OF PROBABILITY

In section I, I rejected those theories which relegated the normative component of a theory of probable inferences to a secondary role.

A substantively normative theory of probable inferences is required. In this respect I am in the tradition of Johnson (1924) and Keynes (1921). However, I differ greatly from Johnson and Keynes in matters of detail. For the Johnson/Keynes approach is to *define* a probability concept in normative terms, whereas I shall make normative judgements about degrees of belief, without building the normative into any definitions of probability. I call the Johnson/Keynes concept of probability the *epistemic probability*. I say that the epistemic probability of p on q, $EP(p/q)$, is equal to α[8] just in case someone whose total evidence consists of knowledge that q would be irrational to have a degree of belief in p other than α.[9] On this approach the epistemic probability of a π-inference 'p_1, p_2, . . ., p_n; therefore r' is $EP(r/p_1 \& . . . \& p_n)$. The aim is to obtain a theory of probable inferences by finding various principles governing epistemic probabilities. Because of the normative character of the concept of an epistemic probability, these principles will be normative ones. Selecting suitable principles we should be able to obtain some intuitively plausible results for the epistemic probabilities of inferences.

I have, however, two reasons for preferring a different normative approach to that of Johnson and Keynes. The *first* is a certain unease about framing principles in terms of something as complex as an epistemic probability. It strikes me as more straightforward to put normative constraints on doxastic changes than to operate with a probability concept which has the normative built into it.

My *second* reason for rejecting the Johnson/Keynes approach is the lack of any simple connection between the epistemic probability of a π-inference and the rationality of coming to have some degree of belief in the π-conclusion as a result of having various degrees of belief in the π-premisses. These difficulties are entirely analogous to the difficulties for the Logical Theory.

The alternative approach is to develop a normative theory of probable inferences by relying on additional principles of rationality, that is principles not required for a theory of deduction. And that is the approach I shall adopt. As a preliminary I ask whether these extra principles concern doxastic consistency. I claim they do not. For if they did, then it would be irrational to maintain a doxastic system consisting of beliefs in propositions which were antecedently jointly improbable, even if the jointly improbable beliefs resulted from observation. For example, if I am certain that there are 100 balls in the urn and I am certain there is only one black one, yet I see I have selected the black one, my beliefs are in antecedently jointly improbable propositions. Yet it is rational not to adjust my system.

III   STOCHASTIC AND RATIONAL IRRELEVANCE

Before I state any extra normative principles I need some definitions. Following de Finetti (1974, volume 1, p. 146) I say that p is *stochastically independent* of q (relative to a given credence function d) just in case $d(p/q) = d(p)$.[10] Since I do not assume the Multiplication Rule, I do not go on to derive the result that if p is stochastically independent of q and the system is δ-consistent then q is stochastically independent of p. And I have no firm intuitions about whether that result is correct.

Related to independence is irrelevance. To judge that q is irrelevant to one's degree of belief in p is, it seems, to judge that one's degree of belief in p should not be affected either by the supposition that q, or by the supposition that not q (or more precisely $\neg q$). Accordingly I say that q is *stochastically irrelevant* to p if p is stochastically independent both from q and its negation $\neg q$. If I were to assume the Multiplication Rule then it would be easy to check that where $d(q) < 1$, stochastic independence of p from q, together with δ-consistency, entails that q is stochastically irrelevant to p. But even with that assumption I would need the definition because of the case in which $d(q) = 1$.

Stochastic irrelevance is not a normative concept, it merely describes a relation between degrees of belief. We may obtain a normative concept by *requiring* stochastic irrelevance for rationality. Now, as I indicated in section II, this would not be a requirement for δ-consistency. I shall construe it as a requirement for the rationality of expansions. Accordingly, I say that q *lacks rational relevance to p* if every rational expansion results in the stochastic irrelevance of q to p; that is, the equality of the degree of belief in p, in p conditional on q and in p conditional on $\neg q$. This lack of rational relevance is itself relative to the doxastic state. For whether there is a rational expansion resulting in stochastic irrelevance may well depend on the doxastic state one starts from. Indeed if one already has attitudes to p, to p conditional on q, and to p conditional on $\neg q$, there is no possibility for an expansion *resulting* in the equality of the three degrees of belief, so the lack of rational relevance is either vacuously true or plain vacuous.

IV   A SPECIMEN PROBABLE INFERENCE

I now return to the paradigm mentioned in section I. We are to suppose that I am certain that the urn contains one black and 99 white balls and that the ball I shall select is within the urn. I come to have a degree of belief (represented by) 0.99 that the ball I select will be white. In this section I provide a non-technical account of the rationality of this inference. This will motivate the more technical sections of this chapter, and the discussion of proportional syllogisms in the next.

Let us suppose that my doxastic system is initially δ-consistent and contains certainty in the π-premises but contains no attitude to the π-conclusion (namely that I shall select a white ball). Let us further suppose that I have no special information about the ball I shall select. Then I shall argue that expansion to a degree of belief 0.99 in the π-conclusion is the one and only rational consistency-preserving expansion to the π-conclusion. By the Principle of the Existence of Rational Consistency-preserving Expansions it suffices to show that there are no other rational consistency-preserving expansions. So we shall suppose one is made to the proposition that the ball I shall select is white. And I shall argue that the final degree of belief in that proposition must be 0.99. Next, by appeal again to the Principle of the Existence of Rational Consistency-preserving Expansions, I can further expand to a consistent system containing attitudes to all the propositions I need to consider. Relying on the Composition Principle I can assume that the overall expansion is both rational and consistency-preserving. Let us concentrate, then, on that overall expansion.

I am certain that there are 100 balls in the urn. So call them ball number one, ball number two etc. Rational changes should, I submit, preserve symmetry. In this case, symmetry and the rationality of the expansion establish that:

(1)   The degree of belief that ball number n is black is the same for all n from 1 to 100. Call this degree of belief y.

Now by the General Addition Rule (thesis 4.9.7):

(2)   The degree of belief that some ball in the urn is black equals $100y$.

But:

(3)   The degree of belief that some ball in the urn is black is certainty.

From (2) and (3):

(4) $y = 0.01$.

At this point I make use of the lack of special information about the ball I select. That ball number n is selected by me should be stochastically irrelevant to whether it is black. Hence, for each n:

(5)   The degree of belief that ball number n is black conditional on its being selected is equal to the unconditional degree of belief that ball number n is black.

From (4) and (5):

(6)   The degree of belief that ball number n is black conditional on its being selected equals 0.01.

Now within the scope of the supposition that ball number n is selected, the proposition that ball number n is black is equivalent to the proposition that the selected ball is black. So by Conditionalization we have from (6):

(7)   The degree of belief that the selected ball is black conditional on ball number n being selected equals 0.01.

And this holds for any n. Since I am certain that, for some n, ball number n is selected, and the system is δ-consistent we can infer from (7) (by the Multilemma Rule, thesis 4.9.11) that:

(8)   The unconditional degree of belief that the selected ball is black equals 0.01.

But the system is δ-consistent. So it follows from (8)[11] that:

(9)   The degree of belief that the selected ball is white equals 0.99.

This shows that the only rational consistency-preserving inference to some degree of belief in the π-conclusion is to a degree of belief 0.99.

But I relied not merely on previously stated principles governing δ-consistency and rationality. A systematic theory will require three additional principles. The first concerns names of stipulated content. 'Ball number n' is a referring expression whose content is only that it refers to one of the balls in the urn, and that 'ball number n' and 'ball number m' refer to different balls if $n \neq m$. We require some principle permitting the introduction of such names. For if we chose the wrong sorts of referring expressions, such as 'the ball I shall select' or 'the black ball' then the above argument would not go through. Secondly I relied heavily on the symmetry of the situation to obtain (1). Some principle governing symmetry needs to be stated. The one I rely on is that if we introduce new names whose content, if any, is stipulated in a suitable fashion, then any expansions to propositions involving these hitherto unconsidered names should be symmetric. That is interchanging these names shall not affect the outcome. I refer the reader to section VI for the details. Because the names have not been considered hitherto no observation or other source of information could rationally oppose this symmetry.

Finally I rely heavily on a judgement of irrelevance to obtain (5). Some principle governing irrelevance is needed for a systematic theory. I discuss it further in section VII. Here it suffices to sketch my account. What we want to know is when a's being an H is required by rationality to be stochastically irrelevant to a's being a G. Here it helps if, once again, 'a' is a name of stipulated content. I proceed in two stages. First I state some circumstances in which there is a presumption in favour of irrelevance. Then I consider what might overcome this presumption. The resulting account is not as systematic as I would have liked and it is improved on in chapter 9. The presumption in favour of irrelevance arises when the predicates 'G' and 'H' do not have (too much) conceptual overlap. This will be defined in section VII. Here I shall just give examples. Let us compare the degree of belief that a is a father with the degree of belief that a is a father conditional on a's being a bachelor. I would not require equality as a condition for a rational expansion to one or both of those attitudes. For the concepts (or stereotypes perhaps) of fatherhood and bachelorhood tell us that it is at least a good bet that a father is male and that a bachelor is male. In that case there is too much conceptual overlap. By contrast, if all we know is that a is a macroscopic object, then there is a presumption that we should expect to have the same degree of belief that a is round as that a is round conditional on its being red. In that case the conceptual overlap between roundness and redness, namely that they both apply to macroscopic material objects, is already covered by our assumption that *a* is a macroscopic material object. This presumption can be overcome. We might for instance have noticed a statistical correlation between roundness and redness. For a systematic theory further principles are needed governing when the presumption is overcome. One of these is that it is overcome if every consistency-preserving expansion resulting in the irrelevance is already excluded as irrational. Let us say that the presumption holds *strongly* if it is not overcome for the above reason. Then it may still be overcome for another reason. For there may be two or more strong presumptions against rational relevance which are incompatible in the sense that any expansion which satisfied all these strong presumptions would either fail to preserve δ-consistency or be excluded as irrational because it failed to satisfy some other principle of rationality, such as the Symmetry Principle. The strong presumption may be overcome, I submit, only in this case. And in that case I say there is a counter-presumption, namely a further presumption that the strong presumption is indeed overcome. In section VII of this chapter I discuss when this counter-presumption is in turn overcome, and I provide an intuitive example in section III of the next chapter.

V NAMES OF STIPULATED CONTENT*

Do English proper names such as 'Mary' have *content*? That is controversial. But I shall need names with very little content. So I shall not rely on English names. Instead I shall *introduce* names with precisely specified content. I shall call them names, but if you think names should have no content, call them referring expressions. Given a count-predicate *F* we can name the *F*s as *F*-number-one, *F*-number-two etc., which in a given context I abbreviate to *1*, *2* etc. We just say 'Let the *F*s be called *1*, *2* etc.'. Of course if there are no *F*s these names will be empty. But within the scope of the supposition that there are precisely *n* *F*s we can name them *1*, *2*, . . . *n* and be sure they all refer and refer to different *F*s. This trick of saying 'Let the *F*s be *1*, *2* etc.' is admittedly artificial and contrived. But it is nonetheless quite legitimate and is like the practice of mathematicians who say 'Let a solution be *x*; then . . .'. Here '*x*' is used not as a variable but as a name. The legitimacy of this practice is expressed in the following principle:

The Naming Principle

Given any count-predicate F, any integer n, and any finite set of propositions $\{p_1, \ldots, p_m\}$, there are names (which I shall often abbreviate to the numerals 1 to m), not already occurring[12] in the propositions $p_1, \ldots, p_m$ such that no credence function d is δ-consistent if:
$d(i$ is an $F/$ There are precisely n Fs$)<1$; or if
$d(i = j/$ There are precisely n Fs$)>0$ if $i \neq j$.

Effectively, what this principle does is ensure that, relative to the supposition that there are precisely n Fs, 'i is an F' is self-evident and '$i = j$' self-refuting if $i \neq j$. This expresses the content which these names have been stipulated to have.

VI THE SYMMETRY PRINCIPLE*

Given two names 'a' and 'b', by exchanging them we transform a proposition p into a proposition $p^{a,b}$. If neither 'a' nor 'b' occur in p then, trivially, $p = p^{a,b}$. But that could occur non-trivially if we assumed that, for instance, 'Jack and Jill love each other' and 'Jill and Jack love each other' express the same proposition. I say a set of propositions is *symmetric* with respect to the exchange of 'a' and 'b' if p is in it just in case $p^{a,b}$ is. And I say a credence function is *symmetric* with respect to the exchange of 'a' and 'b' if its domain is symmetric and $d(p^{a,b}) = d(p)$ for all p in $Dom(d)$.

The significance of symmetry is that it corresponds to a lack of any actual 'information'[13] the person has which distinguishes a from b. Now if the names have content then there may be potential 'information' distinguishing a from b. Whether names ever have content is controversial. But for the moment suppose they have and that English names give clues about sex. Further suppose d^- is symmetric with respect to the exchange of 'Jack' and 'Jill'. All that is required to destroy this symmetry is to consider the propositions 'Jack is female' and 'Jill is female'. For then it is rational to expand

d^- to d^+ where d^+(Jack is female)$<d^+$(Jill is female). The potential 'information' is in the content.

Accordingly I state a principle which is restricted to names of stipulated content. We have:

The Symmetry Principle

Suppose names (abbreviated to *1* to *n*) are introduced as in the Naming Principle. Suppose that d^-/d^+ is a consistency-preserving expansion. And suppose d^- is symmetric with respect to the exchange of two of the names *1* to *n*, but d^+ is not, even though the domain of d^+ is symmetric. Then the expansion is irrational.

In stating this principle I assume that symmetric expansions will not violate the other principles of rationality. In particular I assume that if the system is δ-consistent then there is an expansion preserving δ-consistency and resulting in the required symmetry. This assumption is correct provided the schemata for s-e propositions, s-e inference and self-refuting propositions are all themselves preserved by the transformation of every proposition p into $p^{a,b}$. (Thus if p is s-e then so is $p^{a,b}$.) For then we have the following:

Thesis 7.6.1 (Symmetric Completability)

Suppose all the principles of δ-consistency have been stated. And suppose the schemata for s-e propositions etc. are preserved by the p to $p^{a,b}$ transformation. In that case, given any δ-consistent credence function d symmetric with respect to the exchange of 'a' and 'b', then there is an extension e of d whose domain is the whole object-language, and which is both δ-consistent and symmetric with respect to the exchange of 'a' and 'b'.

Proof Let f be a δ-consistent extension of d to the whole object-language. Then let e be defined by $e(p) = \frac{1}{2}f(p) + \frac{1}{2}f(p^{a,b})$. It is easy to check that e is both δ-consistent and symmetric.

The Symmetry Principle which I have stated is enough for a systematic theory of proportional syllogisms. But it might still appear too restricted. For symmetry considerations are sometimes applicable to names which are not of stipulated content. This appearance of restriction is deceptive. Suppose we have some d^- which is symmetric with respect to the exchange of '*a*' and '*b*'. Then we can treat '$(x = a)\lor(x = b)$' as the predicate $F(x)$. And we can use the Naming Principle to find two arbitrary names, '1' and '2' for *a* and *b*, but without knowing which names which. Then the lack of any actual or potential 'information' distinguishing *a* from *b* will be reflected in various judgements of irrelevance we may make, such as that '*1* is *G*' is not rationally relevant to '*1* is *a*', for any predicate *G*. These judgements of irrelevance combined with the Principle of Symmetry will enable us to develop an adequate theory.

VII   THE PRESUMPTION AGAINST RATIONAL RELEVANCE*

The specimen probable inference I examined showed the importance both of symmetry and of judgements of irrelevance. In the next chapter I shall use the Symmetry Principle to provide a theory of proportional syllogisms. But that theory will only be a *partial* systematization of our particular judgements. For in it I shall assume we make various particular judgements of irrelevance and build my theory on them, rather than relying on general principles governing rational irrelevance. This is because I believe that the most satisfactory handling of irrelevance and independence is within the context of the comparative theory of rationality. However in this section I provide such theory as I can at this stage.

I begin by using names of stipulated content to extend the notion of rational relevance from propositions to predicates. The basic idea behind this definition is that a predicate '*H*' should lack rational relevance to predicate '*G*' if for a suitable name '*a*', '*Ha*' is not rationally relevant to '*Ga*'. But it is convenient to require that if we have several suitable names 'a_1', . . . 'a_n' then a proposition of the form 'Of a_1, . . ., a_n only *these* are *H*' should lack rational relevance to 'Of a_1, . . ., a_n only *those* are *G*'. Moreover, names with the wrong sort of content will not be suitable. For let 'Imo' be a name which can only name immovable objects and 'Irf' a name which can only name irresistible forces. Then, even if, intuitively '*H*' has no connection with '*G*', we might expect 'Imo is an *H*' to be rationally relevant to 'Irf is a G'. Accordingly I require the names only to have content included in 'F', thus:

> A predicate 'H' is said *to lack rational relevance* to predicate 'G', relative to credence function d and count-predicate 'F' if:
> For any integer n, if names abbreviated to '1' . . . 'n' are introduced as in the Naming Principle (either for 'F' itself or for some predicate entailed by 'F') then the proposition 'Of 1 to n precisely the members of A are H' lacks rational relevance to 'Of 1 to n precisely the members of B are G', where A and B are any subsets of $\{1, \ldots, n\}$.

Under what circumstances will 'H' lack rational relevance to 'G' (relative to d and 'F')? I begin with a condition on the predicates 'G' and 'H' themselves, quite independent of the information contained in d. This condition is that either 'G' and 'H' have no conceptual overlap, or that this overlap provides no information about whether a given F which is an H is also a G. That some such condition is typically required is shown by considering predicates such as 'bachelor' and 'father', as in section IV.

To make this more precise I shall assume that each person has a *conceptual scheme*, and that, as part of that scheme, there are various presumptive analyses, such as that fathers are male, mothers are female and so on. Among these I include category-truths such as that something wooden is a material object. Also as part of that scheme I assume there are various determinable/determinate relations among predicates.[14] Paradigms of these are the relations between 'coloured' and 'red' and between 'red' and 'vermilion'. There is at least a strong presumption that what is coloured has some more determinate colour such as red, or blue, and that what is red or blue is coloured. Likewise there is at least a strong presumption that what is red has some more determinate shade such as vermilion or scarlet, and that to be vermilion or scarlet something must be red. These determinable/determinate relations do not however constitute analyses, for although being coloured may be part of the concept of being red, we can find no other part to the concept in any natural way.

Given any predicate 'P' we can associate with it a set of predicates $Ast(P)$ obtained by adjoining to 'P' all the predicates occurring in its analysis, any further determinates of those predicates, and finally the negation of the predicates obtained in this way.[15] This is all relative to a conceptual scheme, and may all be construed as based on purely presumptive analyses. I then say that $Ast(G) \cap Ast(H)$ is the *conceptual overlap* of 'G' and 'H'. Now two predicates which are only applicable to particulars of a certain category C will have 'C' in their overlap. For example, even though 'wooden' and 'heavy' are not strongly linked conceptually their conceptual overlap would seem to include 'is a material object'. But if the predicate 'F' itself only applies to members of the category, then that a given FH is a C provides no information about whether it is also a G. To put this more succinctly I say that predicate 'P' entails predicate 'G' if it is part of the conceptual scheme that a P is a G. I now have a non-redundant part of a sufficient condition for 'H' not to be rationally relevant to 'G' relative to 'F' and d, namely that either $Ast(G) \cap Ast(H)$ is empty or every member is entailed by 'F'. It might happen that we have a lack of rational relevance even without this condition. But such situations are, I suspect, rare and I shall call them cases of *lucky irrelevance*. Conversely, if we do have the requisite conceptual independence then, I submit, there is a presumption against rational relevance, regardless of the credence function d^-. I state this as:

The Presumption Against Relevance

If either $Ast(H) \cap Ast(G)$ is empty or every member is entailed by 'F', then there is a presumption against 'H' being rationally relevant to 'G' (relative to 'F' and to any credence function d^-).

If the system is initially δ-consistent, then the presumption will be overcome if every rational consistency-preserving expansion in accordance with the presumption is already excluded as irrational. By 'already excluded' I mean excluded by principles other than those concerning relevance. If the presumption is not overcome in this way then I say it is a *strong* presumption. And, as I indicated in section IV, I believe the strong presumption is overcome only in the case where there is a strong presumption in favour of several incompatible judgements of irrelevance. In that case I say that there is a counter-presumption that the initial presumption is overcome.

A sufficient condition for overcoming the counter-presumption and so restoring the initial presumption sometimes occurs when we have two incompatible judgements which differ only in the predicate they are relative to. That is, we have strong presumptions against 'H' being rationally relevant to 'G' relative both to 'F' and to 'F^*', but these are incompatible. In that case, I submit, if 'F' entails 'F^*' the initial presumption is renewed for the judgement relative to 'F', the stronger of the two predicates. The justification for this is that it provides intuitively correct results for proportional syllogisms (see section IV of the next chapter). There remains the possibility of such renewed strong presumptions being incompatible (for example, if F and F^* are equivalent). In that case the renewed strong presumption may, in its turn, be overcome. The epicycles could go on indefinitely. And that is one reason for being dissatisfied with the theory I have developed. I avoid epicycles in the comparative theory of rationality.

8

Proportional Syllogisms

In the previous chapter I stated two principles (Symmetry and the Presumption against Relevance) which were not required for a theory of deductions. Equipped with them I shall now discuss an especially simple, but important, class of probable inferences, the proportional syllogisms, and I shall rely on the comparison between their theory and that of deductions to combat Deduction Chauvinism.

I THE IMPORTANCE OF PROPORTIONAL SYLLOGISMS[1]

By a proportional syllogism I mean a π-inference whose first premiss is about the proportion of Fs which are Gs, whose second tells us that some designated item is an F, and whose conclusion tells us it is a G. For example:

> There are n Fs precisely m of which are Gs.
> a is an F.
> So a is a G.

Here I take 'F' to be a count-predicate and 'a' to be a referring expression. It is convenient to introduce a predicate 'H' as an abbreviation for 'is identical to a'. By so doing we may assimilate the above to:

> There are n Fs precisely m of which are Gs.
> There is some FH.
> So there is some FGH.

Often we assume referring expressions refer uniquely. So there is some motivation for strengthening the second premiss to 'There is precisely one *F* which is an *H*'. This version is slightly easier to deal with, and I shall consider it first. Another variation is obtained by weakening the first premiss to 'The proportion of *F*s which are *G*s is at least α', where we have no precise information about the total number of *F*s.

Proportional syllogisms seem the simplest π-inferences once we leave behind provability. Thus they lack that peculiar intellectual opacity characteristic of naive induction. If we cannot give a theory of proportional syllogisms, how can we expect to provide any theory of non-deductive inferences? Strangely their theory has largely been neglected. In part this is because their very lack of intellectual opacity makes them uninteresting to philosophers, especially those with sceptical leanings; their non-deductive character puts logicians off; and statisticians are, rightly, interested in more challenging questions. But I suspect there is a further reason for their neglect. For in the classical period of probability theory much was made of the notorious Principle of Insufficient Reason, which, in my terminology, tells us to have an equal degree of belief in every member of a set of alternatives unless we have some ground for choosing between them. Now either a Symmetry Principle or something like it is required for a theory of proportional syllogisms. And this would be a special case of the Principle of Insufficient Reason. Unfortunately, when the more general principle fell into deserved disrepute even its innocent special cases were, I suspect, condemned by association. Consequently, theorists have tended to build the equiprobability of alternatives into the conditions under which various special results hold, rather than into the general theory. Now, where the results are mathematically sophisticated that piece of nervousness does not rob them of interest. But it does tend to trivialize the proportional syllogism. An important exception here is Carnap (1962) who built symmetry into his probability theory. It is no accident that Carnap obtains results about proportional syllogisms (1962, section 94).[2]

There is, then, a surprising need for a theory of proportional syllogisms. But even if the topic were more widely discussed I would still have two reasons for developing my own theory. The first is that the framework I have set up differs sufficiently from other approaches for me to need to check that I can obtain satisfactory results. Secondly it may come as a surprise that I am able to obtain these results without the Multiplication Rule.

II AN INFORMAL EXPOSITION

I begin by considering the most straightforward case, in which the π-inference is:

> *P:* There are n *F*s precisely m of which are *G*s.
> *Q:* There is precisely one *F* which is an *H*.
> So *R:* There is an *F* which is a *GH*.

Here I assume '*F*' is a count-predicate. My first result (formalized as thesis 8.5.1) is that the following conditions are jointly sufficient for the rationality of an (expansive) inference from certainty in *P* and certainty in *Q* to a degree of belief (represented by) m/n in *R*:

(1)   The system is initially δ-consistent and is finite.
(2)   The predicate '*H*' lacks rational relevance to the predicate '*G*' (relative to the initial system and the predicate '*F*').

Moreover, in these circumstances, coming to have a degree of belief m/n is the only rational consistency-preserving expansion to some attitude to *R*. Condition (2) explicates the intuitive requirement that we have no special information about the *FH* which is relevant to whether or not it is a *G*. This result may be compared to those for deductive expansions from δ-consistent systems stated in chapter 5 (see thesis 5.4.1). It differs in that we have the irrelevance requirement (2) and, in that the degree of belief in *R* is m/n instead of certainty.

A formal proof of the result stated above is to be found in section V. Here I present an informal discussion. First consider the special case in which $m = 1$. This special case covers the specimen probable inference discussed in the previous chapter. And the proof of the required result is essentially that provided in chapter 7, section IV. So I shall not repeat it. Now consider the case where m is greater than one. Then I am certain there are m *FG*s. So using the Naming Principle I may call them *FG-1*, *FG-2*, . . ., *FG-m*. Because the predicate '*H*' is irrelevant to the predicate '*G*' relative to '*F*' it will also be irrelevant to each of the predicates 'being *FG-i*' for $i = 1 . . . m$.[3] So, by the special case, in which $m = 1$, we obtain the requirement that the expansion be to:

(1) $d^+(FG\text{-}i \text{ is an } H) = 1/n$

But 'There is an F which is a GH' is provably equivalent to the disjunction of 'The $FG\text{-}i$ is an H' for $i = 1 \ldots m$. So by the General Addition Rule and (1) we have:

(2) d^+ (There is an F which is a GH) $= m/n$

And this is the required result.

If the π-premisses are not believed with certainty, but the other circumstances are the same as above, then we can obtain the result that there is some rational consistency-preserving expansion to R, and that for any such, the measure of doubt in R will not exceed the sum of the measures of doubt in the π-premisses plus $(1 - m/n)$. This is a natural extension of the result obtained for deductions (thesis 5.4.1). We add an extra term $(1 - m/n)$ to the measure of doubt because the π-inference is probable rather than provable. Once again I refer the reader to section V for a formal proof. Here I merely sketch it. We can obtain the first result of this section within the scope of the supposition that $P\&Q$. So the degree of belief in R conditional on $P\&Q$ should be m/n. The required result then follows from the assumption that δ-consistency is preserved.

In the π-inference 'P, Q; therefore R' considered so far, the second π-premiss, Q, is of the form 'Precisely one F is an H'. But we may relax that condition. All we require is that at least one F is an H. Intuitively a degree of belief that there is more than one FH should increase the degree of belief we have that some FH is a G. Once again I refer the reader to section V (thesis 8.5.3) for a more formal treatment. Like the first result this may be generalized to cover the case where the person is not certain of the π-premisses.

Finally we may weaken the first premiss. It is not so much the precise number of Fs and Gs which is important as the proportion. Consider the π-inference:

P_1: There are at most N Fs.
P_2: The proportion of Fs which are Gs is α.
Q^*: There is an FH.
So R: There is an FGH.

Suppose someone is certain of the π-premisses and makes an (expansive) inference to R. Then in the same circumstances as before, there is precisely one rational consistency-preserving expansion to R, namely to a degree of belief α. Likewise if the degrees of belief in the π-premisses are not all certainty there is at least one rational consistency-preserving expansion to R, and the measure of doubt in R should not exceed the sum of the measures of doubt in the π-premisses plus $(1 - \alpha)$.

These results are obtained by considering degrees of belief within the supposition that there are precisely n Fs. Now 'There are at most N Fs' is the disjunction of 'There are precisely n Fs', for $n = 1 \ldots N$. So using the Multilemma Rule we can pass from the results conditional on there being precisely n Fs to the unconditional ones.

The results we have obtained cover all normal applications of proportional syllogisms. But what happens if we drop P_1? I can only speculate. One piece of speculation concerns two mathematical formulae 'A' and 'B' for which all we know is that they refer to unique natural numbers.[4] And we know that much with certainty. But we have no idea of how big they are or how big their ratio is. For the sake of definiteness let us suppose that truths about the size of A and B and about their ratio are unprovable.[5] Then, whether or not A is less than B may be judged irrelevant to whether or not A is even. Now it might seem that by a proportional syllogism we could require a degree of belief one half that A is even, conditional on its being no greater than $2B$. (Since half the numbers no greater than $2B$ are even.) Hence, by the irrelevance, there should be an unconditional degree of belief one half that the A is even. But given the way we can re-arrange the integers as 1, 3, 2, 5, 7, 4, 9, 11, 6, etc., we should hesitate before accepting such a result. This shows I think that we should not demand that the theory of proportional syllogisms be extended to cover the case where we have no idea how many Fs there are.

III THE PRESUMPTIVE CHARACTER OF
PROPORTIONAL SYLLOGISMS

The theory of proportional syllogisms which I have provided depends heavily on various judgements of lack of relevance. When we make proportional syllogisms we do, almost invariably, choose a referring expression, 'the H' such that 'H' has the appropriate lack of conceptual overlap with 'G'. Indeed often we have in place of the referring expression, 'the *H*', a proper name. So in typical cases there is a presumption against rational relevance and hence in favour of the rationality of making the proportional syllogism. It is worth noting that in cases where we have the wrong sort of conceptual overlap we do not, intuitively, think of there being any such presumption. For example, consider:

> 90 per cent of doctors are rich.
> The poorest doctor in Sydney is a doctor.
> So the poorest doctor in Sydney is rich.

Now the conceptual overlap of 'poorest' and 'rich' contains 'rich', which is not entailed by 'doctor'. So there is not even a presumption that it is rational to make this proportional syllogism. And that accords with our intuitive judgements. One of the more interesting ways in which the presumption, when there is one, is overcome is where there are rival proportional syllogisms. Here I distinguish two situations. In the first, precisely one proportional syllogism is a rational one to make, and must indeed be made if the inference is both to be rational and to preserve δ-consistency. In the second case there is no such salience.

A well-known example of the first case is provided by the proportional syllogisms:

(1)   Tex is a Texan;
(2)   90 per cent of Texans are rich; so
(3)   Tex is rich.

This is dominated by:

(4)   Tex is a Texan philosopher;
(5)   90 per cent of Texan philosophers are not rich; so
(6)   Tex is not rich.

Someone who is certain of all of (1), (2), (4) and (5), and who has no further information, could rationally come to have a degree of belief 0.9 in (6). Indeed if, thinking of (2), the person came to have a degree of belief even a little less than 0.9 in (6) he or she would be irrational.

But now consider:

(7)   Tex is a philosopher;
(8)   90 per cent of philosophers are not rich; so
(9)   Tex is not rich.

Suppose someone is certain of (1), (2), (7) and (8), and has neither an attitude towards, nor any special information relevant to, (5). That person is in a position to make one of the inferences from certainty in (1) and (2) to a degree of belief 0.9 in (3) or from certainty in (7) and (8) to a degree of belief 0.9 in (9). But he or she cannot make both inferences and still preserve δ-consistency. Does one dominate the other? I say not. So if one were rational, then, by parity of reasoning, so would be the other. And it would be more rational to compromise between the two proportional syllogisms, coming to some degree of belief, x, between 0.9 and 0.1, that (3) and a degree of belief $1 - x$ that (9).

In the first example, then, one proportional syllogism dominates the other, and it is irrational to be influenced by the other. But in the second neither dominates the other and compromise is permitted.

In both cases the rationality of making the proportional syllogisms depends on a judgement of lack of rational relevance, for which there is a strong presumption (see sections IV and VII of the previous chapter). But because of the impossibility of making both the proportional syllogisms of each pair considered, there is a counter-presumption that this strong presumption is overcome. In the first case, the counter-presumption is overcome and the inference from certainty in (4) and (5) to a degree of belief 0.9 in (6) is rational but the rival one [from certainty in (1) and (2) to a degree of belief 0.9 in (3)] is not. This is in accordance with the discussion of section VII of the last chapter. For, 'Texan philosopher' entails 'Texan' but not vice versa. However, in the second case the expansions from certainty in (1) and (2) to a degree of belief 0.9 in (3) and from certainty in (7) and (8) to a degree of belief 0.9 in (9) are formally similar. (If we swap 'philosopher' and 'Texan' we can pass from one to the other.) So we should not expect the counter-presumption to be overcome in that case. All this is in accordance with our intuitive judgements.

IV   AGAINST DEDUCTION CHAUVINISM

There is a widespread assumption that in some way deductions are first-class inferences and probable inferences second or even third-class. I now use the results I have obtained in order to resist this. I concentrate on expansions, when making the comparison, because, as I pointed out in chapter 6, deduction has relatively little to do with adjustment.

First I consider the *deductivist*. The deductivist insists that accepting the premisses of a probable inference provides no reason for accepting rather than rejecting the conclusion. Now deductivists may well insist it is nonetheless *all right* to make probable inferences,[6] and hence, presumably, not irrational. How is that possible? It is possible if the requirements of rationality grossly underdetermine the inferences we make. In particular, although making a proportional syllogism may be rational in the circumstances, not making it would, they say, be equally rational in the circumstances. Deductivists, then, need not be sceptical about the rational permissibility of probable inferences. Nonetheless Deductivism is a sceptical position. For the theory I have provided shows how, if we rely on systematized intuitions, it is sometimes irrational not to believe the conclusion of a proportional syllogism (to a suitable degree). Hence the deductivist holds a position contrary to our systematizable intuitions. Therefore Deductivism should be rejected.

More common, I think, than Deductivism is *Deduction Chauvinism*, the view that deductions are first class and probable inferences second class, even though sometimes required for rationality. Once again relying on our pre-critical intuitions, I shall combat Deduction Chauvinism.

I begin by listing four ways in which deductions are purportedly superior to probable inferences.[7] I shall then comment on them.

(1)   Deductions are truth-preserving, but probable inferences are not. So there is no risk in making a deduction, while there is with a probable inference.

(2)   Deductions can be presented as part of a systematic theory, but probable inferences resist systematization:[8]

(3)   Probable inferences are sensitive to the addition of extra premisses in a way that deductions are not. Hence they rely on the Requirement of Total Evidence, which is hard to use.

(4)   If a deduction can be made, there is only one conclusion which is rational. But in the case of probable inferences there can be rival conclusions. For example:

Tex is a Texan philosopher.
At least 90 per cent of Texans are rich.
At most 10 per cent of philosophers are rich.
So (i) Tex is rich; *or*
(ii) Tex is not rich.

(In this example, we do not know the proportion of Texan philosophers who are rich.)

As regards (1), the π-inferences do differ in the way indicated. But by itself that establishes no superiority either way. For it does not follow that there is no risk in making a deduction. The relevant risk involved is the risk of getting a false conclusion; and deductions from false premisses run a risk of getting false conclusions. The risk is far less for an inference of high probability from relatively secure premisses than it is for a deduction from highly conjectural premisses. Compare:

There are a hundred balls in the urn. (I counted them three
   times.)
Of these one is black, the rest are white. (I checked that too.)
So if I select a ball it will be white.

with:

The train left at 8.00 p.m. (According to last year's timetable.)
It is now 8.01 p.m. (By my four-dollar watch.)
So the train has already left.

The former inference runs less risk of having a false conclusion than the latter.

If we are going to draw a first-class/second-class distinction by means of the risk of having a false conclusion, we should draw it between conclusive demonstrations (that is deductions from premisses *known with certainty*) and all others, whether deductions or probable inferences. And, I submit, deduction chauvinists no longer discriminate on that basis.

Next consider (2), the claim that probable inferences resist systematization. First let us note the *limited* significance this would have even if correct. It would merely show that our reliance on them would have to be based solely on particular judgements and not on a combination of particular judgement with systematic theory. But, in any case, I resist the claim that they are not capable of systematization. Progress has and is being made on the theory of probable inferences. It has proven difficult, I admit. That just shows we need to work harder.

As regards (3), I deny there is any relevant difference. Admittedly if the δ-premisses of a deduction are δ-consistent, and if these premisses would be unaltered by a consistency-restoring adjustment, then it is rational to make the deduction. Or if we knew the system was already δ-consistent it would be rational to make the deduction. But to be certain that either condition held would involve a survey of all our doxastic attitudes. And that is not possible. Of course, we have a good idea about what is relevant, we take a bit of a risk, and do not check all doxastic attitudes. But the same goes for the probable inferences. We take into consideration only the premisses we believe relevant.

I now turn to (4). In cases such as these, which I discussed in the previous section, my theory underdetermines what is required for rationality. This may be just a limitation of my theory. But perhaps a whole range of degrees of belief that Tex is rich are all permissible. Admittedly, where the premisses are certain, and where deductive reasoning is appropriate, there is often not such a range of permissible degrees. So what has been shown? That some deductions lead to a more precise range of permissible degrees of belief than some probable inferences. But sometimes, as the results of section II show, a probable inference can lead to a precise degree of belief required for rational expansion. Conversely, where the premisses are not certain, rational deduction is compatible with a range of degrees of belief in the π-conclusion. Even when the contrast can be made it hardly seems an indication of superiority. One might as well argue that being a slave is superior to being free in the respect that a slave's life is more regulated.

I conclude that probable inferences are not second class. At least not unless many deductions are too. But this leaves us with a further question: What are the origins of Deduction Chauvinism? Part of the answer I think lies in a positivist or naturalist inspired nervousness about the normative character of logic. For if we attempt to banish the normative from logic, we shall be left with only positive logic. And while the normative aspects of a theory of deduction are by no means trivial, the theory I have given of proportional syllogisms shows that we require two sorts of judgement which are more clearly normative than those required on a theory of deduction, namely those concerning symmetry and irrelevance. For the normative judgements required in a theory of deduction can be smuggled in by requiring 'consistency' or 'coherence', which have a less normative sound to them.

V A MORE RIGOROUS TREATMENT*

In section II I provided a sketch of the proof of various results concerning proportional syllogisms. Here I provide a more rigorous treatment. In addition to the intrinsic value of rigour, this treatment is necessary if it is to be checked that I do not rely on the Multiplication Rule, or other principles I have not explicitly assumed. First consider the π-inference:

P: There are n $\bar{F}$s precisely m of which are Gs.
Q: There is precisely one F which is an H.
So R: There is an F which is a GH.

Here I assume 'F' is a count-predicate. I state:

Thesis 8.5.1

Suppose the π-inference is 'P; Q. Therefore R', with certainty in P and in Q, but no attitude towards R. Suppose also the system, represented by d^-, is δ-consistent and finite. Finally suppose 'H' lacks rational relevance to 'G', relative to d^- and 'F'. Then there is precisely one rational expansion to R which preserves δ-consistency, and it assigns a degree of belief m/n to R.

Proof By the Principle of the Existence of Rational Consistency-preserving Expansions, there is some rational expansion d^-/d^+ to R which preserves consistency. It suffices to show that any such expansion will have $d^+(R) = m/n$. First I introduce names, which I abbreviate to '1', '2', . . . 'n' for the n Fs, in accordance with the Naming Principle. These names are assumed not to occur in members of $Dom(d^+)$. Then, appealing again to the Existence of Rational Consistency-preserving Expansions, I consider an expansion d^+/e where e is δ-consistent, where $Dom(e)$ is symmetric with respect to the exchange of any two of the names '1', . . ., 'n', and where $Dom(e)$ includes the various propositions considered below. Then by the Composition Principle d^-/e is rational. By the Symmetry Principle e must be symmetric with respect to the exchange of any two of the names '1', . . ., 'n'. Now we may consider all the ways of selecting m out of the n names '1', . . . 'n'. For each of these ways there is a corresponding set of entities. I name the sets A_1, . . ., A_k. Here k is the number of ways of selecting m items out of n. So $k = n!/m!(n-m)!$. For any predicate Z applicable to particulars let Z^F apply to A_u just in case A_u consists of *all* the Fs which are Zs.[9] Then by the symmetry of e with respect to the exchange of any 'i' and 'j' we have:[10]

(1) $e(A_u$ is $G^F) = e(A_v$ is $G^F)$ for all u,v

By the Naming Principle:

(2) $e(i = j /$ There are precisely n Fs$) = 0$, if $i \neq j$

So, since (e There are precisely n Fs$) = 1$, by the Restricted Multiplication Principle:

(3) $e(i = j) = 0$, if $i \neq j$

Now, if $u \neq v$, then $A_u = A_v$ s-e implies a finite disjunction of propositions of the form $i = j$, where $i \neq j$. So from (3), by the General Addition Rule we obtain:

(4) $e(A_u = A_v) = 0$ if $u \neq v$

Again, $(A_u$ is $G^F)\&(A_v$ is $G^F)$ s-e implies $A_u = A_v$. So, from (4):

(5) $e[(A_u$ is $G^F)\&(A_v$ is $G^F)] = 0$ if $u \neq v$

From (1) and (5), by the General Addition Rule:

(6) $e[(A_1$ is $G^F)\vee$ . . . $\vee(A_k$ is $G^F)] = k\, e(A_u$ is $G^F)$, for $u = 1, . . ., k$

But relative to 'There are precisely n Fs',
$(A_1$ is $G^F)\vee$ . . . $\vee(A_k$ is $G^F)$ is provably equivalent to 'There are precisely m Fs which are Gs'. So:

(7) $e[(A_1 \text{ is } G^F) \lor \ldots \lor (A_k \text{ is } G^F)/\text{There are precisely } n \text{ } Fs] =$
     $e \text{ (there are precisely } m \text{ } Fs \text{ which are } Gs/\text{There are precisely } n \text{ } Fs)$

Now P s-e implies that there are precisely n Fs and that there are precisely m Fs which are Gs. And we have certainty in P. So:

(8) $e \text{ (There are precisely } n \text{ } Fs) = 1 = e \text{ (There are precisely } m \text{ } Fs$
     which are Gs)

From (7) and (8) using the Restricted Multiplication Principle:

(9) $e[(A_1 \text{ is } G^F) \lor \ldots \lor (A_k \text{ is } G^F)] = 1$

From (6) and (9) we obtain the encouraging result:

(10) $e(A_u \text{ is } G^F) = 1/k, \text{ for } u = 1, \ldots, k$

Now 'H' lacks rational relevance to 'G' relative to d^- and 'F'. So:

(11) $e(A_u \text{ is } G^F/i \text{ is the only } FH) = e(A_u \text{ is } G^F)$

Relative to 'i is the only FH', 'There is an FGH' is provably equivalent to the disjunction of the propositions 'A_u is G^F' for all those subscripts u such that $i \in A_u$. So by the General Addition Rule:

(12) $e(\text{There is an } FGH/i \text{ is the only } FH) = s/k$ where s is the number
     of the A_u which contain i as a member; that is, the number
     of ways of choosing a set of $(m-1)$ items out of $(n-1)$ items.
     So $s/k = [m!(n-m)!/n!)] \times [(n-1)!/(m-1)! \ (n-m)!] = m/n$.

Therefore:

(13) $e(R/i \text{ is the only } FH) = m/n$

By reasoning similar to (2) to (6) we have:

(14) $e(i \text{ is the only } FH \text{ and } j \text{ is the only } FH) = 0, \text{ if } i \neq j$

And:

(15) $e[(1 \text{ is the only } FH) \lor \ldots \lor (n \text{ is the only } FH)] = 1$

From (13), (14) and (15) the required result follows by the Multilemma Rule.

I now obtain the result for the case where the π-premisses are not believed with certainty.

Thesis 8.5.2

Consider the π-inference 'P; Q. Therefore R' as above. Suppose P and Q but not R are in $Dom(d^-)$. Suppose d^- is finite and δ-consistent. Finally suppose 'H' is not rationally relevant to 'G', relative to d^- and to 'F'. Then there is some rational consistency-preserving expansion d^-/d^+ to R, and for any such:
$$1 - d^+(R) \leqslant 1 - d^-(P) + 1 - d^-(Q) + 1 - m/n.$$

Proof All the considerations of the previous proof apply to degrees of belief within the scope of the supposition that $P\&Q$. So we eventually obtain, for a suitable extension e of d^+:

(1) $e(R/P\&Q) = m/n$

So by the Material Conditional Rule (thesis 4.9.1):

(2) $e[(\neg(P\&Q)\vee R])\geqslant m/n$

The disjunctive syllogism '$P,Q,\neg(P\&Q)\vee R$. Therefore R' is self-evident. So by the Subadditivity Rule (thesis 4.9.9):

(3) $[1 - e(R)] \leqslant [1 - e(P)] + [1 - e(Q)] + [1 - e(\neg(P\&Q)\vee R]$

From (2) and (3):

(4) $1 - e(R)\leqslant 1 - e(P) + 1 - e(Q) + 1 - m/n$

Hence:

(5) $1 - d^+(R)\leqslant 1 - d^-(P) + 1 - d^-(Q) + 1 - m/n$

In theses 8.5.1 and 8.5.2, the second π-premiss of the proportional syllogism was of the form 'Precisely one F is an H'. But we can relax the uniqueness condition. All that we require is that at least one F is an H. We have:

Thesis 8.5.3

Suppose the π-inference is:

P: There are n Fs precisely one of which is a G.
Q^*: Some F is an H.
So $R:$ There is an F which is a GH.

And suppose $d^-(P) = 1 = d^-(Q^*)$, but R is not in $Dom(d^-)$. Suppose also d^- is δ-consistent and finite. Finally suppose 'H' is not rationally relevant to 'G', relative to d^- and 'F'. Then there is a rational expansion d^-/d^+ to R which preserves δ-consistency, and as such assigns a degree of belief at least m/n to R.

Proof The proof is as for thesis 8.5.1 as far as:

(10) $e(A_u$ is $G^F) = 1/k, \ u = 1, \ . \ . \ ., \ k$

But instead of (11) we obtain, from the irrelevance condition:

(11*) $e(A_u$ is G^F/B_w is $H^F) = e(A_u$ is $G^F)$ where B_w is any non-empty subset of $\{1, \ . \ . \ ., \ n\}$

Now relative to 'B_w is H^F', 'There is an FGH' is provably equivalent to the disjunction of the propositions 'A_u is a G^F' for all those u such that $A_u \cap B_w \neq \phi$.

So, by the General Addition Rule:

(12*) $e(\text{There is an } FGH/B_w$ is $H^F) = s^*/k$

Where s^* is the number of the A_u which have non-empty intersection with B_v. Hence $s^* \geqslant s$. And we have:

(13*) $e(R/B_w$ is $H^F) \geqslant s/k = m/n$

We can also derive the analogues of (5) and (9) with H replacing G, namely:

(14*) $e[(B_w$ is $H^F)\&(B_v$ is $H^F)] = 0$, if $w \neq v$

And:

(15*) $e[(B_1$ is $H^F)\vee(B_2$ is $H^F)\vee \dots] = 1$

From (13*), (14*) and (15*), by the Multilemma Rule:

(16*) $e(R) \geqslant m/n$

Hence we have the required result:

(17*) $d^+(R) \geqslant m/n$

Thesis 8.5.3 may be generalized as was thesis 8.5.1, to obtain an analogue of thesis 8.5.2.

Finally, we only need consider proportions, not the number of Fs and of Gs.

Thesis 8.5.4

Suppose the π-inference is:

P_1: There are at most N Fs.
P_2: The proportion of Fs which are Gs is at least α.
Q^*: There is an FH.
So R: There is an FGH.

Suppose $d^-(P_1) = d^-(P_2) = 1 = d^-(Q^*)$ and the other conditions of thesis 8.5.1 hold, then the same result holds, with ' $\geqslant \alpha$' in place of 'm/n'.

Proof We apply thesis 8.5.1 to degrees of belief within the scope of the supposition that there are precisely n Fs. Then we apply the Multilemma Rule. (I assume that 'There are precisely n Fs and precisely m Fs' is self-refuting if $m \neq n$.)

Thesis 8.5.4 generalizes as did thesis 8.5.1, resulting in an analogue of thesis 8.5.2.

9

Comparisons of Rationality

In the previous chapters, I systematized judgements of rationality. I now turn to a complementary project, that of providing a system of *comparisons* of rationality. I shall be concerned with the comparison of doxastic changes of the same kind;[1] for instance, with expansions from a given credence function d^- to a given proposition p. And I shall not be considering contractions.[2] Among changes of a given kind, we may judge one to be more rational than another. Thus among rational changes the more rational ones may be called works of rational supererogation, and praised as such. Or again, even among irrational changes some may be less irrational than others.

This comparative approach to rationality is, I admit, not as familiar as that in which one makes judgements of rationality or irrationality. However I have five reasons for considering it. *Firstly*, comparisons of rationality are of intrinsic interest. *Secondly*, the comparative theory helps provide a less idealized theory of rationality, one which is relative to an individual's ability. A theory of rational comparisons which is not itself person-relative will rank the changes possible for X. Then a sufficient condition for a change to be rational for X is that it is the most rational change among those possible for X. *Thirdly*, the theory of rational comparisons is, in one respect, more satisfactory as a theory than that of rationality itself; it has greater unity, involving as it does a single quantity of logical disvalue, called stress, which is to be minimized.[3] *Fourthly*, I suspect that the comparative approach is the more fundamental. For I see no way of accounting for the comparisons in terms of a flat rational/irrational distinction. But it is fairly plausible that the rational/irrational distinction is derived from the comparisons of rationality. For instance, assuming that fairly simple principles will, more or less roughly, pick out a class of changes which in normal circumstances[4] contain the most rational ones, it is convenient that we impose a flat rational/irrational distinction on the grades in accordance with such principles. *Fifthly*, and most importantly, I

consider comparisons of rationality because there are areas, such as
the theory of adjustments, which seem to resist a simple non-
comparative approach.

I shall develop the theory of comparisons of rationality by assigning
a numerical measure to the logical disvalue of a system. I call this
the *stress*. Then, of expansions of a given kind, or of adjustments of
a given kind, the ones which result in less stress will be the more
rational. Because the comparative theory is less familiar than the non-
comparative, I permit myself a more discursive and less rigorous
approach. I see no obstacle, other than the reader's and my own
patience, to a much longer, more detailed, and more rigorous
development. But I think that could properly await the time, if it should
ever come, when my theory has found favour.

Although the comparative and non-comparative theories have
different topics, there is still a threat of incompatibility. For we have
the requirement that if one change is rational, any change which is
no less rational must also be rational. In section XI I argue that no
such incompatibility arises.

I   STRESS

Consider a doxastic change d^-/d^+, where d^+ is δ-inconsistent, or
where the change breaks some symmetry. Then d^+ has some logical
disvalue. It is not as it should be. Further, the amount of logical
disvalue which d^+ has depends on how far d^+ departs from δ-
consistency or symmetry. We may make, then, various comparisons of
logical disvalue. Among these is one to the effect that significant
departures from δ-consistency are worse than the breaking of
symmetry. So sometimes disvalues with different sorts of origin are
nonetheless comparable. Just as I did for doxastic systems, I *represent*
these comparisons numerically. I assume there is a (non-negative)
numerical measure of logical disvalue, which I call *stress*. And as with
doxastic systems we have a superfluity of representations. Just as the
superfluity of representations of doxastic systems by credence functions
was lessened by requiring that the Addition Rule hold for consistent
systems, likewise the superfluity of representations of the comparisons
of logical disvalue will be lessened by assuming that stress depends
on the defects in an especially simple fashion, described below. That
the stress *can* be so measured is a hypothesis, justified by its ability to

systematize the data simply; but that it is, given that it can be, is a stipulation which restricts the range of possible representations.

I write the stress of a system represented by d as $\text{Str}(d)$.[5] Part of this stress is implicit stress, due to the impossibility of extending d without new logical disvalue. But part of it, which I call the explicit stress, $\text{EStr}(d)$, is due to the various logical defects which the system actually has. As I said above, I seek an especially simple way of describing stress. I assume that the explicit stress is the sum of various *components*, each of which is the stress due to some particular defect. In part, this assumption is justified on the grounds of simplicity. For I am setting up a hypothesis and so may help myself to the usual criteria in selecting hypotheses. However, the assumption is also partly stipulative. For what is to count as a single defect is constrained by this additivity requirement. If the disvalue is incapable of being expressed as the sum of other disvalues then the defect is taken to be a single one. The basic form, then, of the stress is that it is derived, in a manner to be discussed in section III, from explicit stress, which in turn is the sum of various stress-components, each of which is due to a single defect of the system.

To illustrate the concept of stress, and to anticipate some of the themes of this chapter, I shall consider Sir T. Rasa. Initially he is doxastically passive. That is, his various beliefs come about entirely as a result of influences external to reason, among which I include observation, testimony and memory. Sir Rasa, in need of a garden ornament to put among his rhododendrons, buys a copy of the Venus de Milo, and is assured by the supplier that it is a faithful reproduction. On the supplier's testimony he comes to have full belief that it is. But he then recalls, having seen the original somewhere, that it is somewhat lacking when it comes to arms. Inspection reveals, however, that his Venus has the number of arms appropriate to a Greek goddess, namely two. Any normal person would begin adjusting his or her doxastic system so rapidly that it would be unclear where memory and observation ended and inference began. But it is not so with Sir Rasa. He makes no adjustment and so comes to have full belief in each of three members of an inconsistent triad:

P_1: My Venus is a faithful copy of the original.
P_2: The original does not have two arms.
P_3: My Venus does have two arms.

The result is that his doxastic system has a large amount of disvalue, or stress as I call it. This is due to its doxastic inconsistency. If he draws conclusions such as that his Venus both does and does not have two arms then the stress will be explicit. Otherwise it is implicit.

To further illustrate the concept of stress, let us now suppose that Sir Rasa, while away from home, rhododendrons and statue, learns the need for adjustment. He might remove the stress due to δ-inconsistency by rejecting what he has seen, namely the two-armed character of his Venus. But that would result in almost as great stress, perhaps even greater, due to the rejection of what you (seem to) perceive. Here I am considering stress due to an external factor, namely observation, even though I am giving a theory of internal changes. External factors can rationally influence internal changes.

However if he merely comes to have a slight loss of confidence in what he saw ('Perhaps I imagined the arms'), the disvalue, that is stress, from that source, would not be as great as in the case of disbelief. Likewise rather little stress would be caused by disbelieving the supplier. Indeed if he had other grounds for rejecting the supplier's evidence, such as a belief that many salesmen hold a *pragmatic* theory of truth, this would cause no stress at all. But I shall assume he has no such grounds. Again he might reject what he seems to remember. That too, I submit, would result in stress. Yet again – in accordance with my judgement of rationality – he could compromise, retaining almost full belief in P_3, having considerable doubts about P_2 and disbelieving P_1 but not with full disbelief. The compromise, even if it is the most rational adjustment, does not remove all disvalue. It merely minimizes it. This is borne out by the felt need to investigate further, and so acquire new external sources of information in the hope of removing the stress. Sir Rasa, in pursuit of such information, rings up his supplier and calls him a scoundrel. The supplier remarks that Sir Rasa had only seen the original in damaged form, which damage occurred in antiquity. So how does he know his copy is not faithful? Sir Rasa then comes to disbelieve P_2, believing P_1 after all. Has he removed all stress? No. For he has various *a priori* intuitions. And these, if relied on, would result in a belief that no one knows quite what the missing bits and pieces looked like, and hence disbelief in P_1. So his present doxastic state still contains stress, though not due to inconsistency, namely that due to a rejection of what is *a priori* intuitable. There is a felt need for yet further investigation. He rings up his supplier again. Eventually all is revealed: so many customers used to complain about incomplete Venuses that they are now made 'complete'. Finally Sir Rasa can rest, free from doxastic stress.

This example illustrates the way stresses can differ in strength. In addition it shows how even the most rational adjustment can leave a residue of stress, which only further enquiry and subsequent external change can remove.[6]

II UNAVOIDABLE STRESS

One of the marks of inconsistency, by which it is distinguished from other logical defects, is its removability. Other logical defects may not be removable by a rational adjustment. Hence the minimal stress may be greater than zero. Curiously, it is this which gives the comparative theory its power. For it enables us to handle rational *tendencies*, and compromises between such tendencies. Consider, for example, the Presumption Against Relevance. Sometimes, as when we have two rival proportional syllogisms, this presumption is overcome. But there should still, I judge, be a tendency towards irrelevance. And the most rational doxastic change should reflect the overall result of these tendencies. By introducing suitable components of stress, conflicting tendencies can be treated as tendencies to minimize stress-components. And to minimize the total stress we should, I shall argue, compromise between the tendencies. The areas where the non-comparative theory was inadequate turn out to be those in which even rationality, and not merely maximal rationality, is a matter of balance or compromise between opposing tendencies.

We have, then, various tendencies, with differing epistemic strengths. On a given occasion, one tendency may be almost entirely overcome. For example, at one stage it seemed that Sir Rasa would have almost completely to ignore testimony. It is tempting to say, when this happens, that the defeated party, here testimony, has been shown to be unreliable and should have less epistemic importance (i.e. contribute less stress) in future. But that, I claim, is a mistake. Simply to have to concede the most, or even everything, in such a compromise should not result in a loss of epistemic importance. I call this the No Dishonour in Defeat Principle. And I attach much importance to it. Without it the compromise strategy would be unstable because we could re-negotiate, as it were, using revised epistemic importances.

III   STRESS DUE TO INCONSISTENCY

With the exception of Completability the principles of δ-consistency specify various equalities or inequalities which the credence function should satisfy. For example, the Addition Principle requires that $d(p \lor q) + d(p \& q) = d(p) + d(q)$. For each of these principles there will be a component of the explicit stress. The stress-component will be zero if the principle is satisfied, and the greater the violation of the principle the greater the stress. Thus if $d(p \lor q) + d(p \& q)$ is very near $d(p) + d(q)$ the stress due to the violation of the Addition Principle will be very small. (I postpone the mathematical details until section IX.) The sum of these stress-components will be zero if and only if all the principles of δ-consistency, except perhaps Completability, are satisfied. (Although there may be other non-zero components arising from other sources.)

To handle a tendency towards Completability we need to consider the implicit stress. Suppose we are considering extensions of the credence function d to some finite set P of propositions. There should be a tendency towards d having a δ-consistent extension e to P. We could ensure this by defining the implicit stress of d as the minimum value of all the explicit stresses of extensions e to P. Then minimizing the implicit stress of d will involve a tendency towards d having a δ-consistent extension to P. Unfortunately if P is no longer finite this will give us infinite stresses. We have two options here. The first is to abandon the idealization of logical omniscience, which is no longer required for the comparative theory, in favour of a weaker idealization, namely the assumption that δ-consistent systems can be extended δ-consistently to very large but still finite systems. In that case we no longer have a tendency towards Completability. The second option is to retain a tendency towards Completability but assume that the greater the extension the less significant it is when calculating implicit stress. (See section IX for the details.) This ensures that the implicit stress is finite. The tendency towards having δ-consistent extensions will then be stronger for the smaller extensions.

Given this way of calculating the implicit stress due to δ-inconsistency, expansions will never reduce the total stress, and may even increase it. So why are they ever preferable to simply not changing the system? The reason, I believe, is that often there is a value to be had in having an attitude to a given proposition. A measure of this value could be subtracted from the stress. And it shows that making the expansion is on balance worthwhile even if it does not decrease the logical disvalue. Further it would seem that we should avoid contracting away from a proposition towards which there is value in having an attitude. In such cases suitable adjustments will be preferable to contractions.

Typically I assume that the stresses due to significant departures from δ-consistency are of especially great magnitude. So, typically, the maximally rational changes will either restore δ-consistency or fail to do so by a negligible amount. But in some cases, as in the example of Dr Methodos (chapter 5, section III), other disvalues may be significant. In such cases the maximally rational expansion might involve the destruction of δ-consistency.

IV   OBSERVATION, TESTIMONY, INTUITION
AND MEMORY

As I indicated in section I, even external factors can result in stress. It is convenient to begin with observation,[7] because that is the clearest case. So suppose I am currently observing that p. Then, I submit, my not having a high degree of belief that p results in stress. So, minimizing stress results in a tendency towards a high degree of belief that p. This tendency may well be opposed by others. In that case the most rational outcome might be a low degree of belief in p in spite of the non-defective character of the observation. But by the No Dishonour in Defeat Principle there will remain a tendency, which may re-assert itself, for a high degree of belief in p. This result falls out of the theory of stresses I am developing, because of the way that theory provides compromises. In addition it is, on reflection, an intuitively acceptable result. It is not the observation's fault that it clashes with other considerations, any more than I am an intrinsically defective predictor if I forecast that you would not win the lottery but you did. To be mistaken is one thing, to have been all along at fault is another. Admittedly it is common sense to take the former as some evidence for the latter, but we should not exaggerate the strength of that evidence. I have laboured this point because it stands in opposite to the tradition of Descartes, who characteristically says:

Now I have sometimes caught the senses deceiving me; and a
wise man never entirely trusts those who have once cheated him.
(1954, pp. 61–2)

The metaphors of deceiving and cheating show how Descartes believes
that being mistaken is a sign of an intrinsically defective character.[8]
I do not think of my senses as swindlers or charlatans.

I shall treat testimony as a source of information similar to
observation. Admittedly this is controversial. For many philosophers
assume that we have to make some inference in order to profit by
testimony, an inference such as:

The witness is reliable.
She or he says p.
So p.

or:

He or she says p.
The best explanation for his or her saying p is that he or she
believes that p. The best explanation for that in turn is . . .

And if some such assumption were correct, then testimony would not
be an independent source of information. Nonetheless the combination
of observation or memory with inference which constituted testimony
would function like a source of information. So my use of testimony
in illustrative examples would not be undermined. With due caution,
then, we may introduce stress-components for testimony as well as
for observation.

A priori intuition I take to be rather like observation. If p is intuited,
then not having a high degree of belief that p will result in stress. Here,
as for observation, the No Dishonour in Defeat Principle tells us that
intuition can be mistaken without thereby being intrinsically defective.
Some of the desire to reject intuition derives, I suspect, from a 'once
bitten twice shy' reaction to mistaken *a priori* knowledge-claims, similar
to that of Descartes to mistaken perception. Although I treat intuition
as analogous to observation, it is also analogous to the knowledge of
self-evident propositions. Indeed I would say the latter was just a
special case of intuition. This suggests quite generally and not just
for logic, that what *could* be intuited should affect the implicit stress.

And that would constitute a disanalogy with observation. I have no strong opinion on this, and in the theory I present I neither assert nor reject that suggestion. But I incline towards the position that a given person has various intuition-schemas and even potential instances of those schemas will affect the implicit stress.

There is one case where testimony should not result in a stress-component, however reliable the witness. Suppose the witness argues saying 'p, q; therefore r'. As a result I might accept p, q and r. But there should be no tendency to believe r over and above that due to the tendency to believe p, and q, combined with the way p and q support r. To be sure, if the witness goes on to say 'And I have other reasons for believing r' then, indeed, we may have a stress-component for r. But otherwise we should not. This is brought out by considering the proper response to the discovery that p and q are false (but not inconsistent with r). Should we still tend to believe r on testimony? Intuitively we should not.

Finally I consider 'memory'.[9] If what is 'remembered' is 'remembered' as held only because of the support of other beliefs, also 'remembered', there is no associated stress-component. Otherwise there is.

The effect of testimony and 'memory' will be a tendency towards intellectual conformism and intellectual conservatism respectively. And that is as it should be. For we should not totally ignore the opinions of others or our own earlier conviction. But this is only a tendency, and will be opposed, for the most part, by other tendencies. I am not providing a charter for intellectual fascism.

The stress-components for observation, testimony, intuition and memory will, like those due to δ-inconsistency, be greater the further removed the system is from certainty in what is observed, attested, intuited or remembered.[10]

V   THE NEED FOR COMPROMISE

Zero stress is not usually attainable. That is partly because of clashes between observation and intuitions, or, more obviously, between observation and testimony ('He says it was square, but I saw it was round'). So maximum rationality will be the result of the minimization of stress, rather than its elimination. In section X I shall show that, depending on the form of the mathematical functions representing the stress, there are three satisfactory hypotheses. These are best illustrated by considering a clash between two sources of stress. Suppose I have two sources of information (say two witnesses), one asserting that *P* the other denying that *P*. And suppose that, as a result, the departure from certainty that *P* results in stress, but so does the departure from contracertainty that *P*. On one theory the correct resolution of the conflict is that the 'winner takes all'. That is, one of the two sources of stress will totally dominate the other. The result then will either be certainty that *P* or contracertainty that *P*. On another theory the proper result is a compromise. The greater the relative strength of the stress-component pushing towards certainty in *P* the nearer the compromise is to certainty that *P*. I am able to assign an index to the strength of a stress-component which I call the *index of epistemic importance*. Then the proper compromise is to a degree of belief x in *P* where $x/(1 - x) = \sigma/\tau$, and where σ and τ are the epistemic strengths pushing towards certainty in *P* and contracertainty in *P* respectively.

The compromise resolution is never contrary to my intuitive judgements. For when one of the indices of epistemic strength is much greater than the others then the compromise closely approximates total domination by the strongest source of stress. However the winner-take-all resolution is often quite contrary to my intuitive judgements. This is especially the case where the two epistemic strengths are almost exactly balanced. Then, on the winner-take-all resolution, the slightest imbalance in favour of *P* warrants certainty in *P* not merely as rational but as maximally rational. I submit that in such cases a degree of belief near ½ is called for, as in the compromise resolution. Therefore the winner-take-all resolution is not always correct. But can we mix resolutions? The results of section IX show that we can, but only in a restricted fashion. On theoretical grounds there are three hypotheses of about equal simplicity:

(1)   The winner-take-all resolution is always correct.
(2)   The compromise resolution is always correct.
(3)   There are two classes of stress-components. In clashes between members of the first class a winner-take-all resolution is correct. In clashes between members of the second class a compromise resolution is correct. Finally suppose a member of the first class clashes with a member of the second. Then if it is strong enough

the correct resolution is for it completely to dominate the other. If not the correct resolution is compromise.

In case (3) I call the first class the *potentially dominant* stress-components. Now I have rejected (1). So we have to decide whether (2) or (3). What candidates are there for potentially dominant stress-components? They would have to form a distinguished class, and one which we intuitively judge should often dominate others. The only class satisfying those constraints are the stresses due to the violation of δ-consistency. So I conclude that for the most part the compromise resolution is correct, the possible exceptions being clashes involving a stress due to δ-inconsistency.

VI THE REVISION OF LOGIC

Quine (1953, p. 43) boldly advocates the empirical revisability of logic. Although he argues in the context of empiricism, the revisability thesis for logic presents a challenge even for the moderate (i.e. non-dogmatic) rationalist. For if we admit the revisability of *a priori* beliefs in general, why should logical beliefs be exempt? I begin by distinguishing two different ways in which we may reject a logical rule, say the principle of non-contradiction. The first, more radical, rejection is to insist that the rule was all along a mistake. In that case one denies it entry into positive logic and hence gives it no place in the theory of δ-consistency. If, for example, the rule were that of non-contradiction one would deny that $p\& \sim p$ is always self-refuting. Hence, for some p, one would insist that there should be no stress involved in being certain of $p\& \sim p$.

By contrast, the moderate revision of logic is based on the need for compromise. Violations of δ-consistency lead to stress. If these stress-components are potentially dominant, then typically, total stress will be minimized by requiring δ-consistency. But on occasion the combination of other stresses will be strong enough for the compromise policy to operate. And, of course, if the compromise resolution is always correct then the compromise policy operates anyway. (Although in typical cases the resulting violation of δ-consistency will be negligible.) Either way, then, there is the possibility of a moderate revision of logic in which the stress-components due to δ-consistency are accepted, but the resulting compromise ensures the (temporary) infringement of the results of positive logic.

An important difference between the radical and moderate revisions is seen when science initially seems to threaten logic but then the threat is removed. In the radical revision of logic science is just a catalyst. Respect for it might have helped us seriously consider whether to accept the logical rule, but having rejected that rule, it stays rejected even if new science removes the threat. Otherwise we have inferred the normative from the non-normative, an 'ought' from an 'is'. But in a moderate revision of logic, removal of the threat enables the old logic to be restored, by the No Dishonour in Defeat Principle.

VII   THE PROBLEM OF THE DIRECTION OF THE ARROW OF *MODUS TOLLENS*

In outline I have already presented my modified Duhem response to this problem. As I argued in chapter 6, the proper policy is, usually, the Compromise Solution; that is, an adjustment which results in compromise. And the comparative theory justifies such compromise as maximally rational and so, *a fortiori*, rational. It only remains to fill in some details. First, compromise is not required where one of the conflicting sources of 'information', say observation, may be condemned as intrinsically defective. And the mark of such defectiveness is that even were the other sources to vanish we could still not trust the observation. In that case the defective source has no epistemic strength. In all other cases we have a genuine problem, and my theory dictates a compromise. Which compromise occurs depends on the relative epistemic strengths of the parties. But it also depends on their number and logical connection, as I show below.

Another detail that might be filled in is the way in which the theories are themselves supported, in one way or another, by further observations. For instance, intuition may result in a stress-component tending towards certainty in T conditional on $P_1 \& \ldots \& P_n$, where T is the theory and $P_1, \ldots, P_n$ are supporting observations or lower-level theories. In that case the clash does not, strictly speaking, involve the theory so much as an intuition and some observations. So my original formulation was a simplified one. Again the auxiliary hypothesis could be a combination of *testimony* and intuition. Because of these ramified complexities, it seems best to abstract away from some of the details of the problem, and also to ignore the fact that conditional degrees of belief may be involved. For those details do not affect results about the way the compromise depends on the number of observations. Again I shall, for simplicity, ignore any revision to logic, which will typically be very slight.

I begin, then, with the simplest situations. We have a provably inconsistent n-ad, $p_1, \ldots, p_n$, such that no $(n-1)$-ad is inconsistent. Initially the person is certain of all of $p_1, \ldots, p_n$. In that case, as I argue in section X, stress is minimized by coming to have a measure of doubt in each of the p_i inversely proportional to the index of the epistemic strength of p_i.

Another interesting case is that in which we have propositions p_0, $p_1, \ldots, p_n$, where for each $i = 1, \ldots, n$, p_0 is provably inconsistent with p_i, and where there are no logical connections not derived from these. This models the case where a theory T clashes with each of n observations, not just with the n taken together. We can show that the degree of belief in p_0, on the maximally rational adjustment, goes down as n increases. And that is as expected: the more conflicting observations, the worse it is for the theory. Quite how rapidly the degree of belief goes down as n increases is not determined by the theory alone. We can arrange for it to go down in a simple inverse proportion to the number, n, of conflicting observations, or more rapidly, or more slowly. For what it is worth a rate of decrease which is inversely proportional to the square root of the number of conflicting observations seems about right to me.

The results I have mentioned accord with a healthy respect for observations. The more of them clash with the theory then the greater should be our doubts. But perhaps I have succeeded *too well*. Surely, this result should only hold for *independent* observations. What if the p_i, for $i = 1, \ldots, n$, are all based on a *single* observation? I seem to be faced with a *reductio* of my theory, namely that merely taking s-e equivalents of a given observation should result in increased doubt in a theory which clashes with it. Fortunately, if the p_i are all based on a single observation, say p_1, then only *that* observation results in a stress-component. Beliefs accepted only because of other beliefs do not have their own stress-components. So the *reductio* is avoided.

The modified Duhem justification, then, works not merely for the very basic intuition that the Compromise Solution is correct, but holds even for the details of that compromise, in so far as we have intuitions about them.

VIII   SYMMETRY AND IRRELEVANCE

There will be stress-components which result in a tendency towards symmetry and towards irrelevance. First consider symmetry. If we exchange two names '*a*' and '*b*' in a proposition *p* then we obtain a proposition $p^{a,b}$ which may or may not be the same as *p* itself. A tendency towards symmetry will be ensured by stress-components which are greater the greater the difference between the degrees of belief in *p* and in $p^{a,b}$ for various propositions *p* and names '*a*' and '*b*'. But for which propositions, and for which names, should we have this component, and the resulting tendency towards symmetry? The occurrence of antecedent symmetry in all the sources of information about *a* and *b* would seem to be relevant here. Those sources of information will, I think, be of two kinds only. The first will consist of any content the names *a* or *b* have. The second will be due to observation, testimony, and memory. But whatever the sources, they have associated stress-components. Adding these up we obtain the partial stress due to various possibly asymmetric sources of information. The difference between this partial stress due to the credence function *d* and the partial stress that would result if we exchanged the names '*a*' and '*b*' gives us a measure of the asymmetry in the sources of information. I propose, then, a stress-component due to asymmetry which is greater the less this measure of asymmetry in the sources of information. The mathematical details will be found in the next section. Here I note that I allow *some* tendency towards symmetry even when we do not have symmetry in the external sources of information. The intuitive justification for this is that there should be a tendency, although a slight one, to introduce symmetry which is not present in what is observed. Suppose I 'remember' having seen a thousand ravens and I 'remember' that one was white and the rest black. There should, I submit, be a slight tendency to have some doubt about whether there was a white raven, even though the external source of information, namely 'memory', is not symmetric with respect to the exchange of the names of the birds. To ensure this, admittedly slight, tendency I think we need some tendency towards symmetry even where there are asymmetric sources of stress. This hypothesis about the stress due to asymmetry is further justified by its ability to systematize our intuitions concerning induction, as I argue in the next chapter.

Although I need a stress-component due to asymmetry, in some circumstances it is redundant in that the other stresses ensure symmetry. For it quite often happens that there is a unique credence function which minimizes stress. Now suppose that there are no sources of information which distinguish *a* from *b*. Then the stress-components will be unaltered by the interchange of '*a*' or '*b*'. So exchanging '*a*' and '*b*' in a credence function which minimizes stress[11] will produce one which also minimizes stress. Given uniqueness, this exchange leaves the credence function unaltered, thus ensuring symmetry. Even if, as I rather doubt, we always had uniqueness, this would not render the stress due to symmetry totally redundant. For the above argument does not apply if we have only an approximation to symmetry in the sources of information.

Independence and irrelevance are easily handled using stress-components. That is because of the presumptive character of considerations of irrelevance. Wherever the only conceptual overlap between the predicates '*G*' or '*H*' is entailed by the predicate '*F*', then I posit a stress-component tending towards the irrelevance of '*H*' to '*G*' relative to '*F*', and in particular to the irrelevance of '*a* is *H*' to '*a* is *G*' where '*a*' is any name whose content, if any, is entailed by '*F*'. The circumstances where the presumption in favour of irrelevance is overcome are just those in which this stress-component is opposed by others, and so some compromise between irrelevance and other considerations is maximally rational.

To illustrate this, consider again the rival proportional syllogisms discussed in the previous chapter. First consider someone who is certain of all of:

(1)   Tex is a Texan philosopher.
(2)   90 per cent of Texans are rich.
(3)   90 per cent of philosophers are not rich.

But the person has no information about the wealth of Texan philosophers. In this case the tendencies towards irrelevance will result in tendencies towards the conclusions of rival proportional syllogisms, and so a compromise should be reached. The person should have a degree of belief between 0.9 and 0.1 that

(4)   Tex is rich.

Next consider someone who is certain of (1) and (2) as before, but also certain that:

(5)   90 per cent of Texan philosophers are not rich.

In this case if we assume δ-consistency is not to be violated it can be shown that the tendency towards the irrelevance of 'is Tex' to 'is rich' relative to 'is a Texan' should be completely resisted in favour of the tendency towards the irrelevance of 'is Tex' to 'is rich' relative to 'is a Texan philosopher'. So it is maximally rational to come to have a degree of belief 0.1 that Tex is rich. This is in accordance with the results of the previous chapter (especially section IV), which tell us that it is irrational to come to have a degree of belief any greater than 0.1 that Tex is rich. The reason why we do not have compromise in this case is that if we had a degree of belief greater than 0.1 that Tex is rich we should have a degree of belief less than 0.1 that some other Texan philosopher is rich. Otherwise δ-consistency would be violated. And that imbalance results in greater overall stress than if both degrees of belief equal 0.1. So the stress is minimized by having the degree of belief equal to 0.1 that any given Texan philosopher is rich. For a more detailed discussion I refer the reader to section XI.

IX   THE MATHEMATICAL FORM OF THE STRESS FUNCTION*

The explicit stress $EStr(d)$ is the sum of various stress-components. Each of these is of the form $\psi(\Delta)$ where Δ measures the departure from the zero-stress state and ψ is an increasing function [i.e. if $x > y$ then $\psi(x) > \psi(y)$] for which $\psi(0) = 0$. If P is self-evident[12] then $\Delta = 1 - d(p)$. If p is self-refuting then $\Delta = d(p)$. If q s-e implies p then $\Delta = 1 - d(p/q)$, and so on. Corresponding to the Addition Principle we have $\Delta = |d(p \lor q) + d(p \& q) - d(p) - d(q)|$, that is, the amount by which d departs from satisfying the Addition Principle. Again
$$\Delta = |d(p \& q) - d(p/q) \times d(q)|$$
would be appropriate if we assume the Multiplication Rule. And it would handle, with other stress-components, departures from the Restricted Multiplication Principle and the Principle of Alternative Supposition. So there is no difficulty in finding *some* stress-component corresponding to those two principles. Now, I have not relied on the

Multiplication Rule in the non-comparative theory. But I may nonetheless hypothesize a stress-component with

$$\Delta = |d(p\&q) - d(p/q) \times d(q)|$$

on the grounds that it is the simplest stress-component which handles departures from the Restricted Multiplication Principle and the Principle of Alternative Supposition. For even the simplest formula which handles departures from these two principles without entailing the Multiplication Rule is quite gruesome.[13] So in a roundabout way the comparative theory of rationality provides a justification of the Multiplication Rule in the non-comparative theory. I did not rely on such a justification for the obvious reason that the reader might – as I myself do – consider the non-comparative theory to be based on firmer intuitions than the comparative.

Similarly, if p is observed with certainty then there is a stress component of the form $\psi(\Delta)$ where $\Delta = 1 - d(p)$. In the case of merely probable observation, and especially in the case of probable testimony and memory, we might have zero stress even if $d(p) < 1$. So for some $\eta < 1$ we would have $\Delta = \eta - d(p)$ if $d(p) < \eta, \Delta = 0$ otherwise. Another subtlety is that there could be conditional testimony. If the witness says 'If the town-hall clock was accurate I saw the accused at ten', this testimony should, I think, result in a stress of the form $\psi(\Delta)$ where $\Delta = 1 - d(P/Q)$, and where P is the proposition that the witness saw the accused at ten and Q the proposition that the clock was accurate.

The tendency towards symmetry should result in a stress-component of the form $\psi(\Delta)$ where $\Delta = |d(p) - d(p^{a,b})|$, and where $p^{a,b}$ is the result of exchanging the names 'a' and 'b' in p. Finally a tendency towards the irrelevance of 'H' to 'G' relative to 'F' should result in a stress component of the form $\psi(\Delta)$ where

$$\Delta = |d(a_1, \ldots, a_m \text{ are the } FGs/a_1 \ldots . a_m \text{ are the } FHs) - d(a_1, \ldots, a_m \text{ are the } FGs)|.$$

All this is straightforward enough and ensures that the greater the departure from zero-stress then the greater the stress. But what of the functions I have represented by ψ? For a start they are not all the same, some stresses are greater than others even for a given value of Δ. But considerations of theoretical simplicity suggest that they all have a common form. Even this underdetermines the choice of the functions. However I shall make an expository idealization and take all the functions to be a constant times a power of Δ. That is $\psi(\Delta) = \lambda\Delta^{\alpha}$. The λ, and perhaps even the α, might vary from case to case, but ψ is always of that common form. The constants λ and

α must both be positive if we are to have $\psi(0) = 0$ and if ψ is to be an increasing function.

In the previous section I indicated that the strength of the tendency towards symmetry should be less the greater the departure from symmetry among the sources of information. To make this more explicit I define the possibly asymmetric stress $\text{PAStr}(d)$ to be the sum of the stress-components such as observation, testimony and memory, and the content of names, which could be asymmetrical. Then given any names 'a' and 'b' and a credence function d we can define a new credence function $d_{a,b}$ by

$d_{a,b}(p) = d(p^{a,b})$; and

$d_{a,b}(p/q) = d(p^{a,b}/q^{a,b})$.

We have symmetry of the sources of information with respect to the exchange of 'a' and 'b' if:

$\text{PAStr}(d) = \text{PAStr}(d_{a,b})$.

So we should ensure that the coefficient λ is greater the less the quantity:

$|\text{PAStr}(d) - \text{PA(Str)}d_{a,b})|$.

Since all the other sources of information are symmetrical

$|\text{PAStr}(d) - \text{PAStr}(d_{a,b})|$ is the same as $|\text{EStr}(d)\text{-EStr}(d_{a,b})|$. So to be on the safe side we could allow $\text{PAStr}(d)$ to be the sum of all the stress-components other than that due to asymmetry itself.

There remains the tendency towards Completability. Roughly speaking, we ensure a tendency towards Completability by defining the stress, $\text{Str}(d)$ in terms of the explicit stress $\text{EStr}(e)$ of extensions e of d, which in turn are defined as the sums of the stress-components for e.

Unfortunately the simple formula:

$\text{Str}(d) = \min \{\text{EStr}(e) \mid d \mathrel{\mathcal{R}} e \text{ and } Dom(e) = L\}$

(where L is the whole object-language) is not satisfactory. For it will lead to infinite stresses whenever d is δ-inconsistent. As such it obliterates all *degrees* of logical disvalue among the inconsistent doxastic systems. It leads to infinite stress because every proposition p in $Dom(d)$ has infinitely many s-e equivalents p_1, p_2, etc. Either the extension e accumulates infinite stress by having $e(p_i) \neq e(p)$, or by repeating for the s-e equivalents the inconsistency in d.

In response to this I assume that potential or implicit logical defects matter less than actual ones, and the further removed from actuality the less they matter. For this purpose I require there to be a recognizable class of *elementary* operations on sets of propositions, operations such as removing the first disjunct (or conjunct), forming the disjunction (or conjunction) of two propositions, negation, removal of negation, quantification, replacement of propositions by obvious synonyms, and swapping terms between two propositions. In this way, given any finite set of propositions A we can form $A^{(1)}$, $A^{(2)}$ etc., where $A^{(n)}$ consists of A and all that is obtainable from A by at most n elementary operations. The $A^{(n)}$ will be finite but the size of the $A^{(n)}$ will rapidly increase as n increases, and also with the size of A itself. We may now define the *implicit stress* for extensions using n elementary operations:

$\text{IStr}_n(d) = \min \{\text{EStr}(e) \mid d \, ℛ \, e \text{ and } Dom(e) = [Dom(d)]^{(n)}\}$.[14] By selecting suitable positive fractions, w_1, w_2, etc., we can ensure that the sum: $\text{EStr}(d) + w_1 \, \text{IStr}_1(d) + w_2 \, \text{IStr}_2(d) + \ldots$

converges for any d with finite domain.[15] I take the sum to be $\text{Str}(d)$. The w_i are weights which reflect the decreasing significance attached to potential stress as we go further from the actual credence function d. In this way we establish a tendency towards Completability. Alternatively we could define the stress as $\text{EStr}(d) + \text{IStr}_1(d) + \ldots + \text{IStr}_N(d)$, for some suitably large integer N. This would be to abandon Completability and the logical omniscience idealization. But although that would result in some dissonance between the comparative and non-comparative theories, it would be a step in the direction of a more realistic, less idealized theory, and so have much to commend it.

X   THE MINIMIZATION OF STRESS*

To find a maximally rational adjustment d^-/d^+ or a maximally rational expansion d^-/d^+ we must find the d^+ which minimizes the stress for some specified class of credence functions. For the case of adjustments the class consists of those credence functions with the same domain as d^-. For expansions we are to consider those credence functions which are extensions of d^- to some specified proposition or set of propositions. There will always be at least one way of minimizing stress. But this minimum depends on very many stress components. Accordingly I need to simplify matters. I do so by considering artificially small systems with very few relevant stresses. These simple systems will model more complicated and realistic ones. Moreover I concentrate on the cases where we can ignore the implicit stress. One such case is when we assume δ-consistency is not violated, or only negligibly so, and that there are no violations of other intuition-schemas adding to the implicit stress. For in that case variations in stress are equal to variations in the explicit stress. Even when we are considering violations of a single principle of δ-consistency (other than Completability) the effect of considering implicit stress would simply be to magnify the stress due to the violation. Since I have not stated any precise numerical comparisons of different stress-components this will not affect my results.

I begin with the simplest situation of all. This is the clash between two stresses, one tending towards certainty in some proposition p, the other towards contracertainty. The first stress is $\lambda[1 - d(P)]^\alpha$, the second $\mu(d(P))^\beta$ where λ, μ, α and β are positive constants.

Let $d(P) = x$. Then we are to find the value of x between 0 and 1 which minimizes:

(1) $\quad f(x) = \lambda(1 - x)^\alpha + \mu x^\beta$

The standard procedure of the Differential Calculus is to investigate the derivative of $f(x)$, namely:

(2) $\quad f'(x) = -\lambda\alpha(1 - x)^{\alpha - 1} + \mu\beta x^{\beta - 1}$

I begin by considering the case where $\beta > 1 > \alpha$. In that case $f'(x) \leqslant 0$ unless:

(3) $\quad \lambda\alpha/\mu\beta \leqslant x^{\beta - 1}(1 - x)^{1 - \alpha}$

Now the maximum value of $x^{\beta - 1}(1 - x)^{1 - \alpha}$ is given by $x = (\beta - 1)/(\beta - \alpha)$ and is $(\beta - 1)^{\beta - 1}(1 - \alpha)^{1 - \alpha}/(\beta - \alpha)^{\beta - \alpha}$. So given any $\beta > 1 > \alpha$ then for ratios of λ to μ less than $\beta(\beta - 1)^{\beta - 1}(1 - \alpha)^{1 - \alpha}/\alpha(\beta - \alpha)^{\beta - \alpha}$ we shall have $f'(x)$ negative at $x = 0$, where it is $-\lambda\alpha$, negative near $x = 1$ where it is arbitrarily large and negative, but positive somewhere in between. Hence as x increases from 0 to 1, the stress $f(x)$ decreases then increases and then decreases again. So as we increase $d(P)$ from 0 to 1 the result initially gets more rational then less rational then more rational again. I find that highly counter-intuitive. The nearer we get to maximum rationality, at least in a simple situation like this, the more rational the outcome should be. I conclude that we should not have a power of Δ less than one for some stress-components and greater than one for others. So we must either always assume the stress is proportional to a power of Δ no less than 1, or always assume it is proportional to a power of Δ no greater than 1.

If $\alpha \leqslant 1$ and $\beta \leqslant 1$ then:

(4) $f'(x) = -\lambda\alpha(1-x)^{\alpha-1} + \mu\beta x^{\beta-1}$

This is the difference between a decreasing or constant term $\mu\beta x^{\beta-1}$ and an increasing or constant term $\lambda\alpha(1-x)^{\alpha-1}$. So $f'(x)$ is either always decreasing or constant. It is constant only if $\alpha = 1 = \beta$, in which case it is $\mu - \lambda$. So in this case the minimum value is always achieved at one or both of $x = 0$ or $x = 1$, with the exception of the case in which $\alpha = 1 = \beta$ and $\lambda = \mu$, where all the values of $f(x)$ are the same. Hence if we take every stress component to be proportional to a power of Δ no greater than one, we ensure the winner-take-all strategy. (Except for the special case where $\alpha = \beta$ and $\lambda = \mu$ in which case all outcomes are equally rational.)

If $\alpha > 1$ and $\beta > 1$ the opposite holds, and $f'(x)$ is always increasing. It starts at a negative value, $-\lambda\alpha$, and finishes at a positive one, $\mu\beta$. So there is a unique minimum somewhere between 0 and 1. Hence if all the powers of Δ are greater than one we always have the compromise resolution.

Finally consider the case of $\alpha = 1$ and $\beta > 1$, which arises if we have some stress-components proportional to Δ and others to a power of Δ greater than one. In that case:

(5) $f'(x) = -\lambda + \mu\beta x^{\beta-1}$

This is increasing from $-\lambda$ to $\mu\beta - \lambda$. So if $\mu/\lambda > 1/\beta$ there is a unique minimum between 0 and 1, giving us the compromise resolution again. But if $\mu/\lambda \leqslant 1/\beta$ the derivative is never positive, and the minimum value occurs at $x = 1$. So if λ/μ is large enough we have a winner-take-all resolution. Hence if some stress-components are proportional to Δ but others proportional to a power of Δ greater than one then the ones proportional to Δ are *potentially dominant*. That is, where they are strong enough they totally dominate opposing stress-components. But otherwise there is a compromise.

The only tenable positions, then, are:

  (i)   All the stress components are proportional to a power of Δ no greater than one, and the winner-take-all resolution always holds;
  (ii)   All the stress-components are proportional to a power of Δ greater than one, and the compromise resolution always holds; or
  (iii) Some of the stress-components are proportional to Δ, others to a power greater than one. In that case the compromise resolution holds among the latter, the winner-take-all among the former, and in a clash between one of the former and one of the latter the former are potentially dominant.

For the remainder of this section I shall assume that we have rejected (i). I assume that the only potentially dominant stress-components, if there are any, are those due to δ-inconsistency. I shall restrict my attention to the case of either no or negligible violations of δ-consistency. Therefore I am able to concentrate on the compromise resolution where all the powers of Δ are greater than one. I make the further simplification that this power is the same for all components. In that case it is convenient to write the constant of proportionality as $\sigma^{\alpha-1}$ for some positive constant σ. So every stress-component is of the form $\sigma^{\alpha-1}\Delta^{\alpha}$ where, however, the constants σ vary from component to component.

In the simple situation considered above we are to minimize:

(6) $f(x) = \sigma^{\alpha-1}(1-x)^{\alpha} + \tau^{\alpha-1}x^{\alpha}$

Here σ and τ are the constants for the two clashing stress-components. The unique minimum occurs for $x/(1-x) = \sigma/\tau$. That is, we divide the range from 0 to 1 in proportion to the constants σ and τ. That is what justifies treating these constants as significant rather than their $(\alpha-1)$th powers. I shall call them the indices of epistemic importance.

Notice that where we have more than one source of information tending towards belief in the same proposition (e.g. observation agrees with testimony) we shall have two components, $\sigma_1^{\alpha-1}[1-d(p)]^{\alpha}$ and $\sigma_2^{\alpha-1}[1-d(p)]^{\alpha}$. These will combine to a resultant $\sigma^{\alpha-1}[1-d(p)]^{\alpha}$, where $\sigma^{\alpha-1} = \sigma_1^{\alpha-1} + \sigma_2^{\alpha-1}$. If $\alpha = 2$, we simply add the indices of epistemic importance. If $\alpha = 3$ we take the square root of the sum of the squares, and so on.

I now discuss the cases where there are more than two stress-components involved in the clash. First consider an inconsistent

n-ad $\{p_1, \ldots, p_n\}$ of which no $(n-1)$-ad is inconsistent. Simplifying the situation as before I assume the stress is given by:

$$(7) \quad \text{Str}(d) = \sigma_1{}^{\alpha-1} [1 - d(p_1)]^\alpha + \ldots + \sigma_n{}^{\alpha-1} [1 - d(p_n)]^\alpha$$

I am interested in which adjustment resulting in consistency will minimize this stress. For consistency we require, by the Inconsistent Polyad Rule:

$$(8) \quad d(p_1) + \ldots + d(p_n) \leqslant n - 1.$$

And I assume, again for simplicity, that (8) suffices for consistency. So we have to minimize $\text{Str}(d)$, given by (7), subject to the constraint (8). This is a straightforward problem in the Calculus and the solution is given by solving (9) and (10):

$$(9) \quad \sigma_1{}^{\alpha-1} [1 - d(p_1)]^{\alpha-1} = \ldots = \sigma_n{}^{\alpha-1} [1 - d(p_n)]^{\alpha-1}$$

and:

$$(10) \quad d(p_1) + \ldots + d(p_n) = (n - 1)$$

So we obtain:

(11) $1 - d(p_i)$, the degree of doubt in p_i, is equal to
      $(1/\sigma_i)/(1/\sigma_1 + \ldots + 1/\sigma_n)$.

Degrees of doubt are, in this admittedly oversimplified case, inversely proportional to the indices of epistemic importance. Moreover, if all the indices of epistemic importance are the same, the degree of doubt decreases as n increases. In spite of the simplifications, this is a satisfactory result, which would be reflected by more complicated analyses.

Also interesting is the case where we have propositions p_0, $p_1, \ldots, p_n$, and for each $i \geqslant 1$, p_0 is provably inconsistent with p_i, and there are no logical connections not derived from these. This models the case where a theory T clashes with each of n observations, not just with the n taken together. To illustrate more closely what is going on, I shall take the $p_1, \ldots, p_n$ to have the same index of epistemic importance, σ. Then, with suitable simplifying assumptions we should minimize:

(12) $\text{Str}(d) = \sigma_0{}^{\alpha-1} [1 - d(p_0)]^{\alpha} +$
      $\sigma^{\alpha-1} [(1 - d(p_1))^{\alpha} + \ldots + (1 - d(p_n))^{\alpha}]$

That is, we should minimize:

(13) $\varrho^{\alpha-1} x_0{}^{\alpha} + x_1{}^{\alpha} + \ldots + x_n{}^{\alpha}$

where $\varrho = \sigma_0/\sigma$, and $x_i = 1 - d(p_i)$ is the degree of doubt in p_i. And we should do this subject to the constraints:

(14) $d(p_0) + d(p_i) \leqslant 1$ for all i.

That is, subject to:

(15) $x_0 + x_i \geqslant 1$

The solution is:

(16) $1 - d(p_0) = d(p_1) = \ldots = d(p_n) = \theta/(\varrho + \theta)$.

where θ is the $(\alpha - 1)$th root of n, and $\varrho = \sigma_0/\sigma$. Thus, as expected, the degree of doubt in p_0 (the theory) decreases as ϱ increases. Furthermore, $d(p_0)$ decreases as the reciprocal of the $(\alpha - 1)$th root of n, for large n. For what it is worth, I think the $\alpha = 2$ gives too rapid a rate of decrease. But if we take $\alpha = 3$ we obtain the more acceptable result that the degree of belief in p_0 (the theory) decreases as the reciprocal of the square root of the number of observations which clash with it. In this way we obtain some clues as to the magnitude of the power of Δ in the stress-component.

XI COMPATIBILITY WITH THE
NON-COMPARATIVE THEORY*

For the comparative and non-comparative theories to be compatible we require that for changes of a given kind (e.g. expansions from d^- to p) no change prohibited as irrational is at least as rational as one permitted as rational.[16] The threat of incompatibility, then, arises where we have a principle prohibiting certain changes of a given kind as irrational. Some of the very general principles stated in chapter 3 such as the Decomposition Principle could be construed as such prohibitions. But they tell us that a certain change cannot be rational unless various others are. So they only threaten us with an incompatibility if combined with other principles. One threat comes from the only categorical prohibition, the Symmetry Principle. This prohibits expansions which do not result in symmetry with respect to exchanges between members of some finite set of names of stipulated content not previously occurring in the system. Let us suppose, then, that $Dom(d^+)$ is symmetrical but the d^+ is not symmetric with respect to the exchange of names 'a' and 'b'. Then we may consider the *symmetrization* of d^+, a credence function, $\text{Sym}d^+$, with the same domain as d^+ which is defined by: $\text{Sym}d^+(p) = \frac{1}{2}d^+(p) + \frac{1}{2}d^+(p^{a,b})$ Now there are no sources of stress themselves asymmetrical with respect to the exchange of 'a' and 'b'. For the names did not occur prior to the expansion. Hence there is no component of stress which assigns a greater value to $\text{Sym}d^+$ than to d^+. Indeed most components will be exactly the same. However the symmetry component will be less for $\text{Sym}d^+$ than for d^+. Hence $d^-/\text{Sym}d^+$ is an expansion resulting in less stress than d^-/d^+. Furthermore, it is easy to check that if d^+ is δ-consistent and I have stated all the principles of δ-consistency, then so is $\text{Sym}d^+$. Therefore, restricting our attention, as in the Symmetry Principle, to expansions from δ-consistency to δ-consistency, the expansion(s) which minimize stress must result in the required symmetry.

Notice, however, that if we attempted to extend the Symmetry Principle to cover expansions which did not preserve consistency, we would be in trouble. For example, there might well be an expansive inference to the best explanation d^-/d^+ which did not preserve δ-consistency but was more rational than any consistency-preserving expansion. Then, even if it also results in the appropriate symmetry, a slightly different expansion which did not would only be a little less rational, and so would still be more rational than any consistency-preserving expansion. But there is a rational consistency-preserving expansion. So this symmetry-breaking expansion would be more rational than some rational expansion, and so rational. I take this as an argument against extending the Symmetry Principle. It illustrates the normative phenomenon that excellence in one respect sometimes outweighs a defect in some other respect, which would otherwise lead to a prohibition. (Moral analogues abound, e.g. stealing a motor-car to save someone's life.)

The only other threat concerns the Presumption against Relevance. Strictly speaking, since it is just a presumption it lacks the teeth to result in an incompatibility. But it would still be embarrassing if intuitively acceptable judgements of irrationality made in accordance with the presumption, or with the counter-presumption, were incompatible with the comparative theory I have developed. There is one place where it might seem that I am thus embarrassed. For when discussing proportional syllogisms (chapter 8, section IV) I considered the case of someone who is certain that Tex is a Texan philosopher, and that 90 per cent of Texans are rich but that 90 per cent of Texan philosophers are poor. In this case I said we should not compromise between two proportional syllogisms but instead come to have a degree of belief of 0.1 that Tex is rich. This looks as if it is contrary to the compromise resolution. Fortunately it is not. Assuming that δ-consistency is not violated we can argue that coming to have a degree of belief greater than 0.1 that Tex is rich would inevitably require a degree of belief less than 0.1 that some other Texan philosopher called, say, Tox, is rich.[17] So although there will be less stress due to the stochastic relevance of 'is Tex' to 'is rich' there would be more stress due to the stochastic relevance of 'is Tox' to 'is rich'.

To exhibit an incompatibility, then, it would have to be demonstrated that the total stress is less in this case than in the symmetric case where the degrees of belief are the same that the various Texan philosophers are rich. However, we have no reason to suspect that this is so. Indeed we have reason to believe that the minimal stress will be given by a unique credence function and so must be symmetric with respect to exchange of 'Tex' and 'Tox'. The grounds for this suspicion are that an, admittedly simplified, model will result in uniqueness. Suppose we work within the scope of the supposition that there are precisely n Texan philosophers. (We could remove this supposition using the Multilemma Rule.) Then there will be $k = n!/m!(n-m)!$ sets of m Texan philosophers, where $m = (0.1) \times n$. Name these sets A_1, . . ., A_k. And there is a unique set B of m rich Texan philosophers. So, relying on the General Addition Rule, we have

(1)　　$x_1 + \ldots + x_k = 1$, where $x_i = d(A_i = B)$

I want to show that all the x_i are equal and so are equal to $1/k$. But I am worried about tendencies to push the x_i up to the value which would be appropriate if we had no information about the wealth of Texan philosophers, but only of Texans. Let this value be γ. I take these tendencies to have the same strength for all x_i. Then we are to minimize

$$(2) \quad \sigma^{\alpha-1}(\gamma - x_1)^\alpha + \ldots + \sigma^{\alpha-1}(\gamma - x_n)^\alpha$$

subject to the constraint (1). Here σ is the index of epistemic importance which, in the simplified model, reflects the (equal) strength of these tendencies. Using the Calculus, the minimum is given, by (1) together with:

$$(3) \quad \alpha\,\sigma^{\alpha-1}(\gamma - x_1)^{\alpha-1} = \alpha\,\sigma^{\alpha-1}(\gamma - x_2)^{\alpha-1} = \ldots = \alpha\,\sigma^{\alpha-1}(\gamma - x_n)^{\alpha-1}$$

There is a unique solution given by putting all the x_i equal. This result should remove any initial plausibility there may have been to the claim that the upward pressures on the x_i due to the rival proportional syllogism would result in inequality between the x_i.

10

Induction

In the previous chapter I applied the comparative theory to the revision of logic and to the Problem of the Direction of the Arrow of *Modus Tollens*. In this final chapter I shall apply the comparative theory to inferences by induction, and to inferences from data to hypotheses ('inferences to the best explanation'). Relying on the stress-components discussed in the previous chapter I shall show that not relying on induction is less than maximally rational. This result can be taken in three ways, depending on which particular judgements you make about induction. First there may be those who are genuinely diffident about judging that some particular inference by induction is required either for rationality or for maximal rationality, however *natural* it might be. If they find the comparative theory I have developed persuasive then the justification I provide should remove such diffidence. Next there may be those who judge that reliance on various cases of induction is required for maximal rationality but not for rationality. Then their intuitive judgements are in good agreement with my systematic theory and each supports the other, as in the modified Duhem justification. Finally there will be those who make the judgement that rationality requires the making of various particular inferences by induction. In that case, since I am not able to establish that rationality requires various inferences by induction, their particular judgements are stronger than my theoretical result that maximum rationality requires such inferences. In that case, what I say is not of much weight as a justification. However, it remains of interest as a theory which partially systematizes intuitions.

I SOME PRELIMINARY REMARKS

To justify induction has come to be thought of as the philosophical analogue of trisecting an angle. And, despairing of a genuine justification, philosophers who resist inductive scepticism have tried alternative tactics. Strawson (1952, chapter 9) suggested that reliance on induction was part of what we *mean* by rationality. Perhaps our language is plastic enough to accommodate such usage. But I could give Strawson the word 'rational' and ask 'Why is induction the inference to make?' The normative won't go away. Other philosophers have thought to *vindicate* induction as the best policy even though it cannot be justified. You might as well call the souls in Dante's first circle of Hell vindicated – they are better off than the others.

Moreover I do not just want to establish the rationality of induction. I am not so tolerant. I also want to show that the refusal to rely on induction is less than maximally rational. Am I then to be counted among the angle-trisectors? Why not? The analogy is a good one. What cannot be done is trisect (some) angles *in a specified way* (i.e. with idealized ruler and idealized compass). Likewise I take Hume to have shown that induction cannot be justified deductively. But there are other ways of trisecting angles and other ways of trying to justify induction. At one extreme there are attempts to derive the rationality of induction from further general principles. Carnap's attempts can be seen as such. My chief criticisms of them are my criticisms of the Carnapian programme in general. But it should also be noted that Carnap is a somewhat aprioristic empiricist, whereas I prefer an empirical rationalism. I shall consider and reject three other attempts at justifying induction from general principles in later sections.

At the other extreme from Carnap is the Duhem-style justification. Good sense (i.e. particular intuitive judgement), it might be said, tells us that it is often irrational not to rely on induction, and so, *a fortiori*, maximal rationality requires the reliance on induction. And that, it might be further said, is all that is required by way of justification. This is a bit like the bare hands trisection of an angle: you just draw the appropriate line. I have already indicated a general worry about the unmodified Duhem approach; namely the fact that a systemic theory should sometimes be retained and recalcitrant data rejected. So there is some need for a systematic treatment.

As a preliminary to considering the justification of our intuitions about induction, I shall reply to a couple of arguments for inductive scepticism. The one which I take most seriously is loosely based on Hume's discussion. It is a thought experiment. Suppose you were agnostic about all causal connections. Then what would be your intuition about induction? Each has to perform the experiment him-

or herself. But it is tempting to say that one's confidence in induction would be shaken, or even totally destroyed. A further thought experiment would establish a similar result even if you believe there are causal connections but treat them as nothing beyond appropriate regularities. This is a prima facie argument for inductive scepticism except where we both believe in a causal connection, and reject a Humean account of causation.

My reply is that the thought experiment is misleading. It frequently happens that there is an obvious, or traditional, justification for something and a less obvious one as well. If both are successful then it is justified twice over. What happens if you demolish the obvious or traditional justification? The temptation is to overlook the other justification and so become a sceptic. I claim that the Humean-style thought experiment trades on this temptation. And the justification I shall give for induction (as required for maximum rationality) will support this claim, because it does not depend on there being any causal connections.

Another line of sceptical argument is based on the way inductive inference seems to be 'opaque to the intellect'. Contrast an inference by *modus ponens* and one by induction. In the first case we can, as it were, just *see* that the inference preserves truth. There is a lack of obscurity or opacity about it. And to almost the same extent, proportional syllogisms have this lucidity, we can just 'see' that the higher the proportion of Fs which are Gs the greater the degree of belief we should have that some particular F is a G. But inferences by induction seem, by contrast, mysterious, even magical. We tend to *believe* they are rational but we cannot see why. They cry out, therefore, for a theoretical framework into which they can be fitted and which will, therefore (partially) explain their rationality. Clearly this line of sceptical argument can be replied to by providing the required theoretical framework, which I shall do.

As a further preliminary, I shall survey some of the types of inference often called induction. First there are inferences from samples to population. These are one of the chief concerns of statisticians, who have developed an elaborate theory of them. But we may concentrate on a paradigm, namely the inference from certainty that of N observed Fs, M were Gs, to various degrees of belief about the proportion of the unobserved Fs which are Gs. In particular, we may consider the case where the reasoner is certain that all of N observed Fs are Gs, and comes to a high degree of belief that a high proportion of unobserved *F*s are *G*s. If we know nothing else about the sample (the observed *F*s) which we do not already know of the whole population of *F*s, then the sample is said to be *epistemically random*. But in practice we almost always do have some extra information about the sample, such as its location in space and time. In such cases the inference involves an element of projection or extrapolation – we assume that this extra information is either irrelevant or only marginally relevant. Even where there is no extrapolation, the inference could still be called induction, although I take that to be a degenerate case. One sort of extrapolation is spatio-temporal. Another sort occurs where instead of degreeless qualities *F*-ness and *G*-ness we consider degrees of *H*-ness and *K*-ness. Then the inference will be from the degrees of *H*-ness and *K*-ness in the members of the sample to some (range of) functional correlation(s) between degrees of *H*-ness and degrees of *K*-ness in the population. If here we ignore the relevance of the magnitude of the degrees in the sample, we make a notoriously risky extrapolation. For instance, suppose in a sample of 100 human beings aged 60 to 65 the average time spent per year in hospital is positively correlated with weight. It would be risky to extrapolate this to men between 25 and 30.

Other inferences by induction are from the observed sample to some particular member of the remainder of the population. This Johnson (1924, p. 43) calls *eduction*. Thus the inference from certainty that all the *N* observed *F*s are *G*s to some high degree of belief that *b*, an unobserved *F*, is also a *G*, would be a case of eduction. As with inferences from samples to populations, we usually have information which we treat as either totally irrelevant or of marginal relevance. For instance, the 'unobserved' *F* might have been observed, but without it being observed whether it is *F*. (I *hear* a raven, and infer by eduction that the bird I hear is black.) Or again we may extrapolate or project. Thus, before European arrival in Australia, all of the swans observed by Europeans lived outside Australia, and were white. An inference that the first swan they saw in Australia would be white, though not perhaps irrational, would have been riskier than the inference that the next swan to be seen in Europe would be white. It is important to be aware of the element of extrapolation or projection in inferences by induction, of whatever sort. For there are two problems, that of justifying induction without extrapolation, and that of justifying extrapolation. Goodman's New Riddle of Induction (1954) concerns the latter. Suppose we had a sample of a million emeralds taken between AD 1960 and AD 2040 without knowing the dates more precisely, and, amazingly, they were all grue (i.e. green before AD 2000, blue thereafter).[1] And suppose we had no further information. Then, I think, it would be rational to come to have a high degree of belief both that a high proportion of emeralds in the temporal interval were grue and that some specified emerald, not in the sample, was grue. But in the case considered in the riddle, the sample of emeralds is taken before AD 2000, but much of the population (or the specified emerald) is after AD 2000. In that case we have the suspicious element of extrapolation, or projection as Goodman calls it.

Finally there are what I call inferences from data to hypotheses. The 'data' here can be observations, but can also be lower-order theories or intuitions. The inferences used by scientific realists who infer, say, that Quantum Field Theory (suitably interpreted) is true[2] because it explains so many diverse phenomena, is of this sort. But so are the inferences made by juries when they convict someone on circumstantial evidence: such inferences are by no means peculiarly *scientific*.

II   INDUCTION VIA THEORETICAL EXPLANATION?

The first strategy I shall criticize is the assimilation of induction to inference from data to theory, and the related justification of eduction. It is observed that Fa_1 & Ga_1, Fa_2 & Ga_2 etc. From those observations some theory is inferred containing a generalization about Fs being Gs, which in turn either entails or makes probable that b, known to be an F, is also a G. Either the theory will be scientific (perhaps at the level of folk science) or metaphysical. As an example of the first, the observation that people have survived on some foods but not on others may result in some theory (at the folk level) about nutrition. Using that theory we can then come to believe that some kind of food not previously eaten is nutritious. Here the predicates 'F' and 'G' are applied to kinds of food, where the kinds are phenomenal ones; that is, foods are classified according to how they appear to us. So the 'particulars' a_1, . . ., a_n and b are in this case not so much the chunks of bread or individual nuts as kinds of bread of a certain appearance and aroma, nuts of a certain shape, and so on. Provided we have an independent justification for the inference to the theory of nutrition, there is nothing wrong with such a procedure. However I have doubts whether at the level of folk and other low-level theories the inference to the theory is anything more than an induction. In that case the attempted justification is circular. A more important objection is that this justification does not cover all cases of eduction which are intuitively rational. That an alarm clock has gone off, in all 100 cases when it was set to go off, is evidence that it will go off the next time it is set, and we do not need to understand anything about how it works to rely on such evidence. No doubt we believe there is some explanatory theory and that this would predict that the alarm will go off next time. But unless we have some idea of the explanation, our expectation that the alarm will go off next time is based solely on eduction. Nor can we explain the alarm clock's going off by pointing out that it was designed to do so. For I shall play the cynic and assume that we have observed that most alarm clocks, likewise designed to go off, fail to do so reliably: it is *this* alarm clock which has been reliable, not alarm clocks in general. Finally, we should resist the claim that the mini-hypothesis that the alarm clock will go off for the most part can be inferred without reliance on induction. For that mini-hypothesis lacks the good-making characteristics of scientific theories which warrant our acceptance of them. In the first place, unless we rashly inferred the clock would *always* go off, the generalization is not even especially simple, having as it does a 'for the most part' qualification. Secondly, it scores poorly on strength, for it concerns such a small range of data. Thirdly, it scores even less on aesthetic grounds: if theories were symphonies, that would be a boy blowing a tin whistle. Fourthly, it scores zero as an explanation. For in this case, it seems, the instances explain the generalization, not vice versa.[3]

More promising is the justification via *metaphysical* explanations, as in Armstrong's theory of laws (1983, pp. 103–4). We observe the past regularity between being an F and being a G, and infer that there is a *necessary connection* between being an F and being a G (or perhaps a *probabilistic connection*). The occurrence of a necessary connection will entail or at least support[4] the prediction that the unobserved F is also a G. (Likewise that there is a probabilistic connection will support the prediction that the unobserved F is a G). This attempt to justify induction requires, of course, that we reject Hume's arguments against such a necessary connection. But that does not worry me.

As with the previous attempt to justify induction via a theory, this attempt presupposes we can justify the rationality of some inferences from data to theory. But I grant that. The difficulty with this attempted metaphysical justification (and one that would apply to almost any justification of induction via inference to a theory) is that induction is quite rational when restricted to atypical populations. Suppose I know that for the population at large there is no correlation between gastric ulcers and rheumatism. Nonetheless I then observe that among a sample of people living on Lord Howe Island there is such a correlation. I infer that someone else living on that island who I know has gastric ulcers has rheumatism also. No doubt I assume there is *something* about Lord Howe Island which explains this. But the necessary connection could not be one simply between the conjunction of having gastric ulcers and living on Lord Howe Island on the one hand, and having rheumatism on the other. It would be *ad hoc* to suggest that. Rather the necessary connection would have to be between the conjunction of having gastric ulcers *and* being *F*, on the one hand, and having rheumatism on the other for some property *F*-ness common on Lord Howe Island. But we do not know what *F*-ness is. And if we say that all the people in the sample have *F*-ness, whatever *F*-ness is, hence so does the other person, we have just made an inference by eduction. In this case, then, the attempted justification becomes circular. I conclude that while in some cases the justification of induction via a theory may succeed by itself, and while it may often play a supplementary role, it does not cover all cases where induction is intuitively required for (maximum) rationality.

III THE BAYESIAN APPROACH

Suppose I observe p, and for simplicity, suppose I am certain that p and this certainty is indefeasible. (Actually this supposition is unlikely: typically my observation that p will merely have high epistemic importance.) Now the following *looks* plausible.

The Conjecture of Temporal Coherence

If I observe p with certainty (and indefeasibly) and if *all* I observe is that p, then the degree of belief I have in some proposition h after the observation should, for rationality, be equal to the degree of belief I have in h before the observation within the scope of the supposition that p. [So $d^+(h) = d^-(h/p)$.]

The qualification that *all* I observe is that p is required to avoid the following sort of counter-example. Suppose h is the hypothesis that all ravens are black and p the proposition that I shall see a black raven today on that tree. Then $d^-(h/p)$, the initial degree of belief within the scope of the supposition that p, might be quite high. But if I simultaneously observe a black raven on that tree and a white one flying past, then $d^+(h)$, the final degree of belief should be (near) zero.

The initial plausibility of this principle derives from the fact that what was supposed, namely p, turned out to be the case. So I should have, it might seem, the same degree of belief in h in the two cases. That is, I should have $d^+(h) = d^-(h/p)$. Subjectivists like de Finetti accept this principle, which is a normative one.

Given Temporal Coherence a whole world of Bayesian inferences opens up. Thus if we assume δ-consistency both before and after the observation, if we assume Temporal Coherence, and if we assume the Multiplication Rule, we have:[5]

(1)   If $d^-(p/h)$ and $d^-(h)$ are both positive then $d^+(h)/d^-(h) = d^-(p/h)/d^-(p)$.

This tells us that the degree of belief in h should be amplified by a factor equal to the ratio between the prior degree of belief in p conditional on h and the prior unconditional degree of belief in p.

Among other applications of this result, we could set about justifying *adjustments* by induction. I shall illustrate this by means of a simple example. Let H_k be the hypothesis that K per cent of Fs are Gs. Suppose I know that $H_{100} \lor H_{50} \lor H_0$. More specifically, suppose I have three piles of cards. I have checked that one contains all spades, one half spades and half hearts, and one all hearts. But now I do not know which pile is which. And to further simplify matters, suppose the sample is of size one. This will illustrate the Bayesian justification, but of course we should not expect a high degree of confidence in the conclusion, since it is based on a unit sample. The sample happens to be a spade. So we can rule out H_0. How does this observation affect $d(H_{100})$ and $d(H_{50})$? Intuitively it should favour H_{100} more than H_{50}. And it does. Indeed the amplifying factor for H_{100} is twice

that for H_{50}.[6] [That is, $d^+(H_{100})/d^-(H_{100}) = 2d^+(H_{50})/d^-(H_{50})$.]
So if initially someone had degree of belief $\frac{1}{3}$ in each of H_{100}, H_{50}
and H_0, then he or she should come to have degree of belief $\frac{2}{3}$ in
H_{100}, $\frac{1}{3}$ in H_{50} and 0 in H_0. Hence the Bayesian approach seems
to justify learning from experience in an inductive fashion.

However I have two criticisms of the Bayesian justification. The
first criticism is that it fails to justify inductive *expansion*. For without
some prior degree of belief in h, (1) is vacuous. The second criticism
is that Temporal Coherence, where it applies at all, is derived from
other judgements of rationality. To develop this criticism I begin with
a common question about Temporal Coherence. Suppose you initially
had a given degree of belief in h conditional on p, but as you observe
that p you just changed your mind. What would be irrational, or even
less than maximally rational, about that?

One, perfectly good, answer is not compatible with the Bayesian
justification of induction. It is that it is required for (maximum)
rationality to make inferences from belief in p to belief in h, and the
degree of belief in h conditional on p is the result of making such an
inference. Quite generally where the degree of belief in h conditional
on p is constrained in a way which does not change with observation,
Temporal Coherence will be a correct but *derived* principle, based on
that constraint. But if Temporal Coherence is to be used to justify
inferences from belief in p to belief in h that justification is not available.
And I can think of only one further justification with any initial
plausibility.[7] It is based on the claim that we should not change a
doxastic attitude without good reason. I shall concede that, at least
for the sake of argument. Then it is further claimed that to change
the degree of belief in h conditional on p just because you have observed
p would be a change for no good reason. And so it would be – except
where the degree of belief in h conditional on p itself depends on the
degree of belief in p. But in that case observing p could well be a good
reason for changing ones degree of belief in h conditional on p. In
what peculiar situation, you ask, would the degree of belief in h
conditional on p itself depend on the degree of belief in p? I say:
Precisely in the application to induction. For (1) is derived using the
following instances of the Multiplication Rule:

(2) $d^-(h\&p) = d^-(h/p) \times d^-(p)$

and

(3) $d^-(p\&h) = d^-(p/h) \times d^-(h)$

From these we derive an equation in which $d^-(h/p)$ is constrained by $d^-(h)$, $d^-(p/h)$ *and* $d^-(p)$, namely:

(4) $\quad d^-(h/p) = d^-(p/h) \times d^-(h)/d^-(p)$

So, peculiar though it might initially seem, the degree of belief in h conditional on p itself depends on the degree of belief in p. The circumstances, then, are precisely those in which Temporal Coherence has no justification independent of any justification for induction.

The initial plausibility of Temporal Coherence can be explained as a combination of two factors. Firstly, *as a rule of thumb*, there is a presumption against changing your mind. For it is likely that your existing belief will have some justification and changing your mind therefore runs a risk of being irrational. Secondly, and more importantly, induction *is*, I claim, required for maximum rationality. So there is, at least in the case being considered, an independent constraint on $d(h/e)$. So the Conjecture of Temporal Coherence, at least in the relevant case, has some rational basis. Its only failing is as an independent principle.

IV   THE WILLIAMS/STOVE ARGUMENT

Another attempt to justify induction is by means of a proportional syllogism. This is due to Williams (1947), and has recently been championed by Stove (1973 and 1985). It is also, I think, essentially the same as Fisher's fiducial method in statistics. But Fisher, to the best of my knowledge, never articulated his method with any clarity.

This method is based on results in pure mathematics which show that the vast majority of large samples (of a given size) closely match the population in their composition, that is, in the proportion of Fs which are Gs. (This is vague, but the mathematical results themselves are precise.) Let us call a sample which closely matches the population a *matcher*. Then if the observed sample is of size N we reason as follows:

The vast majority of samples of the size N are matchers. The observed sample is a sample of size N. So it is a matcher.

This is a proportional syllogism. Hence if the circumstances are appropriate for making it we should come to have a high degree of belief that the observed sample is a matcher. But we know the composition of the observed sample. So we can make an inference to the composition of the population: it must closely match that of the observed sample. The Williams/Stove argument succeeds only if the proportional syllogism is a rational one to make. But is it? To ensure that it was it would suffice that no information we have about the sample is more than marginally relevant to its being a matcher.

The first sort of information we are likely to have is the location of the sample in space and time. Whether this is at most marginally relevant depends on whether extrapolation is justified. And the crucial requirement here is the lack of conceptual overlap between spatio-temporal predicates on the one hand and 'F' and 'G' on the other. But that is ensured, at least relative to a conceptual scheme, provided 'F' and 'G' are not gruey predicates. And, of course, it is where the predicates are not gruey that we have direct intuitive support for induction. The judgements of irrelevance, then, required for extrapolation are quite in order. But there remains a more basic difficulty. For the remainder of the justification to succeed, we must have information about the sample composition. It is not much use believing the sample is a matcher if we have forgotten the proportion of Gs in the sample. Hence, for the justification to succeed we must rationally judge the composition of the sample to be irrelevant (or only marginally relevant) to whether it is a matcher. I shall now argue in two stages that we do *not* have the requisite irrelevance. First I critically examine those lines of reasoning which tempt us to make that judgement of irrelevance. Then I show how the predicate 'is a matcher' is not the sort of predicate for which we would expect irrelevance (or even marginal relevance).

First, then, I suspect that one reason why having such and such a proportion of Gs appears irrelevant to being a matcher is precisely because it would be so *obviously* relevant if we knew the proportion of Gs in the population. Hence that we do not know the proportion removes its *obvious* source of relevance. But that the obvious source of relevance is removed is no argument for irrelevance unless there is a presumption against relevance.

The second line of reasoning is that there is indeed a presumption against relevance: unless relevance can be shown irrelevance is to be assumed. I think the initial plausibility of this line of reasoning is due to its lack of explicitness as to whether we are considering the rational permissibility of stochastic irrelevance or its rational obligatoriness. The presumption is only plausible as part of a general presumption in favour of rational liberty. As such it provides only a presumption against the requirement of relevance. But what is needed for a justification of our intuitions about induction would be a presumptive prohibition against stochastic relevance, or at least a presumption that it is less than maximally rational. Otherwise all we have established is the permissibility of induction.

A third line of reasoning is to say that provided we always work with the minimal evidence we can ignore the problems of relevance. Now the minimal evidence for the case of induction consists of knowledge of the sample size and composition. So if that is all we know, we should be able to perform our probabilistic calculations without worrying about relevance. The mistake in this line of reasoning is that what is minimal for the induction is not minimal for the crucial step in the Williams argument, namely the proportional syllogism. There the minimal evidence is simply knowledge of the sample size. If that is all we know, then, indeed, the only rational inference is that the sample is a matcher. Unfortunately, unless we also know its composition, and hence have more than minimal evidence, this will be of no use when it comes to justifying induction.

Next I point out that the predicate 'is a matcher' has a conceptual overlap with the predicate describing the sample composition. So we should not expect irrelevance. '*S* is a matcher' is analysed as:

For all y, if the proportion in the population is y then the proportion in the sample is within ϵ of y.

Here ϵ is a small number, and the smaller ϵ the better the match. So we have the following dyadic predicate in the conceptual overlap:

The proportion in _____ is less than . . .

Hence we do not have a presumption against rational irrelevance. Indeed suppose the sample proportion is M/N. Then for those y within ϵ of M/N the sample proportion's being M/N entails that it is within ϵ of y, and for those y not within ϵ of M/N, the sample proportion's being M/N is inconsistent with its being within ϵ of y. So if the sample proportion were to lack rational relevance to whether the sample is a matcher this would be the result of quantifying over the y, where for some values of y we have entailment and for others inconsistency.

Quantification would have generated irrelevance from relevance. I see no reason for expecting such good luck.

There is not therefore a strong case for the lack of rational relevance needed for Williams's argument, as stated above. But, as I understand it, Stove (1985) has provided an improved version of the Williams argument. He does not claim that the sample proportion is *always* irrelevant. What he claims is that for some sample proportion we have either irrelevance or else the relevance favours induction. (It favours induction if knowledge of the sample proportion *increases* the probability of its being a good matcher.) And indeed if we rely on the standard calculus of probabilities[8] it can be shown that we must have either irrelevance or relevance favouring induction for some proportion.

Even if the Stove modification succeeded, it would not provide what I want of a justification, only what Stove needs for his purposes. For I think we should be able to justify our intuitions that for *any* fairly high sample proportion it should be maximally rational to make the inductive inference. A more serious criticism of Stove's modification is that the standard calculus of probabilities does not make due allowance for ranges of equally rational degrees of belief. I admit that we cannot have unfavourable stochastic relevance for all sample proportions. But if a whole range of degrees of belief are equally rational, then we could well have no sample proportion for which it is less than maximally rational to assume a relevance unfavourable for induction. I conclude, reluctantly, that the Williams/Stove argument fails.

V   A JUSTIFICATION OF INDUCTION

In the previous three sections I considered, but rejected, the best three attempts I know of in the literature at a justification of induction. I now show how the result that maximal rationality requires reliance on induction can be derived from my systematic theory, without *ad hoc* assumptions. And this holds even where we have no knowledge of causal connections. In this section I shall ignore the complication due to extrapolation. For, as I indicated in the previous section, I think the judgements of irrelevance involved in extrapolation are not problematic. My justification for induction is based on the stress-component due to asymmetry. Recall that there will be a tendency towards symmetry with respect to the exchange of two names '*a*' and '*b*'. This tendency is strongest where all the sources of information are already symmetrical with respect to this exchange. But, as I argued previously, even if the sources are not symmetrical we should still have some tendency towards symmetry. And, I submitted, the index of epistemic importance associated with the stress due to any asymmetry between '*a*' and '*b*' is less the greater the difference between the extrinsic stress in the credence function d and that in $d_{a,b}$, the result of exchanging a and b.

Now consider the case where a has been observed to be a G but it has not been observed whether or not b is a G. Then there is a stress-component tending to produce a high value for the degree of belief that a is G, but no such stress-component for b. Hence we have an asymmetry in the stresses with respect to the exchange of '*a*' and '*b*'. Therefore the stress due to asymmetry will be rather small. Nonetheless it will still be there, tending to pull the degrees of belief that a is G and that b is G together. This combines with the stress which gives a tendency towards a high degree of belief that a is G, to produce a tendency towards a high degree of belief that b is G. So if we expand to some degree of belief that b is G there will at least be a tendency towards expanding by means of an eduction from as being G to bs being G. This will be reinforced if there are many observed items which are observed to be Gs (or for that matter, remembered to be Gs or attested as being Gs). The tendency will be opposed by others due to various observed items not being Gs. The maximally rational degree(s) of belief that b is G will be the result of the number of items observed to be G, the number of them observed not to be G and the relative strengths of the various tendencies towards symmetry. In the very special case where all the strengths are the same, the maximally rational degree of belief that b is a G should depend only on the number, m, of items observed to be G and on the number, n, observed not to be G. A simple model discussed in section VII gives the result that the degree of belief that b is G depends on m and n in an intuitively satisfactory fashion. That is, the higher the ratio of m to n the nearer the degree is to certainty, and if $n = m$ the appropriate degree is one half.

However the situation where all the stresses due to the asymmetry are of equal strength is atypical. Typically some observations will be more significant than others. For instance, if '*b*' is stipulated to entail '*raven*' then observations about other ravens are much more significant than observations about other birds. In part this is due to the influence of a theory, such as that birds come in natural kinds. But something similar holds even without the influence of theories. Suppose we had various sorts of rock described phenomenally and with not even the beginning of a theory of them. Further suppose we have tested the magnetic properties of some of them and that we are to infer whether an untested sample is magnetic. Then we would rightly attach more significance to rocks which resembled the one under consideration. My theory provides a way of measuring such pertinent similarity. For given any two names 'a' and 'b' the difference between the stress of d and of $d_{a,b}$ [where $d_{a,b}(p) = d(p^{a,b})$] will reflect all the relevant differences between 'a' and 'b' due either to the content of the names 'a' or 'b', or to differences in what is observed, remembered or attested to. And the theory of stresses I developed in the previous chapter requires the asymmetry component to be less the greater the difference between the stresses due to d and to $d_{a,b}$. The theory ensures, then, that intuitively more pertinent observations are given greater weight when we make a (maximally rational) inference by induction.

My comparative theory, then, provides a justification for eduction as the only maximally rational change even where there is no inference to a causal connection or to some theory.[9] (But notice that I have not claimed that such reasoning is required for rationality). A corollary of this justification is that, in a rather special case, eduction leads to certainty with maximum rationality. For suppose no observation, testimony or intuition has ever even hinted at a non-G. Then all the tendencies of stress-components due to asymmetry will incline in the same direction. And the upshot will be certainty that some unobserved item is also a G. For example, let us suppose we have a complete list of the ontological categories for which we have evidence. Then we should be *certain* there are no other sorts of entity. This is a justification for a strong version of Occam's razor. And, I claim, it accords with our intuitions *provided* it is remembered that I do not mean by certainty a maximally possible degree of confidence, but rather that paradigm of confidence we had as a result of observation in our days of pre-philosophical innocence. I anticipate an objection to this corollary. It will be said that δ-inferences should not lead to certainty unless based on provable π-inferences. I would like to have pointed to belief in other minds as a counter-example to the objector's claim. But I doubt if that is the result of an inference at all. However, an example that should be persuasive is that of someone who is certain that there are infinitely many Fs precisely one of which is a G. (Say that there are infinitely many spatio-temporal worlds in precisely one of which some physical constant has a specified value.) Intuitively, it seems that in suitable circumstances someone could rationally come to have full belief that some given F (say the world we are in) is not the one which is a G. Yet the π-inference is not provable.

Results about induction to the proportion of unobserved Fs which are Gs follow from those for eduction to a belief that a given F is also a G. (For the details see section VII.)

VI   INFERENCE FROM DATA TO HYPOTHESIS

I now provide a modified Duhem justification of inferences from data to hypothesis. Although, following Harman (1973) these are now often called *inferences to the best explanation*, I shall, among other things, argue that this is a misnomer.

I reject Bayesian attempts to justify inferences from data to hypothesis for the same reason as I rejected the Bayesian attempt to justify induction. Similar to Strawson's attempted solution of the problem of induction is Armstrong's suggestion (1983, p. 59) that 'to infer to the best explanation is part of what it is to be rational. If that is not rational, what is?' If this is an analysis of what 'rational' means, I reply by conceding the analysis if necessary, but insisting that it has not been shown that inference to the best explanation *is to be made*.

I know of no other attempts at justification. But a modified Duhem justification is easily provided. I suggest that *any* hypothesis, whether it fits the data or not, which has various good-making features[10] is intuitively 'seen to be true'. But to avoid lunacy, I admit that much that is intuitively 'seen to be true' is nonetheless rejected because it fails to fit the data. However, by the No Dishonour in Defeat Principle, I claim that such intuitions are not suspect simply because they have often been defeated. Admittedly one should critically examine such intuitions. But if, as I believe, this one survives such examination, it should still provide a tendency towards belief in theories with these good-making features. What I posit, then, is a stress-component[11] tending towards certainty in any hypothesis p with good-making features. And the better the hypothesis the greater its epistemic strength. Now the hypothesis may clash with various data. It may also clash with other hypotheses. So which, if any, hypotheses are to be accepted will be the result of an appropriate compromise between the claims of the individual hypotheses, observations and other considerations. If among hypotheses compatible with (most of) the data one is much better than the others, then the compromise will result in a high degree of belief in it. So in that case 'inference to the best explanation' is not much of a misnomer. (However, I have not mentioned explanatory power. But you may take it either to be a good-making feature or a consequence of one if you wish.) But sometimes several theories will be of comparable goodness. In that case the proper compromise will be one of agnosticism: we should not decide which of the theories is correct, even though one might be somewhat better than the others. That is one reason why I consider the phrase 'inference to the best explanation' to be misleading: the best may not be better by enough. Here, I take it, intuitive judgements support my position.

The justification I have provided has two further interesting features. The first is that it is somewhat Popperian, in that the data do not directly support hypotheses, rather they (tend to) weed them out. On my account, what directly supports a hypothesis is its good-making features.

The second interesting feature is that if two hypotheses are compatible, if they both have good-making features, and if they both fit the data well enough, then I allow that it is maximally rational to believe that both are true. Perhaps you object: How can they both be true? I reply that if there is some good reason for not believing them both to be true then there will be an appropriate stress-component, so the envisaged situation has not arisen. But in the cases being considered there is no such good reason. So why should just one theory be true? For example, why should not both a field theory and a particle theory in physics be correct? Part of the resistance to such multiplication of theories derives, I suspect, from the quest for a theory which tells the whole truth, or the ultimate truth. Now I rather sympathize with this quest: we do and should seek such a unitary theory. But seeking is one thing, finding another. Until we find a theory which excludes all others and is much better than any other excluded by the data, we should not assume we have discovered the whole truth. Another source of resistance to multiple theories comes, I suspect, from the surmise that it leads to Relativism. But that is mistaken. For in any sense in which a *uniquely* supported theory would be absolutely true, all the true theories are absolutely true. This is no more perplexing than the fact that 'Grass is green' and 'Snow is white' are *two* truths. The mistake is facilitated by the way we talk of *the* truth. This suggests there is only one truth; and if by that we mean that whether a proposition is true or false is neither person- nor culture-relative, then I agree. But it, in turn, suggests there can only be one true theory explaining a given body of data. I reject this latter suggestion and that is one of my reasons for not talking of inference to *the* best explanation.

One final comment: but for the logical omniscience idealization, I would have needed to consider the difficulty that we cannot survey all possible theories. How confident should we be that none of the unsurveyed theories is both better than the best we know of, and excludes it? I suspect that this is hardly constrained by rationality at all. It strikes me as rationally permissible to be quite confident that no such possibility has been overlooked. It also strikes me as rationally permissible to be quite confident that some such has been. And I am not even prepared to deny that both positions are maximally rational.

VII   TWO RESULTS CONCERNING INDUCTION*

In the situation discussed in section V, we have observed that $a_1, \ldots, a_m$ are Fs, that $c_1, \ldots, c_n$ are not Fs, and we have not observed whether b is an F. The stresses due to asymmetry are, I assume, rather weak. So they will not significantly affect the degrees of belief in the propositions that $a_1, \ldots, a_m$ are Fs and that $c_1, \ldots, c_n$ are not Fs. So let us assume that $d^-(Fa_i) = d^+(Fa_i) = 1$, $i = 1 \ldots m$, and that $d^-(Fc_j) = d^+(Fc_j) = 0$, $j = 1 \ldots n$. Let $d^+(Fb) = x$. Then the relevant stresses are of the form $\sigma_i^{\alpha-1}(1-x)^\alpha$, for $i = 1 \ldots m$ and $\tau_j^{\alpha-1}x^\alpha$, for $j = 1 \ldots n$.

The σ_i and τ_j are the indices of epistemic importance associated with the asymmetry with respect to the exchange of 'a_i' and 'b', and 'c_j' and 'b' respectively. As indicated in section V, these will be greater the less the difference in stress resulting from the exchange. We have to minimize:

(1) $\sigma_1^{\alpha-1}(1-x)^\alpha + \ldots + \sigma_m^{\alpha-1}(1-x)^\alpha + \tau_1^{\alpha-1}x^\alpha + \ldots + \tau_n^{\alpha-1}x^\alpha$

That is, we have to minimize:

(2) $\sigma^{\alpha-1}(1-x)^\alpha + \tau^{\alpha-1}x^\alpha$

where:

(3) $\sigma^{\alpha-1} = \sigma_1^{\alpha-1} + \ldots + \sigma_m^{\alpha-1}$

and:

(4) $\tau^{\alpha-1} = \tau_1^{\alpha-1} + \ldots + \tau_n^{\alpha-1}$

the minimum is given by:

(5) $(1-x)/x = \tau/\sigma$

Clearly the stronger and more numerous the σ_i compare to the τ_j the smaller τ/σ and hence the nearer x is to 1. If all the σ_i and τ_j are equal we have a special case where the ratio $(1-x)$ to x is the $(\alpha-1)$th root of n/m. In particular if $n = m$ we have $x = \frac{1}{2}$.

I now turn to an inference by induction from the observed proportion of *F*s which are *G*s to the total proportion of *F*s which are *G*s. Recall that in the non-comparative theory I did not rely on the Multiplication Rule, but that in the last chapter I considered it could be justified as giving the simplest formula for stress. Accordingly I shall initially rely on it to show this sort of induction to be required for maximal rationality. But, because of the problematic character of the Multiplication Rule, I shall also discuss what happens if we reject it. Let H, then, be the hypothesis that at least a proportion γ of unobserved *F*s are *G*s. Let b be some arbitrary unobserved *F*. Then by the theory of the proportional syllogism we should expand to:

(6) $d^+(Gb/\!\sim\! H) < \gamma.$

Assume that $H \& \sim\! H$ is self-refuting, $H \vee \sim\! H$ self-evident, and that the Multiplication Rule holds. Then we have:

(7) $d^+(Gb) = d^+(Gb/H)\,d^+(H) + d^+(Gb/\!\sim\! H)\,[1 - d^+(H)]$

From (6) and (7):

(8) $d^+(Gb) \leqslant d^+(H) + \gamma[1 - d^+(H)]$

Therefore:

(9) $d^+(H) \geqslant [d^+(Gb) - \gamma]/(1 - \gamma).$

Given, then, an inference by eduction to a high value for $d^+(Gb)$ we obtain high, but not quite so high values for $d^+(H)$, for suitable γ. For example we have:

	$\gamma = 0.9$	$\gamma = 0.8$	$\gamma = 0.7$
$d^+(Gb) = 0.9$	$d^+(H) \geqslant 0$	$d^+(H) \geqslant 0.5$	$d^+(H) \geqslant 0.66$
$d^+(Gb) = 0.95$	$d^+(H) \geqslant 0.5$	$d^+(H) \geqslant 0.75$	$d^+(H) \geqslant 0.83$
$d^+(Gb) = 0.99$	$d^+(H) \geqslant 0.9$	$d^+(H) \geqslant 0.95$	$d^+(H) \geqslant 0.98$

Abandoning the Multiplication Rule, we have to reason in a less formal fashion. There will be some component of stress corresponding to the Restricted Multiplication Principle and the Principle of Alternative Supposition. This will tend to push $d^+(Gb)$ to a point between $d^+(Gb/H)$ and $d^+(Gb/\sim H)$. (If it is not between the two the Principle of Alternative Supposition will be violated.) Thus we have:

(10) $d^+(Gb) = \lambda d^+(Gb/H) + (1 - \lambda) d^+(Gb/\sim H)$

where $0 \leqslant \lambda \leqslant 1$, and λ depends on $d^+(H)$.
Therefore, from (1):

(11) $d^+(Gb) \leqslant \lambda + (1 - \lambda)\gamma$

So:

(12) $\lambda \geqslant [d^+(Gb) - \gamma]/(1 - \gamma))$

Hence we have obtained the same inequality for λ as we did previously for $d^+(H)$. This shows that λ is high given a high $d^+(Gb)$ and suitable γ. But the stress-component which corresponds to the Restricted Multiplication Rule and the Principle of Alternative Supposition, will, by continuity, allow a high value to λ only given a fairly high value to $d^+(H)$. So in a rather loose and qualitative fashion we obtain justification for inferences from the sample to the population, even without the Multiplication Rule.

APPENDIX 1

Notation

STANDARD SYMBOLS

&	(and)	∩	(union)
∨	(and/or)	<,>	(ordered pair)
~	(not)	<	(strictly less than)
∈	(belongs to)	>	(strictly greater than)
⊂	(is included in)	≤	(less than or equal to)
∪	(intersection)	≥	(greater than or equal to)

SPECIAL SYMBOLS

δ-	Doxastic (1.III)
π-	Propositional (1.III)
d, e, with sub- and superscripts	Used for credence functions (2.III)
$Dom(d)$	The domain of d (2.V)
$d \wedge e$	The meet of d and e (2.V)
$d \, \mathbf{R} \, e$	d is a restriction of e (2.V)
$e \| P$	The restriction of e to P (2.V)
$\daleth p$	The Boolean negation of p (4.IV)
$Ast(P)$	The set of predicates associated with P (7.VII)
$Z^F(X)$	X is the set of all the Fs which are Zs (8.V)
$Str(d)$	The stress due to d (9.I)
$EStr(d)$	The explicit stress due to d (9.I)
$IStr(d)$	The implicit stress due to d (9.III)
σ, τ, with subscripts	Used for indices of epistemic strength (9.V)
$PAStr(d)$	The potentially asymmetric stress due to d (9.III)

Summary of Idealizations

The results I have obtained are within the scope of various idealizations, restrictions of scope, or other similar factors. The chief of these are:

EXPOSITORY IDEALIZATION IN THE THEORY OF STRESSES

Stress-components are taken to be of the simple form $\lambda\Delta^{\alpha}$ where Δ measures the departure from zero-stress and λ and α are both positive. This is a simplification for the purposes of exposition. Other functions such as exponential ones could also have been considered. Chapters 9 and 10 are within the scope of this idealization.

IDEALIZATION OF LOGICAL OMNISCIENCE

The idealization of logical omniscience (see Glossary) is required throughout the non-comparative theory, which may be seen as a first-approximation to a less idealized theory. However we can drop logical omniscience in the comparative theory by taking the weights w_n in the formula for the implicit stress to be zero for large n (see section 9.IX).

NUMERICAL REPRESENTATION OF DOXASTIC ATTITUDES

From chapter 4 on, I consider not doxastic systems themselves so much as the credence functions which represent them. As a result I ignore the possibility that one full belief might be more confident than another. This is a restriction of scope. Likewise in cases where the comparisons of degrees of belief fail to be transitive the credence function will not faithfully represent the doxastic system.

NUMERICAL REPRESENTATION OF LOGICAL DISVALUE

In chapters 9 and 10 I work with the concept of *stress*, which is a numerical measure of logical disvalue. Just as the use of credence functions results in some loss of information about systems, so the reliance on stress in my theory could obliterate some subtleties in the theory of logical disvalue.

RESTRICTION TO DOXASTIC CHANGES

My primary interest is in the rationality of inferences. But, as I explained in section 1.V, I consider these inferences only *qua* doxastic changes. Hence I ignore the dimension of assessment in which we concede that a rational change was made but ask whether it was made for the right reasons.

RESTRICTION TO AN OBJECT-LANGUAGE

Partly to avoid difficulties which might arise when we consider the rationality of changes to judgements of rationality themselves, I restrict my attention to doxastic systems whose propositions are in an object-language. This also enables me to ignore the threat of rational predicaments and to assume that every proposition has a Boolean negation.

Principles Governing the
Rationality of Doxastic Changes

I GENERAL PRINCIPLES

The Principle of Relevant Adjustment (3.IV)

If an expansion represented by d^-/d^+ is rational even though the system represented by d^- is δ-inconsistent, then there must be a rational adjustment represented by d^-/d^*, and a rational expansion represented by d^*/d^+, such that d^* is δ-consistent.

The Composition Principle (3.V)

The composite of two rational doxastic changes would itself be a rational change.

The Decomposition Principle (3.V)

The parts of the canonical decomposition of a rational doxastic change are themselves rational.

II PRINCIPLES GOVERNING DOXASTIC CONSISTENCY

Note 1

These govern the δ-consistency of credence functions. For principles directly governing doxastic systems see section 4.VIII.

Note 2

For derived theses see section 4.IX. Among them are the following named rules:

The Conjunction Rule	(thesis 4.9.6)
The Disjunction Rule	(thesis 4.9.5)
Doxastic *Modus Ponens*	(thesis 4.9.2)
The Equivalence Rule	(thesis 4.9.4)
The General Addition Rule	(thesis 4.9.7)
The Material Conditional Rule	(thesis 4.9.1)
The Multilemma Rule	(thesis 4.9.11)
The Polyad Rule	(thesis 4.9.10)
The Subadditivity Rule	(thesis 4.9.9)

The Addition Principle (4.III)

If p,q, $p\&q$ and $p\lor q$ are all in $Dom(d)$, then either $d(p\&q) + d(p\lor q) = d(p) + d(q)$ or the system is δ-inconsistent.

The Naming Principle (7.V)

Given any count-predicate F, any integer n, and any finite set of propositions $\{p_1, \ldots, p_n\}$, there are names (which I shall often abbreviate to the numerals 1 to n), not already occurring in the propositions $p_1, \ldots, p_n$ such that no credence function d is δ-consistent if $d(i$ is an $F/$There are precisely n Fs$)<1$, or if $d(i=j)/$There are precisely n Fs$)>0$ if $i\neq j$.

The Principle of Alternative Supposition (4.IV)

Suppose $\{r_1, r_2 \ldots r_n\}$ is a *finite* set of alternatives. In that case if p and $<p,r_i>i = 1,2 \ldots, n$ all occur in $Dom(d)$, but *either* $d(p)>d(p/r_i)$ for all i *or* $d(p)<d(p/r_i)$ for all i, then the system is δ-inconsistent.

The Completability Principle (4.V)

If d is δ-consistent then d has a δ-consistent extension to the whole object-language.

The Principle of Conditionalization (4.III)

Suppose r is not disprovable. Let d_r be defined by:

(1) $Dom(d_r) = \{p \mid <p,r> \in Dom(d)\}$; and

(2) $d_r(p) = d(p/r)$ if $<p,r> \in Dom(d)$.

Then given any δ-consistent credence function d, d_r is also δ-consistent, and moreover satisfies the principles of self-evidence and self-refutation even when these are interpreted as relative to r.

The Restricted Multiplication Principle (4.III)

Suppose $p\&q$, $<p,q>$ and q are all in $Dom(d)$. In that case:

(1)   If $d(q) = 1$, but $d(p\&q) \neq d(p/q)$, the system is δ-inconsistent.
(2)   If $d(p/q) = 1$, but $d(p\&q) \neq d(q)$, the system is δ-inconsistent.

The Principle of Self-evidently Equivalent Suppositions (4.II)

If p s-e implies q and vice versa, and if $<r,p>$ and $<r,q>$ are both in $Dom(d)$, then either $d(r/p) = d(r/q)$ or the system is δ-inconsistent.

The Principle of Self-evident Implication (4.II)

If q s-e implies p, and if $<p,q>$ is in $Dom(d)$, then either $d(p/q) = 1$ or the system is δ-inconsistent.

The Principle of Self-evident Propositions (4.II)

If p is a s-e proposition in $Dom(d)$, then either $d(p) = 1$ or the system is δ-inconsistent.

The Principle of Self-refutation (4.II)

If p is a self-refuting proposition and if p is in $Dom(d)$, then either $d(p) = 0$ or the system is δ-inconsistent.

III   PRINCIPLES GOVERNING CONTRACTIONS

The Inconsistency Requirement for Contractions (3.VI)

If a system is doxastically consistent it is irrational to contract it.

The Principle of Minimal Contraction (3.VI)

If a contraction away from a set of propositions *P* would restore rational consistency, then it is irrational to contract away from *Q*, where *P* is a proper subset of *Q*.

The No Obligation Principle for Contractions (3.VI)

A contraction is never required for rationality.

IV   PRINCIPLES GOVERNING EXPANSIONS

The Existence of Rational Consistency-preserving Expansions (from Consistency) (5.III)

Consider any δ-consistent credence function d^- and any proposition *r* not in the domain of d^-. If there is a consistency-preserving expansion to *r* then there is some rational consistency-preserving expansion to *r*.

The Existence of Rational Consistency-preserving Expansions from Inconsistency (5.VI)

Consider any credence function d^- and any proposition *r* not in $Dom(d^-)$. If there is a consistency-preserving expansion to *r* which satisfies the Principle of Relevant Adjustment, then there is a rational consistency preserving expansion to *r*.

The Presumption Against Relevance

If either $Ast(H) \cap Ast(G)$ is empty or every member is entailed by '*F*', then there is a presumption against '*H*' being rationally relevant to '*G*' (relative to '*F*' and to any credence function d^-).

The Symmetry Principle

Suppose names (abbreviated to *1* to *n*) are introduced as in the Naming Principle. Suppose that d^-/d^+ is a consistency-preserving expansion. And suppose d^- is symmetric with respect to the exchange of two of the names *1* to *n*, but d^+ is not, even though the domain of d^+ is symmetric. Then the expansion is irrational.

V PRINCIPLES GOVERNING ADJUSTMENT

The Existence of Rational Minimal Adjustments (6.II)

If d^- is δ-inconsistent there is some rational adjustment d^-/d^+ which is minimal.

The Possibility of Rational Adjustment (6.I)

If d^- is δ-inconsistent then there is some rational adjustment d^-/d^+ which restores δ-consistency.

The Preservation of Consistency by Adjustments (6.I)

If d^-/d^+ is an adjustment, and d^- is δ-consistent but d^+ is δ-inconsistent, then d^-/d^+ is irrational.

The Progress Towards Consistency Principle (6.I)

If d^- is δ-inconsistent then an adjustment d^-/d^+ is irrational unless d^+ is nearer δ-consistency than d^-.

Notes

INTRODUCTION

1 Consider, for instance, the motivation for Gentzen's theory (1969, pp. 68–131).

2 Although I base my positive/normative distinction partly on Johnson's distinction between normative and positive sciences (1921, Part I, pp. 224–6), I reject Johnson's claim that logic is purely normative.

3 Advocates of Psychologism, such as Ellis (1979), treat ostensibly normative logic as a descriptive theory. Provided they put scare quotes around 'normative' they may nonetheless be able to agree with much that I say about normative logic.

4 A class of partial exceptions which I do not discuss, except briefly in chapter 5, are the relevance logicians (see Anderson and Belnap 1975, and Routley et al. 1982). I suspect that their complaints about classical logic are based on discrepancies between the 'valid' inferences of classical logic and inferences which are intuitively rational ones to make. However, they are not explicitly normative in their approach.

5 The use of Bayes' Theorem by subjectivists such as de Finetti (1974, volume II, pp. 195–9) shows this concern with how (the degree of) belief changes with new evidence. But others such as Levi (1980, p. 81), who differ in many ways from the subjectivists, seem to share their concern with the response to new evidence.

6 That is the principle which requires the degree of belief in p after discovering that e to be the same as the conditional degree of belief of p on e prior to the discovery.

7 There will be those who will reply to my rhetorical question, saying that we should consider the practice of great thinkers, especially scientists. But I say that great thinkers are characterized far more by powers of imagination and insight than by rationality.

8 Since I treat the intuitive judgements as data, like scientific observations, a more detailed discussion of methodology can be read off from my discussion of the problem of the direction of the arrow of *modus tollens* in chapter 6.

9 In chapter 9 I call this the No Dishonour in Defeat Principle and I attach considerable significance to it.

10 Goodman (1954, p. 67) states a similar methodology:

> A rule is amended if it yields an inference we are unwilling to accept; an inference is rejected if it violates a rule we are unwilling to amend.

My position is closer to Rawls's and my differences from Rawls's position are also differences from Goodman's.

11 I have in mind adaptations of Mackie's arguments (1977, pp. 36–42).

12 I owe the happy phrase 'iron law' to Armstrong, who took it from La Salle.

13 Ellis concedes that they play a secondarily regulative role.

14 Either the rationality of the change explains, or the features in virtue of which it is rational. Where we take the rationality on authority it must be the former.

15 A device recommended to me by Philip Pettit and inspired by the example of Amartya Sen (Sen 1970).

1 PROPOSITIONS, RATIONALITY AND INFERENCES

1 There has been considerable discussion in the literature about languages of thought. But all I am claiming is that propositions are *like* sentences in a language.

2 Churchland (1981), for instance, seeks to eliminate beliefs. Quine in 'Quantifiers and Propositional Attitudes' (1966, pp. 183–94) analyses beliefs as polyadic relations between believers, objects and predicates. This is most naturally construed as an elimination of propositions in the Cambridge sense.

3 Lycan uses the term 'computational' rather than 'functional'.

4 There is a danger of circularity in both criteria for identity of type. For what constitutes the same function and what constitutes the same truth-conditions may well reflect what we say constitutes the same proposition. However if we start with a somewhat vague intuitive criterion we should then obtain two more precise criteria: a trip round the circle results in greater precision.

5 In addition, one solution to Kripke's puzzle about Pierre (Kripke 1979, pp. 234–83), and one I favour, is simply to deny that translation always preserves belief. I take it that translation preserves truth-conditional types. So the appropriate type for objects of belief is not truth-conditional.

6 Although there may be a fuzzy interface. Sartrean bad faith seems to be intermediate between a moral and a rational defect.

7 I believe that too little emotion can lead to an irrational scepticism as well as too much. Even in the face of considerable evidence there can be a reluctance to *commit* oneself: some emotion, even intellectual violence, may be required to accept the consequences of one's argument.

8 This position was suggested to me by Paul Thom.

9 A theory of degrees of belief without numerical representation is slow going but not impossible (see Forrest 1981, pp. 38–57).

10 As a consequence what I say has surprisingly little contact with the work of Relevance Logicians.

2 DOXASTIC SYSTEMS

1 That they might not be was drawn to my attention by Peter Menzies.

2 I stipulate this usage, rejecting the alternative in which agnosticism is restricted to cases where the degree of belief in p is (approximately) equal to the degree of disbelief in p.

3 We may also sometimes compare degrees of belief for different people. But that is not my present concern.

4 If my degree of belief in q is equal to or higher than my degree of belief in q conditional on p, it would be peculiar to say 'If p then q'. But provided I have a conditional belief in q on p it would not be peculiar to say 'Even if p, then q'.

5 An alternative is to represent the system in a way which results in less loss of information but is not as easy to handle technically. Following Kyburg (1974, p. 247) for instance, we could represent a doxastic system as a pair of credence functions d^L and d^U where the interval $d^L(p)$ to $d^U(p)$ represents the degree of belief in p. Or again, following Levi (1980, p. 78), we could represent a doxastic system as a convex family of credence functions, that is a family such that if d_0 and d_1 belong to it then for all $0 < t < 1$, d_t belongs to it where $d_t(p) = (1 - t)d_0(p) + td_1(p)$. Since my primary reason for considering degrees of belief in the first place is because I need them for a theory of belief, I see little advantage to these alternatives. For the loss of information in the representation I give does not unduly concern me.

6 Alternatively we could enrich the real numbers with infinitesimals. This would enable us to represent comparisons among attitudes of certainty. For we could then represent certainty either by one or by one less an infinitesimal. However I do not need this refinement for my present purpose.

7 We select the α_i recursively. We can find α_1 less that $\frac{1}{4}$. Suppose we have found positive $\alpha_1, \ldots, \alpha_n$, whose sum is less than $\frac{1}{4}$, such that for no

positive or negative integers $m_1, \ldots, m_n$ do we have $m_1 \times \alpha_1 + \ldots + m_n \times \alpha_n = 0$. Then there are uncountably many positive reals less than $\frac{1}{4} - (\alpha_1 + \ldots + \alpha_n)$. But there are only countably many real numbers of the form $-(m_1 \times \alpha_1 + \ldots + m_n \times \alpha_n)/m_{n+1}$ for integers $m_1, \ldots, m_{n+1}$. So we can find a positive real α_{n+1} less than $\frac{1}{4} - (\alpha_1 + \ldots + \alpha_n)$ such that for no positive or negative integers $m_1, \ldots, m_{n+1}$ do we have $\alpha_{n+1} = -(m_1 \times \alpha_1 + \ldots + m_n \times \alpha_n)/m_{n+1}$. Hence for no integers $m_1, \ldots, m_{n+1}$ do we have $m_1 \times \alpha_1 + \ldots + m_n \times \alpha_n + m_{n+1} \times \alpha_{n+1} = 0$. And so we go on.

3   THE FRAMEWORK FOR A DYNAMICS OF BELIEF

1   I use the terms 'contraction' and its converse 'expansion' in much the same way as Levi (1980, p. 25). However he is there considering corpora of knowledge claims rather than doxastic systems.

2   I say a proposition *occurs* in a system if some attitude towards it does, and so it is in the domain of the representing function.

3   If the change is represented by d^-/d^+, the contraction will be $d^-/d^- \wedge d^+$ and the expansion will be $d^- \wedge d^+/d^+$.

4   Di-alethic logicians hold that sometimes p and $\sim p$ are both true (e.g. Priest 1979, pp. 219–24; Routley 1979). Presumably they sometimes believe p and believe $\sim p$.

5   There is nothing, however, to prevent the choice of one expansion from within a range of rational expansions from being affected by whether or not it occurred before or after the restoration of doxastic consistency. The irrelevance that I am considering is rational rather than psychological.

6   The composite of changes represented by d^-/d^0 and d^0/d^+ would be represented by d^-/d^+. Conversely for any d^0, the change represented by d^-/d^+ can be decomposed into one represented by d^-/d^0 and one represented by d^0/d^+.

7   Mathematical reasoning depends crucially on the rationality of processes consisting of chains of rational inferences. Again Descartes' methodological principle of reaching complex conclusions as a result of simple steps (Rule V for the Direction of the Mind) has never been criticized on the grounds that a process composed of individually rational steps might not be overall rational.

8   If no propositions occur in the system before but not after, then the canonical decomposition does not include a contraction. And similarly with the adjustment and the expansion. So the decomposition is into a contraction and/or an adjustment and/or an expansion.

9   Let d^1 be $d^- \| [Dom(d^-) \cap Dom(d^+)]$.
Let d^2 be $d^+ \| [Dom(d^-) \cap Dom(d^+)]$.

Then either $Dom(d^-)$ $Dom(d^+)$, in which case $d^1 = d^-$, or d^-/d^1 is a contraction. And either $d^1 = d^2$ or d^1/d^2 is an adjustment. Finally, either $Dom(d^+)$ $Dom(d^-)$, in which case $d^2 = d^+$, or d^2/d^+ is an expansion.

10 That is, d^-/d^+ is decomposed into $d^-/d^- \wedge d^+$ and $d^- \wedge d^+/d^+$.

11 I assume that sufficient auxiliary hypotheses are built into T to ensure that T, O_1, . . ., O_n form an inconsistent $(n + 1)$-*ad*.

12 Much of the work of the Gärdenfors School concerns contractions (see Makinson 1986).

4 THE PRINCIPLES OF DOXASTIC CONSISTENCY

1 Even representations which preserve as much information as possible. For suppose we have a representation of a finite system, such that $d(P\&Q) + d(P\vee Q) = d(P) + d(Q)$, where none of the degrees of belief in $P\&Q$, $P\vee Q$, or P are τ-equal to that in Q. And suppose that the attitude to Q is neither certainty nor contracertainty. Then by thesis 2.6.2 there is another representation e, satisfying the conditions of thesis 2.6.1, which differs from d only in the value assigned to Q and those propositions τ-equal to Q. Clearly $e(P\&Q) + e(P\vee Q) \neq e(P) + e(Q)$.

2 As di-alethic logicians claim. See for instance Priest (1979, pp. 219–24) and Routley (1979, pp. 301–31).

3 Here I allow infinite disjunctions. They are, I suggest, in perfectly good order provided they are not used as a substitute for existential quantification. For they may be interpreted by quantifying, in a suitable meta-language, over the subscripts.

4 It can also be considered the finite case of a property called *conglomerability* by de Finetti (1974, pp. 98–9). This is rejected by him, in the infinite case, for good reasons.

5 Throughout section V I am heavily indebted to Brian Ellis's treatment of completability (1979, pp. 9–16).

6 In addition there are objections to it (see de Finetti 1974, p. 91).

7 This is essentially Ellis's requirement A4 (1979, p. 12).

8 This is analogous to thesis 4.9.3, which, however, I derive from the Addition Principle.

9 Named after the Archimedean Principle for real numbers, which tells us that for any positive number x there is some integer n such that $nx > 1$, and so excludes infinitesimals.

10 Notice that this is a necessary, not a sufficient, condition for p to be believed.

11 Here I introduce some obvious notation. D is the degree of belief in S, D^* in S^* etc.

12 Again, the notation is obvious, D is the degree of belief in S, D_i in S_i etc.

13 Although I try not to beg any questions about the connection between self-evidence and truth, this claim is most easily supported by assuming that a self-evident inference is one which self-evidently preserves truth. Since I am working with a Boolean negation, not the ordinary English negation, I claim that disjunctive syllogisms do self-evidently preserve truth.

5 DEDUCTIVE EXPANSIONS

1 The obvious derivation is:
   (1) p
   (2) $\sim p$
   (3) $p \lor q$, from (1)
   (4) q, from (2) and (3) by disjunctive syllogism.

6 TOWARDS A THEORY OF ADJUSTMENTS

1 If you insist that agnosticism involves a lower degree of belief than ⅔, then I would have to consider the case where O and T form a provably inconsistent dyad. This is less realistic than the $O\ T, H$ case, but it would still serve to show that we should not always assume that the adjustment preserves belief in all members of the inconsistent polyad.

2 Safe, that is, from *significant* adjustment. I discuss revisions to logic in chapter 9.

3 Chalmers (1976, p. 64) provides the example of the kinetic theory of gases. He says: 'When Maxwell published the first details of the kinetic theory of gases in 1859, in that very same paper he acknowledged the fact that the theory was falsified by measurements of the specific heats of gases.' Another example, though admittedly a rational reconstruction, is Lakatos's example of Prout's research programme, which he describes as 'progressing in an ocean of anomalies' (Lakatos 1970, pp. 138–40).

4 In some later work (Gärdenfors 1986), he considers 'probability functions' in his account of 'revisions' (i.e. adjustments). But even there he is only concerned with the case where some specified proposition is adjusted to certainty. This is appropriate given his interest in a theory of conditionals, but it still does not provide a satisfactory solution to the Problem of the Direction of the Arrow of *Modus Tollens*.

5 This is further discussed in chapter 9.

6 It is always vulnerable from the threat that there might be markedly better systematic theory. I shall ignore this threat until a better systematization is produced.

7 Whether or not there exists a minimum depends on the principles of δ-consistency. Given only the principles I have stated, it can be shown a minimum exists. First define a topology on the space of the credence functions with the same domain as d^-, by stipulating that a sequence d_1, d_2 etc. converges to d if and only if $d_n(p)$ converges to $d(p)$ for all p in $Dom(d^-)$. Then it can be shown that $\{d|Dom(d) = Dom(d^-)$ and d is δ-consistent$\}$ is topologically *compact*. And dist(d_1,d) is a continuous function of d. These two results show a minimum exists. I do not think it would matter much if a minimum did not exist. Instead of minimal adjustments we could consider ones within η of being minimal, for some very small η (say $\eta = 10^{-10}$).

7 PROBABLE INFERENCE

1 At least not by Reichenbach. See 'The Semantic and the Object Conceptions of Probability Expressions', reprinted in Reichenbach (1978), volume 2.
2 The difference between *propensity* and *objective chance* is not crucial here. Following Mellor (1971) I would say that the objective chance is a property of the total set-up (urn, ball-selector and all) and the propensity a property of the urn and balls alone. Clearly the objective chance would depend *in part* on the propensity.
3 This can be weakened in various ways. For instance we can ignore some evidence as irrelevant. But this weakening does not affect my criticism.
4 The literature on the subject of the theory-laden character of perception (e.g. Hanson 1958) suggests that we cannot sharply separate evidence from other beliefs.
5 Such as the evidence of introspection that I seemed to make the observation. For often we are aware of what we observe without being aware that we observe it.
6 My criticism would be weakened if the acceptance of testimony was not an external change but rather an inference from the observation of what someone says. Sometimes it will be like that. But typically to accept what someone says seems no more an inference from a belief about the words said than to believe what you see is an inference from a belief about what you seem to see.
7 Or *exchangeability* as it is sometimes called. See de Finetti (1974, volume II, chapter 11).
8 For simplicity I ignore the possibility that the epistemic probability will be a range from α to β.

9 This is a reconstruction. What Keynes actually says is:

> The terms *certain* and *probable* describe the various degrees of rational belief about a proposition which different amounts of knowledge authorise us to entertain (Keynes 1921, p. 3).

10 Since even the best representations fail to represent one full belief being greater than another, this is, strictly speaking, an absence of *representable* dependence.

11 Assume that I am contracertain that the selected ball is both white and black, and certain that it is one or the other. Then apply the Addition Principle.

12 Of course the abbreviations may already occur, but the names do not.

13 I use scare-quotes because I wish to remove the restriction that information is always correct.

14 For the details of the determinable/determinate relation see Johnson (1921, pp. 173–6).

15 I assume that if a predicate only applies to items of a certain category so does its negation. So, typically, $(\sim F)a$ will not be equivalent to $\sim (Fa)$.

8 PROPORTIONAL SYLLOGISMS

1 I owe my awareness of their importance largely to David Stove.

2 However, in addition to my criticisms of the whole Carnapian approach, his theory suffers from its high degree of idealization. This removes it somewhat from the inferences people actually make.

3 Some work would be required to show this rigorously, although it is intuitively plausible. So when I provide more formal proofs I use a different method, which does not involve naming the *FG*s.

4 This is based on de Finetti's discussion of a paradox due to Levy (see de Finetti 1974, pp. 98–9).

5 This is a strong supposition. But all I am doing here is *speculating* about what might, for all I know, happen.

6 Inspired, perhaps, by Hume's sceptical solution of his sceptical doubts (*Enquiry*, section 5).

7 Deduction Chauvinism is never explicitly presented as a thesis – its proponents probably think it too obvious. But, by intellectual osmosis, I can suggest the reasons that would be put forward for the superiority of deduction.

8 That a deduction chauvinist might perhaps produce this as a reason is a point I owe to John Mills of Sydney University.

9 The proposition that a_u is Z^F can be expanded as a disjunction in such

a way as to avoid any use of 'A_u' as a referring expression. The only names are the ones abbreviated to '1', . . . 'n'.

10 A_u may be transformed into A_v by means of a series of exchanges of just two of 1, . . ., n at a time.

9　COMPARISONS OF RATIONALITY

1 I say that the initial credence function, d^- and the final domain $Dom(d^+)$, but not of course d^+ itself, specify a kind of change.

2 There is only one contraction from d^- with a specified domain for d^+. So there can be no non-trivial comparisons among them.

3 But the cost of this is greater idealization. For perhaps the logical disvalues are only partially ordered; yet stress is completely ordered. Hence minimum stress is a sufficient but not a necessary condition for maximum rationality. The unity is obtained by ignoring this divergence between minimum stress and maximum rationality.

4 In the abnormal situation of a rational predicament even the most rational might be irrational.

5 An elliptical notation. For the stress might partly depend on external factors such as observation operating at the time at which the person has the system represented by d.

6 Herein lies the germ of an account of explanation as the removal of stress which cannot be removed simply by being rational.

7 I take it that I can observe what is not the case. If you disagree put scare-quotes around 'observe'.

8 We can interpret Descartes in a bland fashion by restricting our attention to the question of certainty. In that case his remarks might not be inaccurate. I do not so interpret him, but this is no place for Descartes scholarship.

9 I assume that you cannot remember what you have not experienced (where the experience need not, however, itself be veridical). So I put scare quotes around 'memory' to indicate that it includes apparent memory.

10 There are a few obvious exceptions to this. For example if the witness says 'Probably p', thereby expressing only a high degree of belief in p, the tendency should not be towards certainty, but only towards a high degree of belief.

11 That is, we obtain $d_{a,b}$ from d, where $d_{a,b}(p) = d(p^{a,b})$.

12 'Self-evident' is, recall, a term of art. As argued in section VI, we could rationally come to reject what we acknowledge to be self-evident in this sense.

13 Here is a recipe for constructing such a formula. Let
$\Delta = |d(p\&q) - Td(q)|$ where T always lies between $d(p)$ and $d(p/q)$ and

equals $d(p/q)$ when $d(q) = 0$ or 1. We could, for instance, have $\mathbf{T} = \ominus d(p) + (1 - \bigcirc)d(p/q)$, where $\ominus = d(q)[1 - d(q)]$. Writing all this out we obtain a stress component of the form $\psi(\Delta)$ where

$\Delta = |d(p\&q) - d(q)^2 + d(q)^3 + [1 - d(q) + d(q)^2] \times d(p/q)d(q)|$.

14 The space of credence functions whose domain is $Dom(d)^{(n)}$ is finite dimensional. Given a suitable topology it is compact. The subset consisting of $\{e|d \quad e\}$ is closed and so also compact. And $\text{EStr}(e)$ is a continuous function of e. So the minimum exists.

15 This is not trivial. The finite subsets of the object-language form a countable set. So we may index them, A_1, A_2 etc. For any given n there will be a maximum explicit stress for the set of all credence functions with domain consisting of one of $A_1^{(n)} \ldots A_n^{(n)}$. Call that Str_n. Then let $w_n = 1/(n^2\text{Str}_n)$. It follows that, given any d with finite domain, for some m, $Dom(d) = A_m$, and for all $n \geqslant m$, $\text{IStr}_n \leqslant \text{Str}_n$. Hence $w_n \times \text{PStr}_n(d) \leqslant 1/n^2$ and the series converges.

16 At least if we ignore rational predicaments.

17 The calculations are similar to those used in the theory of proportional syllogisms of chapter 8, section V.

10 INDUCTION

1 As customary, I alter Goodman's dates.

2 Intellectual modesty, or else what Newton-Smith calls the *pessimistic induction* (Newton-Smith 1981, p. 14), results in some qualification, such as 'approximately true'. I assume such verisimilitudinous slop has already been put in the theory.

3 I owe this point to David Stove.

4 Armstrong allows there to be exceptions to laws; the necessity is a necessity *nihil obstat*. Hence there might not be entailment.

5 Relying on the Multiplication Rule we find that:
$d^-(p/h) \times d^-(h) = d^-(h/p) \times d^-(p)$. By Temporal Coherence $d^+(h) = d^-(h/p)$. So $d^-(p/h) \times d^-(h) = d^+(h) \times d^-(p)$. The required result now follows.

6 The ratio of the amplifying factor is $d^-(P/H_{100})$ to $d^-(P/H_{50})$ where P is the proposition that the sample is a spade. H_{100} entails P, and so $d^-(P/H_{100}) = 1$. By the theory of proportional syllogisms $d^-(P/H_{50}) = \frac{1}{2}$.

7 Ignoring, that is, the Dutch Book Argument, which I rejected in chapter 4.

8 If $q_1, \ldots, q_n$ are pairwise inconsistent then, relying on the Addition and Multiplication Principles for probability,
$\Pr(p/q_1 \vee \ldots \vee q_n) \times [\Pr(q_1) + \ldots + \Pr(q_n)] = \Pr(p/q_1) \times \Pr(q_1) + \ldots +$

$\Pr(p/q_n) \times \Pr(q_n)$. So unless all the $\Pr(q_i) = 0$, $\Pr(p/q_i \vee \ldots \vee q_n)$ cannot be greater than all the $\Pr(p/q_i)$. For a sample of size $(n-1)$ let Q_i be the proposition that it contains precisely i Gs, for $i = 0, \ldots, (n-1)$. Let P be the proposition that the sample is a matcher. Then $\Pr(P/Q_1 \vee \ldots \vee Q_n)$ cannot be greater than $\Pr(P/Q_i)$ for all i. So for some sample composition we have either irrelevance or favourable relevance.

9 At least if the judgements of rationality are all relative to a conceptual scheme. There may be difficulties about the justification of reliance on a green/blue rather than grue/bleen scheme, difficulties which lead us to a theory of universals. But that is not my present concern.

10 For what it is worth I claim to 'see' *a priori* that what is valuable exists and what exists is valuable. This leads to a presumption in favour of the existence of a maximally valuable being ('whom all men call God'), without appeal to the Ontological Argument. Compare but also contrast Leslie's Axiarchism (1979).

11 It will be of the form $\sigma^{\alpha-1}[1 - d(p)]^{\alpha}$, where σ is the index of epistemic strength.

Works Cited

Adams, Ernest (1965) 'The Logic of Conditionals', *Inquiry*, 8, pp. 166–97.

Anderson, A. R. and Belnap, N. D. Jr (1975) *Entailment*, vol 1, Princeton University Press.

Armstrong, D. M. (1983) *What is a Law of Nature?* Cambridge University Press.

Carnap, Rudolph (1942) *Introduction to Semantics*, Harvard University Press.

Carnap, Rudolph (1962) *Logical Foundations of Probability* (2nd ed.), Chicago University Press.

Carnap, Rudolph (1968) 'Inductive Logic and Inductive Intuition', in *The Problem of Inductive Logic* (edited by Lakatos, Imre), North Holland.

Carnap, Rudolph (1971) 'Inductive Logic and Rational Decisions', in *Studies in Inductive Logic and Probability*, vol 1 (edited by Carnap, Rudolph and Jeffrey, Richard C.), University of California Press.

Chalmers, A. F. (1976) *What is this thing called Science?* University of Queensland Press.

Church, Alonzo (1951) 'The Weak Theory of Implication', in *Kontrolliertes Denken, Untersuchungen zum Logikkalkül und zur Logik der Einzelwissenschaften* (edited by Menne, A., Wilhelmly, A. and Angsel, H.), Komissions-Verlag Kurt Alber, pp. 22–37.

Churchland, Paul M. (1981) 'Eliminative Materialism and the Propositional Attitudes', *The Journal of Philosophy*, 78, pp. 67–90.

Dennett, Daniel (1978) *Brainstorms*, Bradford Books.

Descartes, René (1954) *Descartes' Philosophical Writings* (translated and edited by Anscombe, Elizabeth and Geach, Peter Thomas), Nelson.

Deutscher, Max (1983) *Subjecting and Objecting*, University of Queensland Press.

Duhem, Pierre (1954) *The Aim and Structure of Physical Theory* (translated by Wiener, Philip P.), Princeton University Press.

Ellis, Brian (1973) 'The Logic of Subjective Probability', *British Journal for the Philosophy of Science*, 24, pp. 125–52.

Ellis, Brian (1979) *Rational Belief Systems*, Basil Blackwell.

Feller, William (1968) *An Introduction to Probability Theory and its Applications*, vol I (3rd ed.), John Wiley & Sons.

de Finetti, Bruno (1974) *Theory of Probability: a Critical Introductory Treatment* (translated by Mackie, A. and Smith, A.), John Wiley & Sons.

Forrest, Peter (1981) 'Probabilistic Modal Inferences', *Australasian Journal of Philosophy*, 59, pp. 38–53.

Forrest, Peter (1985) 'Antinomies and Rational Predicaments: an Inescapable Labyrinth', *Logique et Analyse*, 112, pp. 375–84.

Frege, Gottlob (1977) *Logicial Investigations* (edited by Geach, P. T. and translated by Geach, P. T. and Stoothoff, R. H.), Basil Blackwell.

Gärdenfors, Peter (1982) 'Imaging and Conditionalization', *The Journal of Philosophy*, 79, pp. 747–60.

Gärdenfors, Peter (1984) 'Epistemic Importance and Minimal Changes of Belief', *Australasian Journal of Philosophy*, 62, pp. 136–57.

Gärdenfors, Peter (1986) 'The Dynamics of Belief: Contractions and Revisions of Probability Functions', to appear in *Topoi*.

Gentzen, Gerhard (1969) 'Investigations into Logical Deductions', in *The Collected Papers of Gerhard Gentzen* (edited by Szabo, M. E.), North Holland, pp. 68–131.

Goodman, Nelson (1954) *Fact, Fiction and Forecast*, Athlone Press.

Hanson, N. R. (1958) *Patterns of Discovery*, Cambridge University Press.

Harman, Gilbert (1973) *Thought*, Princeton University Press.

Hume, David, *Enquiry concerning Human Understanding* (edited by Selby-Bigge, L. A.), Oxford University Press, 1946.

Husserl, Edmund (1970) *Logical Investigations* (translated by Findlay, J. N.), Routledge & Kegan Paul.

Jeffrey, Richard C. (1968) 'Probable Knowledge', in *The Problem of Inductive Logic* (edited by Lakatos, Imre), North Holland.

Johnson, W. E. (1921) *Logic Part I*, Cambridge University Press.

Johnson, W. E. (1924) *Logic Part III*, Cambridge University Press.

Keynes, John M. (1921) *A Treatise on Probability*, Macmillan.

Kripke, Saul (1979) 'A Puzzle about Belief', in *Meaning and Use* (edited by Margalit Avishai), North Holland, pp. 234–83.

Kuhn, T. S. (1970) *The Structure of Scientific Revolutions*, University of Chicago Press.

Kyburg, Henry E. Jr (1974) *The Logical Foundations of Statistical Inference*, Reidel.

Koopman, B. O. (1940) 'The Axioms and Algebra of Intuitive Probability', *Annals of Mathematics*, 41, pp. 259–92.

Lakatos, Imre (1970) 'Methodology of Scientific Research Programmes', in *Criticism and the Growth of Knowledge* (edited by Lakatos, Imre and Musgrave, Alan), Cambridge University Press.

Leslie, John (1979) *Value and Existence*, Basil Blackwell.

Levi, Isaac (1980) *The Enterprise of Knowledge*, MIT Press.

Lycan, William C. (1981) 'Toward a Homuncular Theory of Believing', *Cognition and Brain Theory*, 4, pp. 139-60.

Mackie, J. L. (1977) *Ethics: Inventing Right and Wrong*, Penguin.

Makinson, David (1985) 'How to Give it up: a Survey of Some Formal Aspects of the Logic of Theory Change', *Synthese*, 62, pp. 347-63.

Mellor, D. H. (1971) *The Matter of Chance*, Cambridge University Press.

Moore, G. E. (1922) 'Conception of Intrinsic Value', in *Philosophical Studies*, Routledge & Kegan Paul, pp. 197-219.

Newman, John Henry (1947) *An Essay in Aid of A Grammar of Assent* (2nd ed.), Longman, Green & Co.

Newton-Smith, W. H. (1981) *The Rationality of Science*, Routledge & Kegan Paul.

Popper, Karl R. (1963) *Conjectures and Refutations*, Routledge & Kegan Paul.

Popper, Karl R. (1972) 'Conjectural Knowledge', in *Objective Knowledge* Oxford University Press.

Priest, Graham (1979) 'The Logic of Paradox', *Journal of Philosophical Logic*, 8, pp. 219-29.

Prior, Arthur (1976) *The Doctrine of Propositions and Terms* (edited by Geach, P. T., and Kenny, Anthony), Duckworth.

Quine, W. V. O. (1953) 'Two Dogmas of Empiricism', in *From a Logical Point of View*, Harvard University Press.

Quine, W. V. O. (1966) *Ways of Paradox*, Random House.

Ramsey, F. P. (1931) *The Foundations of Mathematics, and other Logical Essays*, Routledge & Kegan Paul.

Rawls, John (1972) *A Theory of Justice*, Oxford University Press.

Reichenbach, Hans (1949) *Theory of Probability: an Inquiry into the Logical and Mathematical Foundations of the Calculus of Probability* (translated by Hutton, E. H. and Reichenbach, Maria), University of California Press.

Reichenbach, Hans (1978) *Selected Writings* (edited by Reichenbach, Maria and Cohen, Robert S.), Reidel.

Routley, Richard (1979) 'Dialectical Logic, Semantics and Metamathematics', *Erkenntnis*, 14, pp. 301-31.

Routley, Richard (1980) *Exploring Meinong's Jungle and Beyond*, Departmental Monograph 3, Philosophy Department, RSSS, Australian National University.

Routley, Richard et al. (1982) *Relevant Logics and their Rivals*, Ridgeview.

Savage, L. J. (1954) *Foundations of Statistics*, John Wiley & Sons.

Sen, Amartya (1970) *Collective Choice and Social Welfare*, Holden-Day.

Stout, G. F. (1923) 'Are the Characteristics of Particular Things Universal or Particular?' *Proceedings of the Aristotelian Society*, supp. vol. 3.

Stove, D. C. (1973) *Probability and Hume's Inductive Scepticism*, Oxford University Press.

Stove, D. C. (1985) *The Rationality of Induction*, Oxford University Press.

Strawson, P. F. (1952) *An Introduction to Logical Theory*, Methuen.

Williams, Bernard (1979) 'Conflicts of Value', in *The Idea of Freedom* (edited by Ryan, A.), Oxford University Press, pp. 221–32.

Williams, D. C. (1947) *The Ground of Induction*, Harvard University Press.

Glossary

Adjustment (3.X). A doxastic change (q.v.) in which various doxastic attitudes (q.v.) are altered, without any new propositions being considered or old ones being excised. (See also contraction and expansion.)

Agnostic attitude (2.I). Any doxastic attitude (q.v.) too small to be belief but too large to be disbelief.

Anti-conservative δ-inference (5.II). A δ-inference (q.v.) in which the degree of belief in the π-conclusion (q.v.) is less than or equal to the sum of the measures of doubt (q.v.) in the π-premisses (q.v.).

Between (6.VI). Credence function (q.v.) e is said to be between credence functions d_1 and d_2 if e, d_1 and d_2 are distinct, if they all have the same domain, and if for all p in that domain $e(p)$ is either equal to or between $d_1(p)$ and $d_2(p)$.

Boolean negation (4.IV), A Boolean negation, $\neg p$, of p is any proposition such that p & $\neg p$ is self-refuting (q.v.) and $p \lor \neg p$ is self-evident (q.v.).

Canonical decomposition (3.V). A specified decomposition of a doxastic change (q.v.) into a contraction followed by an adjustment followed by an expansion.

Certainty (2.I). Full belief, the proper result of normal perception. (See also contracertainty.)

Coherence, temporal (10.III). See temporal coherence.

Compromise resolution (9.IV). Achieving minimal stress (q.v.) by compromising between various sources of stress.

Compromise solution (6.V). The solution to the Problem of the Direction of the Arrow of *Modus Tollens* in which the degree of belief is lessened in more than one conflicting party.

Conceptual overlap (7.VII). The conceptual overlap of two predicates is the intersection of the predicates associated with them by the conceptual scheme.

Conditional (degree of) belief (2.II). A (degree of) belief within the scope of some supposition.

Conservative δ-inference (5.II). A δ-inference (q.v.) in which the measure of doubt (q.v.) in the π-conclusion is less than or equal to the sum of the measures of doubt in the π-premisses (q.v.).

Consistency-preserving δ-inference (5.III). A δ-inference (q.v.) which preserves the δ-consistency (q.v.) of all δ-consistent subsystems of the initial doxastic system (q.v.).

Contracertainty (2.I). Full disbelief. (See also certainty.)

Contraction (3.I). A doxastic change consisting solely in the excision of various doxastic attitudes (q.v.). (See also adjustment and expansion.)

Contra-deduction (5.II). An anti-conservative (q.v.) δ-inference whose π-inference (q.v.) is a provably inconsistent polyad (q.v.).

Contra-inference (5.II). Coming to disbelieve the π-conclusion (q.v.) as a result of believing the π-premisses (q.v.).

Credence function (2.III). A function whose values are real numbers from 0 to 1 and whose domain (q.v.) is some set of propositions and/or pairs of propositions.

Deduction (5.II). A conservative (q.v.) δ-inference (q.v.) whose π-inference (q.v.) is provable (q.v.).

Degree of belief (2.I). Any attitude of belief, agnosticism (q.v.) or disbelief considered as a member of a doxastic system (q.v.).

Disprovable proposition (4.II). A proposition which is the π-premiss (q.v.) of a provable (q.v.) π-inference whose π-conclusion (q.v.) is self-refuting (q.v.).

Domain of a credence function (2.V). The set of propositions or pairs of propositions for which the credence function (q.v.) is defined; that is, the set of propositions to which there is some attitude in the doxastic system (q.v.) being represented (q.v.).

Doubt, measure of (5.II). See measure of doubt.

Doxastic attitude (1.I). Any attitude of either belief, agnosticism (q.v.) or disbelief.

Doxastic conclusion (δ-conclusion) (1.II). The doxastic attitude (q.v.) reached as a result of a doxastic inference (q.v.).

Doxastic consistency (δ-consistency) (3.II). A doxastic system (q.v.), or a credence function (q.v.) representing it (q.v.), is said to be δ-consistent if it would be rational (q.v.) to maintain it indefinitely in the absence of external changes (q.v.).

Doxastic inconsistency (δ-inconsistency) (3.II). Lack of δ-consistency (q.v.).

Doxastic inference (δ-inference) (1.III). Coming to have some doxastic attitude (q.v.), the δ-conclusion, by means of reasoning, and as a result of having various other doxastic attitudes, the δ-premisses.

Doxastic premisses (δ-premisses) (1.III). The doxastic attitudes (q.v.) from which one reasons in a δ-inference (q.v.).

Doxastic system (1.I). A system consisting of various doxastic attitudes (q.v.) together with various structures, the chief of which are that some beliefs are picked out as certain (q.v.), that some disbeliefs are picked out as contracertain (q.v.) and that some attitudes are greater than or equal to others.

Eduction (10.I). An induction whose conclusion concerns some specified item not a whole population.

Epistemic importance (4.V). See index of epistemic importance.

Expansion (3.I). A doxastic change (q.v.) in which new doxastic attitudes (q.v.) are acquired without any old ones being altered or excised. (See also adjustment and contraction.)

Explicit stress (9.I). The sum of the stress-components (q.v.). (See also implicit stress.)

Extension (2.V). Credence function (q.v.) e is said to be an extension of credence function d if the domain of d is included in that of e and they agree on that domain. (See also restriction.)

External change (3.I). A doxastic change (q.v.) not due to reasoning but to other factors such as observation. (See also internal change.)

Implicit stress (9.I). The stress (q.v.) which a doxastic system (q.v.) has as a result of the inevitability of accumulating explicit stress (q.v.) if the system were expanded.

Inconsistent polyad (4.II). See provably inconsistent polyad.

Index of epistemic importance (9.V). A measure of the strength of a stress-component (q.v.).

Inference (1.III). See doxastic inference and propositional inference.

Internal change (3.I). A doxastic change (q.v.) which is the result of reasoning. (See also external change.)

Logical omniscience (1.IV). The idealization that the person can survey all possibilities and all the results of positive logic.

Measure of doubt (5.II). One minus the numerical representation (q.v.) of the degree of belief (q.v.).

Meet (2.V). The meet $d\wedge e$ of credence functions (q.v.) d and e is the restriction (q.v.) of either of them to the set of propositions on which they agree.

Minimal adjustment (6.II). An adjustment (q.v.) by only as much as is required to restore δ-consistency (q.v.). That is, d^-/d^+ is minimal if d^+ is δ-consistent and there is no δ-consistent d between (q.v.) d^- and d^+.

Nearness to δ-consistency (6.VI). The credence function (q.v.) d is at least as near δ-consistency as the credence function e if either d is δ-consistent or d is between (q.v.) e and some δ-consistent credence function.

Potentially dominant stress-components (9.V). The class, if there is one, of stress-components which offer a partial exception to the compromise resolution (q.v.) because in many clashes with other stress-components they should yield nothing.

Proportional syllogisms (8.I). An inference from the proportion of Fs which are Gs to the conclusion that some designated F is a G.

Propositional conclusion (π-conclusion) (1.III). The proposition towards which the δ-conclusion (q.v.) of a δ-inference (q.v.) is an attitude.

Propositional inference (π-inference) (1.III). A sequence of propositions all but the last of which are the π-premisses (q.v.), and the last of which is the π-conclusion (q.v.).

Propositional premisses (π-premisses) (1.III). The propositions towards which the δ-premisses (q.v.) are attitudes.

Provably inconsistent polyad (4.II). A set of propositions which form the π-premisses (q.v.) of a π-inference (q.v.) whose π-conclusion (q.v.) is self-refuting (q.v.).

Rational (1.II). Rationally permissible, that is, not irrational.

Rational predicament (1.III). A situation in which some change required for rationality is also prohibited as irrational.

Rational relevance (7.III). Proposition p lacks rational relevance to proposition q, in the circumstances, if no rational expansion (q.v.) results in the stochastic relevance (q.v.) of p to q. (Rational relevance is extended to predicates in section 7.VII.)

Representation (2.III). A credence function (q.v.) is said to be a representative of a doxastic system (q.v.) if its domain is the set of all the propositions or pairs of propositions occurring in the system and it satisfies various constraints, the chief of which is that representation should preserve the relation of being greater than or equal to.

Restriction (2.V). A credence function (q.v.) d is said to be the restriction of credence function e to a set of propositions P ($e = d \| P$) if the domain of d is P, which is included in the domain of e, and if e is an extension of d. In any case, if e is an extension of d, d is said to be a restriction of e.

Self-evident (s-e) implication (4.II). Proposition p s-e implies proposition q if it is δ-inconsistent (q.v.) to have a degree of belief (q.v.) less than certainty (q.v.) in q conditional on (q.v.) p.

Self-evident (s-e) proposition (4.II). A proposition is said to be self-evident if it is δ-inconsistent (q.v.) to have a degree of belief (q.v.) less than certainty (q.v.) in it.

Self-refuting proposition (4.II). A proposition is said to be self-refuting if it is δ-inconsistent (q.v.) to have a degree of belief (q.v.) greater than contracertainty (q.v.) in it.

Set of alternatives (4.IV). A set of propositions p_1, p_2, etc. whose disjunction is self-evident (q.v.) and such that the conjunction of any pair is self-refuting.

Stochastic independence (7.III). Proposition p is said to be stochastically independent of proposition q if $d(p) = d(p/q)$. (This is a descriptive, not a normative concept.)

Stochastic irrelevance (7.III). Proposition q is said to be stochastically irrelevant to proposition p if p is stochastically independent (q.v.) of both q and its Boolean negation (q.v.).

Stochastic relevance (7.III). Lack of stochastic irrelevance.

Stress (9.I). A numerical measure of the logical disvalue of a doxastic system (q.v.). (See also explicit and implicit stress.)

Stress component (9.I). The stress due to a single source of logical disvalue other than lack of completability.

Tau ordering (τ-ordering) (2.VI). A partial ordering of the doxastic attitudes (q.v.) obtained from the greater than or equal to relation by ensuring transitivity.

Temporal coherence (10.III). Temporal coherence is satisfied by hypothesis h and observation e if the degree of belief (q.v.) in h after the observation that e equals the conditional degree of belief (q.v.) in h on e prior to the observation.

Index

Addition Principle, 48-9, 53, 64-5, 67-70, 97, 134-8, 148, 184, 192, 195
Addition Rule, *see* Addition Principle
adjustment, 3, 10, 33-47, 85-98, 144-5, 151, 185, 203
  minimal, 88-9, 94, 96-8
Adjustment One at a Time Conjecture, 44, 86
agnosticism, 14, 22, 25, 29, 30, 46, 62, 91, 203
Alchourron, C., 2
Alternative Supposition, Principle of, 55, 58, 60, 67, 72, 184
alternatives, set of, 55, 207
  see also equal alternatives
apologia, 17
Archimedean Principles, 61-4, 192
argument, 16
Armstrong, D. M., 165, 175, 189, 197
arrow of *modus tollens*, 14, 96, 144-5, 188, 193, 203
associated set of predicates, *see* predicates
asymmetry, *see* symmetry
attitude, agnostic, *see* agnosticism
attitude, doxastic, 11-15

Bayesian, 3, 103-4, 167-9, 175, 188
belief, degree of, 9
bivalence, 51, 55
Boolean Negation Principle, 60, 63

Carnap, R., 25, 57, 101, 103, 118, 161
Cautious Deduction Conjecture, 80
certainty, 22, 23, 25, 27, 29-30, 74, 80, 174, 203

degrees of, 26, 190
  see also contracertainty
Chalmers, A., 193
chance, objective, 100-1; *see also* probability
change
  external doxastic, 33, 34, 37, 135, 194
  internal doxastic, 33, 34, 37, 45, 136
chiliad, inconsistent, 44, 48
Church, A., 81
Churchland, P., 189
closure, logical, 2, 23, 48
coherence, 103, 104, 127
  see also consistency
comparative theory, *see* comparison, of rationality
comparison, of degrees of belief, 21-4, 25-7, 30-1, 59, 61, 63, 66
  non-representable 30-1
  of rationality, 7, 10, 18, 21, 38, 50, 96, 113, 133-79
Completability, Principle of, 48, 55-6, 60, 61, 64, 68, 71, 76, 98, 138, 150-1, 152, 184
completability, symmetric, 112
composition, 33, 40-2
Composition Principle, 40-2, 107, 128, 183
Compromise Solution, 95, 144-5, 203
conceptual overlap, *see* overlap, conceptual
conceptual scheme, *see* scheme, conceptual
conclusion
  doxastic, 16, 74, 204
  propositional, 16, 74, 206

truth-conditional type, 12
type, *see* functional type, proposition-
type, truth-conditional type

use criterion, Church's, 81

validity, 9, 72–4, 85, 90, 188
vindication, of induction, 161

weights, in stress-formula, 151, 181
Williams, D. C., 169, 172
Williams/Stove Argument, 169, 172